...OD AFFECT OUR ABILITY TO HAVE FAITH IN HIM? • HOW CAN I BREAK BAD HABITS? • HOW CAN I LEARN TO CONTROL ...MPER? • HOW SHOULD I ACT IF I FEEL THAT I WAS "BORN WITH" THE SOURCE OF MY TEMPTATIONS—IF IT'S JUST THE W... ...AM? • HOW CAN I BETTER CONTROL MY LANGUAGE? • HOW CAN I REALLY REPENT? • HOW CAN I KNOW WHAT SIN... ...HOULD REPENT OF? • HOW CAN I KNOW WHEN I NEED TO CONFESS SINS TO THE BISHOP, OR JUST CONFESS THEM TO GO... ...HOW DOES REPENTANCE APPLY TO ME IF I HAVEN'T DONE ANYTHING THAT BAD? • HOW CAN I KNOW WHEN I'VE BEEN F... ...VEN? • HOW CAN I ENJOY THE BLESSINGS OF FORGIVENESS IF I STILL REMEMBER MY SINS? • HOW CAN I FORGIVE OTH... ...THEY AREN'T SORRY FOR WHAT THEY'VE DONE? • HOW CAN I MAKE THE TEMPLE A MORE IMPORTANT PART OF MY LIFE... ...OW CAN THE TEMPLE GIVE ME INCREASED POWER? • HOW CAN ATTENDING THE TEMPLE HELP ME RECEIVE ANSWERS TO... ...ROBLEMS? • HOW CAN I PREPARE FOR AN ETERNAL MARRIAGE? • HOW CAN I KNOW IF THE PERSON I LIKE IS MY "SO... ...ATE"? • HOW CAN I KNOW WHEN I'M READY TO BE MARRIED? • HOW CAN I KNOW WHEN I'M IN LOVE? • HOW CAN I WA... ...O START A FAMILY WHEN THE WORLD TODAY SEEMS LIKE SUCH A TERRIBLE PLACE? • HOW CAN I STRENGTHEN MY TE... ...ONY? • HOW CAN I KNOW IF SOMETHING I LEARN IN SCHOOL IS TRUE OR FALSE? • HOW COME I CAN'T TRY THE BAD ST... ...IN) TO LEARN IF IT'S BAD AND GAIN MY TESTIMONY THAT WAY? • HOW CAN I KNOW WHEN THE HOLY GHOST IS SPEAK... ...O ME? • HOW LONG WILL IT TAKE FOR AN ANSWER TO COME OR FOR ME TO RECEIVE THE REVELATION I NEED? • HOW... ...ESIRE AND WORTHINESS AFFECT MY ABILITY TO RECEIVE REVELATION ON A DAILY BASIS? • HOW CAN I AVOID BE... ...ECEIVED WHEN RECEIVING REVELATION? • HOW CAN I BE SURE IF SOMETHING IS "EDIFYING" OR RIGHT? WHAT IF I'M N... ...URE? • HOW CAN I TELL THE DIFFERENCE BETWEEN MY OWN THOUGHTS AND THE HOLY GHOST? • HOW SHOULD I ACT... ...EEL I HAVEN'T RECEIVED AN IMPRESSION OR AN ANSWER AT ALL? • HOW CAN I RECOGNIZE AND DEVELOP SPIRITUAL GIF... ...HOW CAN I KNOW IF I SHOULD GET MY PATRIARCHAL BLESSING? • HOW CAN I CHOOSE A MEANINGFUL COLLEGE MAJOR... ...AREER? • HOW CAN I TELL THE DIFFERENCE BETWEEN RIGHT AND WRONG? • HOW CAN I TELL WHAT MEDIA ARE APPRO... ...TE? • HOW CAN I SET STANDARDS THAT WILL KEEP ME SPIRITUALLY SAFE? • HOW CAN I SET A STANDARD I WILL KEEP F... ...HE REST OF MY LIFE? • HOW STRICT SHOULD I BE WHEN I SET A STANDARD FOR MYSELF? • HOW CAN I STAY MORA... ...LEAN? • HOW CAN I AVOID MORALLY COMPROMISING SITUATIONS? • HOW CAN I RESPOND IF SOMEBODY IS TRYING TO... ...E AND I DON'T WANT THEM TO? • HOW DOES MORAL PURITY APPLY TO THOSE WHO HAVE BEEN VICTIMS OF SEXUAL ABU... ...HOW CAN I RESIST AND OVERCOME PORNOGRAPHY? • HOW ARE YOUNG WOMEN BEING TARGETED BY PORNOGRAPH... ...OW DO SOME YOUNG WOMEN BECOME PART OF THE PORNOGRAPHY PROBLEM, AND MAYBE DON'T EVEN KNOW IT? • H... ...AN I HONOR MY PARENTS? • HOW CAN I RESPOND TO MY PARENTS IF I DON'T AGREE WITH WHAT THEY WANT ME TO DO... ...OW CAN I INITIATE A HEART-TO-HEART CONVERSATION WITH MY PARENTS? • HOW CAN I HAVE A FUN AND CLEAN DATE... ...OW CAN I APPROPRIATELY TELL MY DATE THAT I'M NOT COMFORTABLE WITH THE ACTIVITY WE ARE DOING? • HOW SHO... ...REACT IF NOBODY ASKS ME OUT? • HOW CAN I FIND OTHER DATING IDEAS? • HOW CAN I HAVE MORE MEANINGFUL PRAYE... ...HOW DO I KNOW IF I SHOULD KNEEL, STAND, OR SIT WHEN I PRAY? • HOW CAN I START PRAYING IN THE MORNING, AND... ...UST AT NIGHT? • HOW CAN I GET MORE FROM MY SCRIPTURE STUDY? • HOW CAN I GET ANYTHING FROM MY SCRIPT... ...TUDY IF I DON'T UNDERSTAND ALL THE BIG WORDS? • HOW CAN I HELP MY FAMILY STUDY THE SCRIPTURES? • HOW C... ...ET AN AUDIO COPY OF THE SCRIPTURES TO LISTEN TO ON MY IPOD? • HOW CAN I FIND ANSWERS IN THE SCRIPTURE... ...OW DO I KNOW WHERE TO LOOK IN THE SCRIPTURES TO FIND THE ANSWERS I NEED? • HOW CAN I MAKE MORE TIME... ...TUDY THE SCRIPTURES? • HOW CAN HAVING A SPECIFIC QUESTION IN MIND HELP MY SCRIPTURE STUDY? • HOW CAN I K... ...HE SABBATH DAY HOLY? • HOW SHOULD I DRESS ON THE SABBATH? • HOW DOES DOING HOMEWORK ON SUNDAY AFF... ...Y ABILITY TO KEEP THE SABBATH DAY HOLY? • HOW SHOULD I RESPOND WHEN MY EMPLOYER WANTS ME TO WORK... ...UNDAY? • HOW CAN I GET MORE FROM MY CHURCH MEETINGS? • HOW CAN I HELP OTHERS IN MY CLASSES BE MORE REV... ...NT? • HOW CAN I MAKE PARTAKING OF THE SACRAMENT MORE MEANINGFUL? • HOW CAN I KEEP A MEANINGFUL JOURN... ...HOW CAN I MAKE USE OF TECHNOLOGY IN JOURNAL KEEPING? • HOW CAN I CREATE A LIVING AREA THAT INVITES THE H... ...HOST? • HOW CAN I HAVE A GOSPEL-CENTERED ROOM IF I SHARE IT WITH SOMEONE ELSE? • HOW CAN I HAVE A GOSP... ...ENTERED CAR, BACKPACK, LOCKER, COMPUTER, OR CELL PHONE? • HOW CAN I STAY FAITHFUL WHEN LIFE IS HARD? ... ...AN GOD LOVE US IF HE LETS BAD THINGS HAPPEN TO US? • HOW CAN I OVERCOME FEELINGS OF INGRATITUDE? • HOW... ...OVERCOME FEELINGS OF FEAR AND DOUBT? • HOW CAN I WORRY LESS AND STRESS LESS? • HOW SHOULD I RESPOND... ...AVE DOUBTS ABOUT THE CHURCH? • HOW CAN I BE HAPPY? • HOW CAN I HANDLE ANTI-MORMON TEACHINGS IN A CHR... ...KE WAY? • HOW SHOULD I RESPOND IF I SEE PEOPLE PROTESTING AGAINST THE CHURCH? • HOW SHOULD I RESPOND... ...EAR AN ANTI-MORMON STATEMENT THAT BRINGS UP SOMETHING I'VE NEVER HEARD OF BEFORE? • HOW CAN I SET... ...NGFUL PERSONAL GOALS? • HOW CAN I KNOW WHERE TO BEGIN SETTING GOALS? • HOW OFTEN SHOULD I SET GOAL... ...OW CAN I RESIST NEGATIVE PEER PRESSURE? • HOW SHOULD I RESPOND WHEN OTHERS ASK IF THEY CAN COPY MY HO... ...VORK OR CHEAT OFF MY TEST? • HOW CAN I KNOW IF I SHOULD STOP HANGING OUT WITH A CERTAIN FRIEND OR GROUP... ...RIENDS? • I'VE BEEN MAKING CHANGES IN MY LIFE AND BECOMING A BETTER PERSON, BUT MY FRIENDS MAKE FUN OF... ...OR BEING TOO GOOD. HOW SHOULD I RESPOND? • HOW CAN I HELP FRIENDS AND FAMILY WHO ARE STRUGGLING WITH... ...US PROBLEMS? • HOW SHOULD I RESPOND IF MY FRIENDS WANT ME TO "COVER" FOR THEM? • HOW CAN I KNOW... ...HOULD TELL ON MY FRIEND? • HOW CAN I HELP FRIENDS OR FAMILY MEMBERS WHO DON'T ATTEND CHURCH? • HOW C... ...EAR A POWERFUL TESTIMONY? • HOW CAN I BEAR MY TESTIMONY WHEN I DON'T FEEL VERY CONFIDENT IN IT? • ... ...HOULD I RESPOND IF I FEEL I SHOULD BEAR MY TESTIMONY, BUT I DON'T KNOW WHAT TO SAY? • HOW CAN I PREPARE... ...IVE A POWERFUL YOUTH TALK? • HOW CAN I FIND GOOD QUOTES THAT GO ALONG WITH A SCRIPTURE I WANT TO SHAR... ...OW CAN I USE ONLINE RESOURCES TO HELP PREPARE A TALK? • HOW CAN I SHARE THE GOSPEL WITH OTHERS? • HOW... ...PREPARE TO SERVE A MISSION? • HOW CAN I KNOW IF I SHOULD SERVE A MISSION? • HOW CAN I INCREASE MY FAI... ...ESUS CHRIST? • HOW IS FAITH RELATED TO TESTIMONY? • HOW DOES KNOWING ABOUT GOD AFFECT OUR ABILITY TO... ...AITH IN HIM? • HOW CAN I BREAK BAD HABITS? • HOW CAN I LEARN TO CONTROL MY TEMPER? • HOW SHOULD...

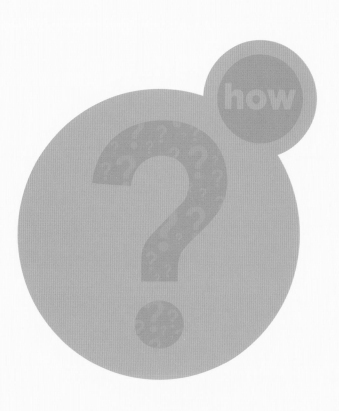

ESSENTIAL SKILLS FOR LIVING THE GOSPEL

JOHN HILTON III AND ANTHONY SWEAT

DESERET
BOOK

SALT LAKE CITY, UTAH

Design by Ken Wzorek and Barry Hansen

Visit us at DeseretBook.com

Library of Congress Cataloging-in-Publication Data
Hilton, John, III.
How? : essential skills for living the gospel / John Hilton III, Anthony Sweat.
p. cm.
Includes bibliographical references.
ISBN 978-1-60641-789-8 (hardbound : alk. paper)
1. Mormon youth—Religious life—Juvenile literature. 2. Christian
life—Mormon authors—Juvenile literature. I. Sweat, Anthony. II. Title.
BX8643.Y6H545 2010
248.8'3088289332—dc22   2010011106

Printed in China
R. R. Donnelley, Shenzhen, China
10 9 8 7 6 5 4 3 2 1

To our parents, who first showed us through
their examples HOW to live the gospel

"Once we . . . understand the importance and meaning of [a] commandment, we need to learn how to do it."

—Elder Russell M. Nelson

contents

Acknowledgments

No book is the result of the work of the authors only. We would like to thank the many hands at Deseret Book who have contributed their talents to this project: Sheri Dew, Chris Schoebinger, Lisa Mangum, Leslie Stitt, Derk Koldewyn, Tonya Facemyer, Richard Erickson, Kayla Hackett, Patrick Muir, Brian Clark, and Bryan Beach.

We would also like to thank the many teachers who have shared great ideas with us. We are grateful for their permission to use some of those ideas in this book.

Last, we would like to thank our spouses, Lani Hilton and Cindy Sweat, and our children for allowing us the time to write this book, and for giving us the opportunity to try to live and teach these gospel principles in our own families.

Introduction: "For *How* to Act I Did Not Know"

You are on a family vacation at the beach and enjoying the ocean water. You effortlessly bob up and down as you play in the waves. Suddenly you notice that you can't touch the bottom anymore. You look back to shore only to see that you are being pulled farther and farther away from land. You put your head down and start to swim back toward the beach, but after thirty seconds of swimming, you are even farther away. Someone yells to you from the shore that you are caught in a rip current. Would you know *how* to get back to shore?

"If caught in a rip current:
- "Remain calm to conserve energy and think clearly.
- "Never fight against the current.
- "Think of it like a treadmill that cannot be turned off, which you need to step to the side of.
- "Swim out of the current in a direction following the shoreline. When out of the current, swim at an angle—away from the current—towards shore."[1]

You have recently become caught up with friends in some activities that you know are wrong. You feel yourself getting pulled away from the safety of the gospel shore and out into the depths of sin. You try to break free from your actions for a time, but your efforts don't seem to get you closer to where you want to be. You are caught in a current of sin, and you want to get out of it. Would you know *how* to get back to the safety of the gospel shore?

"There are those who were once warm in the faith, but whose faith has grown cold. Many of them wish to come back but do not know quite *how to do it*." —President Gordon B. Hinckley[2]

One truth regarding the gospel of Jesus Christ is that it is not enough to know something, or even believe it. No, the gospel is meant to be lived. Jesus himself said, "Not every one that saith unto me, Lord, Lord, shall enter into the kingdom of heaven; but he that *doeth* the will of my Father which is in heaven" (Matthew 7:21; emphasis added). It is not necessarily what we know that brings us blessings, but what we do and become. But what if we know we should do something, but don't know *how* to do it? What if we know we should keep the Sabbath day holy, but don't really know *how* to make that day more meaningful? What if we know we need to be led by the Spirit in our day-to-day lives, but don't really know *how* that works? What if we think we've repented, but aren't quite sure *how* to know if we've been forgiven?

"TEACH ME ALL THAT I MUST DO"

"At the request of President Spencer W. Kimball, . . . the words in a LDS children's hymn ["I Am a Child of God"] were changed from 'Teach me all that I must know' to 'Teach me all that I must do,' because it is not enough just to know [the gospel]; [we] must *do* [what the gospel teaches]."[3]

Fourteen-year-old Joseph Smith faced a similar situation in his quest for truth. He knew he needed to do something about the religious excitement in his area, but he said, *"How* to act I did not know" (Joseph Smith–History 1:12; emphasis added). Joseph knew to pray for help, though, and as President Henry B. Eyring, then a member of the Quorum of the Twelve, said, "The Father and His Beloved Son appeared to him in answer to his prayer. And *he was told how to act,* as he had desired."[4]

The Lord tells *us* how to act as well. The scriptures are full of "how to" formulas to help us live the gospel. For example, the Lord told scattered Israel "how to come unto him and be saved" (1 Nephi 15:14). He answered the question of Thomas the apostle, "How can we know the way?" (John 14:5). King Benjamin told us how to retain a remission of our sins (see Mosiah 4:26). Jesus Christ also told the early saints "how to govern my church" (D&C 41:3), "how to organize this people" (D&C 51:1), and "how to worship" (D&C 93:19). Actually, the Lord is so intent on having us know *how* to act and live the gospel that he gave his saints a commandment regarding it: "And now, behold, I give unto you a *commandment,* that when ye are assembled together ye shall instruct and edify each other, *that ye may know how to act and direct my church, how to act upon the points of my law and commandments,* which I have given" (D&C 43:8; emphasis added).

Not only do we have the words of the ancient prophets to tell us how to live Christ's teachings, but we also have the words of the living prophets to give us specific direction concerning the "how's" of the gospel. Consider the following:

- President Dieter F. Uchtdorf answered the question, "How do we become true disciples of Jesus Christ?"[5]

- Elder Robert D. Hales discussed "how do we know what really is true?"[6]

- Elder David A. Bednar taught "how to invite the constant companionship of the Holy Ghost."[7]

- Elder Richard G. Scott shared "how to prepare to be a full-time missionary."[8]

- Elder Russell M. Nelson taught us "how to pray."[9]

- President Henry B. Eyring told us "how to get protection and help from the Lord."[10]

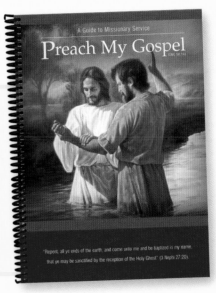

PREACH MY GOSPEL . . . A "How to" Guide for Missionaries AND MEMBERS

Preach My Gospel contains chapters such as

- "How Do I Study Effectively and Prepare to Teach?"
- "How Do I Develop Christlike Attributes?"
- "How Do I Use Time Wisely?"
- "How Can I Improve My Teaching Skills?"

This book attempts to compile many of the "how to" teachings from the scriptures and the words of the prophets so we can know "how to act upon the points of [Christ's] law" (D&C 43:8). We hope that this book will help you learn how to receive the blessings of *doing, living,* and *obeying* the gospel. We testify that the Lord will bless us as we learn *how* to live his gospel and implement it in our life, because ultimately, as Elder Dallin H. Oaks has said, "The gospel of Jesus Christ is a plan that shows us *how to become* what our Heavenly Father desires us to become."[11]

BUT HOW DO I . . . ?

In this book we have tried to address general "how-to" questions. For example,

"How can I help friends and family who are struggling with serious problems?"

It's important to know that in many cases we will need the personal guidance of the Spirit to teach us *how to act*. We've tried to give general principles to act upon, but don't forget to go to the Lord for specific direction regarding the personal challenges you face (see Conclusion: The Holy Ghost Will Tell You *How*).

HOW TO SNEEZE INTO THE WIND WITHOUT GETTING WET

If you enter "how to" into a book search on Amazon .com, there are more than 292,000 results, ranging from the classic *How to Win Friends and Influence People,* to the intense *How to Survive the End of the World as We Know It.* You can also find books on *How to Raise the Perfect Dog* and *How to Read Literature Like a Professor* (have fun with that one!). Of all the things we could learn how to do, learning how to live the gospel may be the most important because it has eternal significance.

HOW to Get the Most Out of This Book

Please note a couple of important features of this book. In each chapter you will find a "Do Try This at Home!" activity. This activity is designed to help you do something active that will help you understand the principles from the chapter. In each chapter you will also find an "Invitation to Act." This is a specific invitation for us to *do* something as a result of what we've discussed in the chapter. Elder David A. Bednar said, "As disciples of the Savior, we are not merely striving to know more; rather, we need to consistently *do* more of what we know is right and become better."[12] We hope you will try these activities at home and accept these invitations to act, as they will strengthen your faith and allow the Holy Ghost to testify to you that the gospel principles are true.

DO TRY THIS AT HOME!

Invitation to Act

How Can I Increase My Faith in Jesus Christ?

> "Remember that faith and doubt cannot exist in the same mind at the same time, for one will dispel the other. Cast out doubt. Cultivate faith." —President Thomas S. Monson[1]

A young man named Junior recently shared in a testimony meeting his experience attending a soccer camp in North Carolina. He impressed the coaches there and was offered a full-ride scholarship. When he asked about the timing of the scholarship in regards to serving a mission, he was told that if he accepted the scholarship he would have to play four years in a row—and then go on his mission. "But you won't want to go," the coach told him, "because after four years I guarantee that you'll get picked up by a professional team." This was very tempting for Junior because playing professional soccer was his dream. After fasting and praying, he called the coach back and said, "I'm sorry, I won't be joining your team. I'm putting my mission as my top priority."

Although Junior might not have realized it at the time, when he made the decision to decline the scholarship, he was exercising faith in Jesus Christ—the first principle of the gospel.

In the book *True to the Faith,* we read, "Having faith in Jesus Christ means relying completely on Him—trusting in His infinite power, intelligence, and love. It includes believing His teachings."[2] But how do we develop faith in our Savior that allows us to trust him completely? This chapter will focus on three primary elements of developing and increasing our faith: creating *hope* in, taking *action* on, and seeing the *evidence* of the promises of Jesus Christ's atonement and teachings. Using the life of Joseph Smith as an example, we can see how, even as a teenager, he implemented all three of these elements to increase his faith in Jesus Christ.

Create Hope through Hearing the Word of God

Paul taught that "faith cometh by hearing, and hearing by the word of God" (Romans 10:17). Hearing, reading, and learning about the promises of God are critical steps in increasing our faith because it naturally creates hope. One reason for this is because the scriptures and words of the prophets are full of promises for the faithful. Jacob wrote, "We search the prophets, . . . and having all these witnesses we obtain a hope, and our faith becometh unshaken" (Jacob 4:6). As we search the scriptures we will find promises that God has made to us—promises that create hope.

WHAT SCRIPTURES CREATE HOPE FOR YOU?

Do you have a favorite scripture that gives you hope? One that promises you blessings if you act in obedience and faith? E-mail us your favorite verses at answers@ldswhy.com

Joseph Smith understood how the scriptures can create hope. During his time of confusion regarding which church was true, he came across the Epistle of James and read this now-famous verse: "If any of you lack wisdom, let him ask of God, that giveth to all men liberally, and upbraideth not; and it shall be given him" (James 1:5). Reading the promise in that verse created hope for Joseph—hope that his question would be answered. This was a critical first step for him, and for us, toward increasing faith.

EVER HAD EXPIRED MILK? HOW ABOUT EXPIRED FAITH?

"Great faith has a short shelf life." —President Henry B. Eyring[3]

Just as milk goes bad after a short amount of time, our faith must continually be renewed or it can sour as well.

Faith

Must be replenished each day

Take Action and Experiment upon the Word

All promised gospel blessings are conditional upon our obedience (see D&C 130:20–21). In other words, if we hope to obtain any blessing, we need to take action and obey what the gospel requires of us to obtain that blessing. This truth is one reason why Joseph Smith said that faith is "the principle of action in all intelligent beings."[4] Elder David A. Bednar said, "True faith . . . always leads to action."[5] It is kind of like the scientific method used in experiments: After a hypothesis is formed, then a righteous experiment must be performed to test it. Our hope in Jesus Christ naturally leads us to act and conduct our own spiritual experiments. The prophet Alma tells us that if we want to increase our faith, we must "awake and arouse [our] faculties, even to an *experiment* upon my words, and *exercise* a particle of faith" (Alma 32:27; emphasis added).

The Spiritual-ific Method

Take a look at the scientific method below. Instead of using it to test *scientific* truths, we can do what Alma says and use the steps to test *spiritual* truths. Notice how Joseph Smith's experience could follow this spiritual-ific method

Ask a question
Which church is true? (Joseph Smith-History 1:10)

Do background research
Study the scriptures (Joseph Smith-History 1:8, 11)

Construct hypothesis
If I ask God in faith, he'll answer my question
(Joseph Smith-History 1:12-13)

Test with a righteous experiment
Go to the woods and pray (Joseph Smith-History 1:14)

Analyze results/draw conclusions
Received a vision of the Father and the Son
(Joseph Smith-History 1:17-19)

Hypothesis is *true*
"I had found the testimony of James to be true"
(Joseph Smith-History 1:26)

Report results
"I then said to my mother, 'I have learned for myself that Presbyterianism is not true'" (Joseph Smith-History 1:20)

HOW *is faith related to testimony?*

When Lehi and his family left Jerusalem, his wife, Sariah, did not know for sure that it was the right thing to do. However, she followed in faith anyway. She experimented upon the word and waited for the evidence. Notice what she says when her sons return with the brass plates: "And she spake, saying: *Now I know of a surety* that the Lord hath commanded my husband to flee into the wilderness" (1 Nephi 5:8; emphasis added). If we obey in faith like Sariah did, *then* our testimonies will be confirmed so we too can say, "Now I know of a surety."

As a teenager, Joseph Smith took his hope from a scriptural promise that God would answer his questions, and he decided to act on it. He *did something* with what he had learned. He said, "I at length came to the determination to 'ask of God.' . . . I retired to the woods to make the attempt. . . . I kneeled down and began to offer up the desires of my heart to God" (Joseph Smith–History 1:13–15). It is our "attempts" in righteous experiments that will produce the results that lead to increased faith, for "faith without works is dead" (James 2:20).

"Faith is like the muscle of your arm. If you exercise it, it grows strong. If you put it in a sling and leave it there, it becomes weak." —*True to the Faith*[6]

Which is more like your faith?

DO TRY THIS AT HOME!

You know how in movies, people can move things with their mind? Have you ever wished you could do that? Did you know that if you have enough faith, Jesus says you can move things—even entire mountains (see Matthew 17:20)? Take a look around you and locate an object (like a lamp or a book or something on the table). Now, move it with your faith!

What happened? Did the object move? We're guessing not. We're guessing all that happened is that you got a headache from focusing your eyes like laser beams really hard.

Moving an object with your faith doesn't have to do with mental focusing or laser-beam eyes. Elder James E. Talmage said, "Faith implies such confidence and conviction as will impel to action. . . . [F]aith is active and positive, embracing such reliance and confidence *as will lead to works*."[7]

In other words, faith is doing something. That is why the apostle James says, "Faith without works is dead" (James 2:20).

So, what's the easiest way to move the object with your faith? Get up and move it!

GET IN THE WHEELBARROW!

There is an apocryphal story of a famous tight-rope walker who walked on a tightrope across the Niagara Falls. The story goes that crowds gathered around to watch the man, who not only made it across the rope, he also did it blindfolded! Then he walked back along the tightrope, across the Falls, but this time, wheeling a wheelbarrow. He said that for his next stunt, he would cross the rope with the wheelbarrow again, but this time he would safely carry a person in the wheelbarrow.

"Do you think I can do it?" he asked the crowd.

The crowd cheered and shouted, "We believe you can do it!"

"Okay," the man said. "Who is willing to get in the wheelbarrow?"[8]

The moral of the story is obvious—we may say that we believe, but true faith requires action. Do we believe enough to "get in the wheelbarrow" and experiment on God's word?

Look for Evidence of Its Truthfulness

Just like in a science experiment, we must look at the results of our obedience. We must analyze the evidence of our faithful action and determine if our hope is confirmed. The scriptures tell us that "faith is . . . the *evidence* of things not seen" (Hebrews 11:1; emphasis added). As you look back over your life, you can probably see a lot of evidence that will strengthen your faith. Can you remember a time when a prayer was answered? When a priesthood blessing provided comfort or healing? When you felt peace while reading the scriptures? That is evidence!

Alma taught us what type of evidence to look for after we have performed our "experiment" upon the word (see Alma 32:27):

"Now, if ye give place, that a seed may be planted in your heart, behold, if it be a true seed, . . . behold, it will begin to *swell* within your breasts; and when you feel these swelling motions, ye will begin to say within yourselves—It must needs be that this is a good seed, or that the word is good, for it beginneth to *enlarge* my soul; yea, it beginneth to *enlighten* my understanding, yea, it beginneth to be *delicious* to me" (Alma 32:28; emphasis added).

The spiritual evidences to look for can easily be remembered and understood by the acronym **SEED:**

S—Swell within us. Look at the evidence of our *feelings.* Does the action produce the fruits of the Spirit, such as love, joy, and peace (see Galatians 5:22)? If it does, it is a good seed.

E—Enlarge our soul. Look at the evidence of what the action does to us as a person. Are we more kind, more energetic, less selfish? Has the action helped us put off the natural man and become more of a spiritual man (see Mosiah 3:19)? If it does, it is a good seed.

E—Enlighten our understanding. Look at the evidence in our mind. Does the action help us see things more clearly? Does it help us understand more deeply? Does it help us have "Aha!" moments of pure knowledge and enlightenment (see D&C 6:15)? If it does, it is a good seed.

D—Delicious to our souls. Look at what kind of appetite the action creates in us, and what kind of hunger it fills. Does the experiment feed us spiritually (see John 6:35)? Does it help us "hunger and thirst after righteousness" (Matthew 5:6)? If it does, it is a good seed.

When we have these feelings it is evidence that what we are experimenting on is true.

? HOW *does knowing about God affect our ability to have faith in him?*

The degree to which we have a correct understanding of God significantly affects our ability to have faith in him. For example, if we mistakenly believe that anything bad that happens in our life is a sign that God is angry with us, then when things go wrong, we might become angry toward God and lose faith. *Lectures on Faith* states that in order to exercise faith in God we must have a correct idea of the kind of being he is.[9] As we come to better know God's true nature and character, we will be able to exercise more faith in him.

"Every time you *try your faith,* that is, act in worthiness on an impression, you will receive the confirming evidence of the Spirit. Those feelings will fortify your faith. As you repeat that pattern, your faith will become stronger."
—Elder Richard G. Scott[11]

Look at the evidence of the SEED in Joseph Smith's words of his First Vision. He said, "My Soul was filled with love and for many days I could rejoice with great joy and the Lord was with me."[10] We know that Joseph's mind was enlightened from the answer he received (see Joseph Smith–History 1:16–18), but his soul was also filled with joy. If we act in righteousness and spiritually discern the evidence of our action, our faith will be confirmed and increase as well.

Elder David A. Bednar called this three-step process a "helix" of faith. He said, "These three elements of faith—assurance [hope], action, and evidence—are not separate and discrete; rather, they are interrelated and continuous and cycle upward. . . . As we again turn and face forward toward an uncertain future, assurance [or hope] leads to action and produces evidence, which further increases assurance. Our confidence waxes stronger, line upon line, precept upon precept, here a little and there a little."[12]

THE HELIX OF FAITH
How to increase your faith

Hope (assurance) in something unseen
Action (experiment) and put it to the test
Evidence (results) of your action

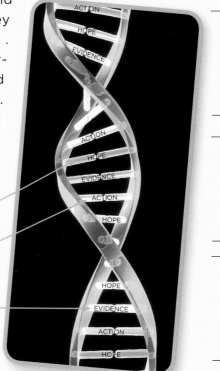

increase in faith

increase in faith

increase in faith

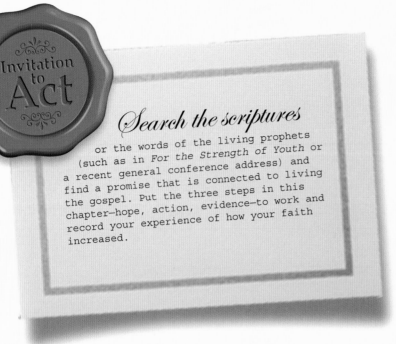

Invitation to Act

Search the scriptures

or the words of the living prophets (such as in *For the Strength of Youth* or a recent general conference address) and find a promise that is connected to living the gospel. Put the three steps in this chapter—hope, action, evidence—to work and record your experience of how your faith increased.

Ultimately faith is a gift that comes from God. As we continue to create *hope* in, take *action* on, and see the *evidence* of the promises of Jesus Christ's atonement and teachings, our faith will grow bit by bit, brighter and brighter until we have a sure knowledge for ourselves. As Alma observed, "Now behold, would not this increase your faith? I say unto you, Yea" (Alma 32:29).

TELL ME ONE MORE TIME!

How Can I Increase My Faith in Jesus Christ?

- **Create hope through hearing the word of God**
- **Take action and experiment upon the word of God**
- **Look for evidence of its truthfulness**

How Can I Break Bad Habits?

Swearing. Complaining. Being critical of others. Losing your temper. Being late. Overeating. Procrastinating your homework. Squeezing the toothpaste tube from the top.

Bad habit #64: There is a lot of toothpaste in the bottom of the tube . . . maybe I should rethink this . . .

DO TRY THIS AT HOME!

Fold your arms. Take a look at how they are folded. Did you fold your left arm over your right arm, or your right arm over your left?

Now, try folding your arms, but put the opposite arm on top than the one you naturally did. How did that feel? How long do you think it would it take before that didn't feel weird anymore and just became natural?

Remember, when breaking a bad habit, you are going to feel a little different at first. Stick with it, and soon enough the positive habit will feel normal and natural.

There are all kinds of bad behaviors that people try to overcome. Most of us have some sort of habit or sin that we have tried to break in our lives—over and over and over again. Yet sometimes we struggle to actually get over it. While squeezing the toothpaste from the top of the tube might not be a big deal, there are bad habits that are sinful in nature. We want to stop repeating our bad behavior—but how can we do it in such a way that we don't start it up again? Elder Richard G. Scott tells us how:

"Suppose a small child were to run in front of your car. What would you do? Careful analysis of each step taken will teach you how to overcome your serious habit:

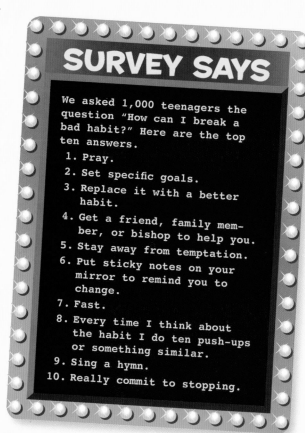

"First your mind decides to stop. Nothing else can happen until that decision is made.

"Then you take your foot off the acccererator. Can you imagine stopping a car with one foot on the accelerator and the other on the brake?

"Finally you firmly apply the brake.

"The same pattern is followed to overcome your entrenched habit. Decide to stop what you are doing that is wrong. Then search out everything in your life that feeds the habit, such as negative thoughts, unwholesome environment, and your companions in mischief. Systematically eliminate or overcome everything that contributes to that negative part of your life. Then stop the negative things permanently."[1]

Decide to Stop

As Elder Scott said, the first thing we can do to change a negative behavior is to decide to stop the bad behavior. And then we must desire to change. Not merely say, "I'd like to change," but seriously decide that change is necessary. One message that is often repeated in the scriptures is what the Lord said to Enos: "I will grant unto thee according to thy desires" (Enos 1:12, see also Alma 29:4–5; D&C 7:8). Notice that it doesn't say, "I will grant unto thee according to thy *wishes*" or "according to thy dreams." Do we *really* desire to change our behavior? Until we see that the benefits of breaking the habit outweigh the gratification that comes from the behavior, we will have little desire to change.

SURVEY SAYS

We asked 1,000 teenagers the question "How can I break a bad habit?" Here are the top ten answers.

1. Pray.
2. Set specific goals.
3. Replace it with a better habit.
4. Get a friend, family member, or bishop to help you.
5. Stay away from temptation.
6. Put sticky notes on your mirror to remind you to change.
7. Fast.
8. Every time I think about the habit I do ten push-ups or something similar.
9. Sing a hymn.
10. Really commit to stopping.

HOW can I learn to control my temper?

Many of the things we'll talk about in this chapter can help you in controlling your temper. But more important than any technique is the understanding that you *can* control whether or not you get angry. President Thomas S. Monson taught, "To be angry is to yield to the influence of Satan. No one can *make* us angry. It is our choice. If we desire to have a proper spirit with us at all times, we must choose to refrain from becoming angry."[2] Perhaps the best way to learn to control our temper is to first understand that nothing can make us angry—it is our choice.

Change the Environment

After we decide to stop a bad habit, Elder Scott tells us to "search out everything in your life that feeds the habit, such as negative thoughts, unwholesome environment, and your companions in mischief."[3] In other words, we need to change the stimulus that prompts the habit. Studying Ivan Pavlov's famous psychology experiment on conditioned responses can help us learn how to break bad habits. Pavlov noticed that dogs began to salivate when those who were to feed them appeared. He predicted that if a stimulus (like ringing a bell) was present when the dogs were given food, then soon the dogs would associate the sound of a bell ringing with getting food. Sure enough, after a few repetitions, the dogs began to salivate when hearing the bell, even if no food was present.[4]

Many of our bad habits are Pavlovian in nature: a conditioned stimulus leads to a conditioned response. When the bell rings, dogs salivate. When we come home, we turn on the television (thus procrastinating our homework). When we hang out with certain friends, we swear or drink. If we can change the environment—change the stimulus (going to the library to study for an hour after school, or changing the group of friends we hang out with)—we will find it easier to change the response and thus, change the habit.

PAVLOV'S DOG AND HABITS

Change the stimulus—change the response!

Make It Difficult to Continue the Bad Habit

Elder Scott mentions another key to help us stop doing bad things: make those bad things difficult to do, or, as he says, "systematically eliminate or overcome everything that contributes to that negative part of your life."[5] For example, if we are trying to eat less candy or sweets, we could put them in a hard-to-reach place.

CHOCOLATE!

One study showed that when chocolates were placed on a worker's desk, that worker would eat more than twice as much chocolate each day compared to when the chocolates were six feet away from the worker's desk.[6]

On desk   Six feet away

The Anti-Nephi-Lehis provide a powerful example of this principle in action. They made a choice to never take another person's life. Notice what they did to make it more difficult for them to change their minds later: "We will hide away our swords, yea, even we will bury them *deep in the earth,* that they may be kept bright, as a testimony that we have never used them, at the last day; and if our brethren destroy us, behold, we shall go to our God and shall be saved" (Alma 24:16; emphasis added).

The weapons were buried *deep in the earth,* or in other words, they were very difficult to access. What would have happened if the Anti-Nephi-Lehis had buried their weapons shallowly in the earth? It might have been much more tempting for them to reach for their weapons when they were faced with opposition. Take a look at how this might be applied to us today:

Bad habit	Bury it shallowly	Bury it deep
Watching bad movies	Hide them under your bed	Dump, delete, discard them
Eating junk food	Put it in the cupboard	Give it away or don't buy it
Visiting bad Internet sites	Decide not to visit them	Install a filter with a password only your parents know

Think for a moment about a bad habit you have. What would it take to bury it deep? Now, go do it!

Get Help from Friends, Leaders, and God

Finally, Elder Scott tells us to "stop the negative [habit] permanently."[7] Seeking help from those around us, and from God, greatly contributes to our ability to stop our habit permanently. There are many different ways we can get others to help us overcome our negative behavior. One approach is to find a friend who is also trying to stop the same habit and work together. Friends can report to each other and set goals together (see chapter 27).

HOW STEEP IS THIS HILL?

The *New York Times* reported on a 2008 study in which students were taken to the base of a steep hill and asked to estimate how steep the hill was. Some students stood by themselves while others had a friend standing by them. Those who had friends standing by them estimated that the hill was less steep than did those students who were standing alone. In other words, having a friend close by made the challenging hill—or for us, the challenging habit to break—appear to be less difficult.[8]

Another powerful key for breaking bad habits completely is to seek heavenly help. Heavenly Father wants to help us overcome the bad habits we have, and the atonement of Jesus Christ can give us the strength to change our habits. Some of us might say, "I can't change!" and we might agree with you! Maybe we *aren't* strong enough to change—by ourselves. However, with the help and power of Jesus Christ, we can change. Elder David A. Bednar taught, "The enabling and strengthening aspect of the Atonement helps us . . . to become good in ways that we could never recognize or accomplish with our limited mortal capacity."[9]

? HOW should I act if I feel that I was "born with" the source of my temptations—if it's just the way I am?

Just because we feel we are born with certain sources of temptation doesn't mean we have to act on those temptations. Elder Dallin H. Oaks taught:

"Perhaps there is an inclination or susceptibility to such feelings that is a reality for some and not a reality for others. But out of such susceptibilities come feelings, and feelings are controllable. If we cater to the feelings, they increase the power of the temptation. If we yield to the temptation, we have committed sinful behavior. That pattern is the same for a person that covets someone else's property and has a strong temptation to steal. . . .

". . . [F]eelings can be controlled and behavior can be controlled. The line of sin is between the feelings and the behavior."[10]

OH, NO! TOOTH DECAY!

Tooth decay isn't pretty. How does one prevent it? By brushing and flossing regularly. But what happens if one slips out of the habit of brushing and flossing? The tooth decay grows and, over time, becomes progressively worse. Simple good habits like brushing and flossing can help prevent tooth decay.

Similarly, simple good habits like sincere prayer and scripture study can help prevent the *spiritual* decay of forming bad habits.

Replace Bad Habits with Good Ones

Fill the empty space with something good before it gets filled back up with junk.

President Boyd K. Packer said, "Do not try merely to *discard* a bad habit or a bad thought. *Replace* it. When you try to eliminate a bad habit, if the spot where it used to be is left open it will sneak back and crawl again into that empty space. . . . When you discard it, fill up the spot where it was. Replace it with something good. Replace it with unselfish thoughts, with unselfish acts. Then, if an evil habit or addiction tries to return, it will have to fight for attention. . . . You are in charge of you. I repeat, it is very, very difficult to eliminate a bad habit just by trying to discard it. Replace it."[11]

IT'LL COST YA!

Another way to break bad habits is to create consequences for yourself. For example, you might have heard of a "Swear Jar" where you put a set amount of money into the jar every time you swear. You can have a similar jar for any kind of habit you're trying to break. If you're trying to stop complaining, you could make a commitment to yourself that every time you complain you'll put a quarter into the jar—and at the end of the month you'll use the money to buy something for someone else.

The consequences don't always have to be negative though. You can also give yourself positive consequences when you make good choices that move you toward breaking your bad habits. For example, if you're trying stop being sarcastic, reward yourself with a treat when you go for two days without making a sarcastic comment.

HOW can I better control my language?

When it comes to changing the words we say, Elder L. Tom Perry offers this suggestion, "If you slip and say a swear word or a substitute word, mentally reconstruct the sentence without the vulgarity or substitute word and repeat the new sentence aloud."[12] So, for example, suppose you're walking and you stub your toe and say a swear word on accident. What should you do? Stop, think about what you could say differently, and then repeat the new sentence out loud. Perhaps, "Ouch. That hurt." ☺ If we consistently do this, Elder Perry tells us, "Eventually you will develop a non-vulgar speech habit."[13]

Study Matthew 4:1-11

(and pay attention to the Joseph Smith Translation in the footnotes). Analyze and highlight how the Savior implemented the following principles in overcoming his temptations:

1. Following the whisperings of the Holy Ghost
2. Fasting
3. Leaving the place of temptation
4. Memorizing scriptures
5. Standing in holy places

How can you apply these same principles to the bad habits you have? Take action!

Invitation to Act

TELL ME ONE MORE TiME!

How Can I Break Bad Habits?

- **Decide to stop**
- **Change the environment**
- **Make it difficult to continue the bad habit**
- **Get help from friends, leaders, and God**
- **Replace bad habits with good ones**

How Can I Really Repent?

A girl is caught stealing from her employer at work. She says she is sorry and pays the money back. Has she repented?

A young man has a problem with viewing pornography online. His parents find out and take away his Internet access, so now he doesn't view it anymore. Has he repented?

A junior high student feels bad about cheating on a test. He knows he needs to tell his teacher and make it right, but he's afraid if he tells her that he'll receive a failing grade. So he decides to wait until he has finished junior high and has been promoted to high school—then he'll go back and tell her. Has he repented?

A girl knows she is being immoral with her boyfriend. She calls her bishop and schedules an interview to talk with him. The day before the meeting with the bishop, the girl does the same thing with her boyfriend one last time. She tells her bishop everything the next day. Has she repented?

A young man sees the bishop and boastfully tells him, "There isn't anything I *haven't* done." Has he repented?

Some may review those situations and think that, yes, some of the people in those scenarios have repented. They confessed, they stopped doing the sin, they felt bad, they met with the bishop—isn't that repentance? Although these may be *parts* of the repentance process, doing them doesn't necessarily mean the person has repented. What is real repentance then? The Bible Dictionary teaches, "[Repentance] denotes a *change* of mind, i.e., a fresh view about God, about oneself, and about the world. . . . Repentance comes to mean a turning of the heart and will to God."[1] In one simple word, repentance is *change*—specifically change toward God through the atonement of Jesus Christ.

"Real repentance goes far beyond simply saying, 'I'm sorry.'"
—Elder Neal A. Maxwell[2]

Repentance Is **CHANGE**

Read Mosiah 27:24–26 about the repentance of Alma the Younger. Highlight in your scriptures all the words that imply *change*: "For, said he, I have repented of my sins, and have been *redeemed* of the Lord; behold I am *born* of the Spirit. And the Lord said unto me: Marvel not that all mankind, yea, men and women, all nations, kindreds, tongues and people, must be *born* again; yea, born of God, *changed* from their carnal and fallen *state,* to a *state* of righteousness, being *redeemed* of God, *becoming* his sons and daughters; And thus they *become new* creatures; and unless they do this, they can in nowise inherit the kingdom of God" (emphasis added).

Sometimes we might think that repentance is like a checklist—the 5 Rs of repentance: recognize, remorse, reveal, restitution, and resolve never to do it again. However, it is possible for someone to follow all of the "R"s in that list and not *change* their hearts. For example, the girl who got caught stealing could recognize she had done wrong, feel remorse because she might lose her job and her reputation, reveal and confess to her employer she took the money, make restitution by paying the money back, and resolve not to steal again. But has she changed her heart from being dishonest and wanting to steal to an honest heart, or is she just trying to save her job? For this reason Elder Neal A. Maxwell said, "Real repentance involves not a mechanical checklist, but a checkreining of the natural self."[3] So how can we really repent and have a change of heart? The following elements of real repentance are taken from the book *True to the Faith*:

- Exercise faith in Heavenly Father and Jesus Christ
- Feel godly sorrow for sin
- Confess sin
- Abandon sin
- Make restitution
- Live righteously

"There can be no real repentance without personal suffering and the passage of sufficient time for the needed cleansing and turning."

—Elder Neal A. Maxwell[4]

BOAT YOUR ROW, ROW, ROW

Try to sing the song "Row, Row, Row Your Boat" backwards. Here are the lyrics:

Dream a but is life
Merrily, merrily, merrily,
Merrily, stream the down gently
Boat your row, row, row

Even though you probably know the song by heart, it was difficult to sing it backwards. Keep practicing it. Remember, repentance is "change," and sometimes change takes time.

DO TRY THIS AT HOME!

Take a permanent marker and put a dot on your hand. Now, you have one minute to get the dot off. Go!

How is this activity like repentance? How is it not?

Exercise Faith in Heavenly Father and Jesus Christ

Elder Richard G. Scott taught, "Formulas have been crafted to help remember some of the essential actions required for full repentance. While these can be helpful, generally they ignore the most fundamental aspect of repentance—that it is centered in Jesus Christ and in His Atonement."[5] We must remember that real repentance is based on faith in the Lord Jesus Christ and his Atonement's ability to pay the price of sin, and cleanse, change, and heal us. As *True to the Faith* says, "Repentance is an act of faith in Jesus Christ—an acknowledgment of the power of His Atonement."[6]

Feel Godly Sorrow for Sin

Notice that this element is sorrow for the sin—not sorrow because we got in trouble, or got hurt, or because of worldly consequences for our poor choices. No, we are sorry because we have offended God, broken his commandments, are no longer worthy of the companionship of the Holy Ghost, and caused suffering for our Savior. This kind of sorrow is called "godly sorrow," which "worketh repentance to salvation" as opposed to "the sorrow of the world" (2 Corinthians 7:10). *True to the Faith* says, "Godly sorrow does not come because of the natural consequences of sin or because of a fear of punishment; rather, it comes from the knowledge that you have displeased your Heavenly Father and your Savior."[8]

? HOW can I know what sins I should repent of?

Elder Neil L. Andersen said, "How do we decide where our repentance should be focused? . . . [H]umbly petition the Lord: 'Father, what wouldst Thou have me do?' The answers come. We feel the changes we need to make. The Lord tells us in our mind and in our heart."[7] Talk to Heavenly Father directly. Ask him what things you should repent of—and listen carefully for answers.

GET REVENGE!

In 2 Corinthians, Paul taught us about what it means to have godly sorrow. He said, "For behold this selfsame thing, that ye sorrowed after a godly sort, (1) what carefulness it wrought in you, yea, (2) what clearing of yourselves, yea, (3) what indignation, yea, (4) what fear, yea, (5) what vehement desire, yea, (6) what zeal, yea, (7) what revenge! (8) In all things ye have approved yourselves to be clear in this matter" (2 Corinthians 7:11; numbering added). Consider what godly sorrow might mean for somebody trying to repent of pornography use. The phrase "what carefulness it wrought in you" could signify that a person with godly sorrow would be extremely careful to stay far away from pornography. "What clearing of yourselves" could imply that the person would completely get rid of anything associated with pornography. But what about the phrase, "What revenge!"? How could a person "get revenge" on the sin of pornography? One way might be for a person to do everything possible to persuade others *not* to participate in that sin. This could be one of the few times it's okay to "get revenge!"

Confess Sin

The Lord said, "Wherefore, I command you again to repent . . . and that you confess your sins" (D&C 19:20). *For the Strength of Youth* says, "You always need to confess your sins to the Lord. You should also confess your sins to those you have wronged. If you have committed serious sins, such as immorality, you need to confess them to your bishop."[9] Your priesthood leader does not forgive your sins, but he can help you to overcome your sins by providing you help, encouragement, and counsel.

HOW can I know when I need to confess sins to the bishop, or just confess them to God?

Even if you don't feel you need your bishop's counsel, remember that your bishop and stake president have been given a divine calling to "serve as watchmen and judges in the Church."[10] Part of a bishop's responsibility as a judge in Israel is determining the worthiness of an individual to participate in gospel ordinances and hold Church callings.

One simple question you could ask yourself is, "Will this sin affect my ability to attend the temple?" For example, sins involving the law of chastity or the Word of Wisdom affect your ability to hold a temple recommend and would need to be confessed to the bishop. In general, if you are wondering if you should confess something to your priesthood leader, it is usually a sign that you should do it. Share your concerns with your bishop. He will help you.

Invitation to Act

If there is a sin that is troubling your mind that you have delayed speaking with your bishop about, put this book down and call him right now. Remember, Satan wants us to think we can hide our sins from God and our priesthood leaders. He does this simply as a deceptive way to keep us from repenting and overcoming the sin. Don't give in to the lies the adversary whispers! Call your bishop and schedule an appointment so you can confess the unresolved sin and begin to overcome it.

"I SHOULD HAVE CONFESSED SOONER"

A young woman named Jessica had been avoiding her bishop for months. She would make up excuses to miss trips to the temple because she didn't want to disappoint her bishop by telling him some of the bad things she had done. She babysat for her bishop a lot, and he thought she was perfect. As the anguish she felt for her sins increased, she decided to confess. To her surprise, her bishop was loving, kind, and understanding. Over a period of time she was able to repent completely and felt good about herself. She said, "I should have confessed sooner." If you're in doubt about whether or not you should confess something to your bishop—just do it!

ARE YOU AN OSTRICH?

Elder Richard G. Scott said, "Do not take comfort in the fact that your transgressions are not known by others. That is like an ostrich with his head buried in the sand. He sees only darkness and feels comfortably hidden. In reality he is ridiculously conspicuous. Likewise our every act is seen by our Father in Heaven and His Beloved Son. They know everything about us. . . .

"If you have seriously transgressed, you will not find any lasting satisfaction or comfort in what you have done. Excusing transgression with a cover-up may appear to fix the problem, but it does not. The tempter is intent on making public your most embarrassing acts at the most harmful time."[11]

Don't be an ostrich by trying to hide your sins!

Abandon Sin

The Lord has said, "By this ye may know if a man repenteth of his sins—behold, he will confess them *and forsake* them" (D&C 58:43; emphasis added). If repentance is change, then it becomes necessary to change our behavior toward righteous living and begin to leave the sinful behavior behind. In the Book of Mormon we read of individuals who "did *forsake* all their sins, and their abominations, and their whoredoms, and did serve God with all diligence day and night" (3 Nephi 5:3; emphasis added).

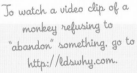

To watch a video clip of a monkey refusing to "abandon" something, go to http://ldswhy.com.

Are You a Monkey?

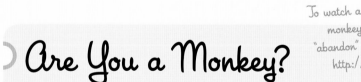

Elder Robert L. Backman of the First Quorum of the Seventy said, "In Africa, the natives have a unique, effective way to capture monkeys. They lop the top off a coconut, remove the meat, and leave a hole in the top of the coconut large enough for the monkey to put his paw in. Then they anchor the coconut to the ground with some peanuts in it. When the natives leave, the monkeys, smelling those delicious peanuts, approach the coconuts, see the peanuts in them, put their paws in to grasp the nuts, and attempt to remove the nuts—but find that the hole is too small for their doubled-up fists. The natives return with gunny sacks and pick up the monkeys—clawing, biting, screaming—but they won't drop the peanuts to save their lives."[12]

Do we ever get caught in monkey traps where we don't want to abandon a certain "favorite" sin, even though we know we should? If so, that sin is preventing us from having a measure of the Lord's Spirit to be with us. The more obedient we are, the more frequently we will have the Holy Ghost with us. If we want to have the Spirit with us in more abundance on a daily basis, we need to repent, abandon the sin, and drop that peanut!

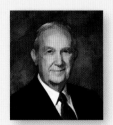

"Do not make the mistake to believe that because you have confessed a serious transgression that you have repented of it. That is an essential step, but it is not all that is required. Nor assume that because someone did not ask you all the important details of a transgression, that you need not mention them. You personally must make sure that the bishop or stake president understands those details so that he can help you properly through the process of repentance for full forgiveness."—Elder Richard G. Scott[13]

Make Restitution

True to the Faith teaches, "You must restore as far as possible all that has been damaged by your actions, whether that is someone's property or someone's good reputation. Willing restitution shows the Lord that you will do all you can to repent."[14] Moses taught, "If fire break out, and catch in thorns, so that the stacks of corn, or the standing corn, or the field, be consumed therewith; he that kindled the fire shall surely make restitution" (Exodus 22:6).

Some sins are so serious that we often can't make restitution, like sins of immorality. Elder Neal A. Maxwell taught a great principle connected to this idea: "Sometimes, however, restitution is not possible in real terms, such as when one contributed to another's loss of faith or virtue. Instead, a *subsequent example of righteousness provides a compensatory form of restitution.*"[15]

A SATANIC SUCKER PUNCH . . . HOW LONG WILL IT TAKE TO REPENT?

Depending on the seriousness of the sin, repentance may take time—but in at least one sense of the word "repentance," we can repent very quickly. Elder Jeffrey R. Holland, then the Commissioner of the Church Education System, said, "You can change anything you want to change, and you can do it very fast. That's another satanic sucker punch—that it takes years and years and eons of eternity to repent. It takes exactly as long to repent as it takes you to say, 'I'll change'—and mean it. Of course there will be problems to work out and restitutions to make. . . . But change, growth, renewal, and repentance can come for you as instantaneously as for Alma and the Sons of Mosiah."[16]

Repentance MATH

If one person commits five small sins a day for seventy years that would be about 127,750 sins. Multiply that by say, 200 people in your ward, that equals 25,550,000 sins. If there are ten wards in your stake, that's more than two hundred and fifty-five million sins, just in your stake! The great news is that the Savior atoned for *all* of those sins—and every other sin in the world. He simply invites us to repent (see D&C 19:15-19).

HOW *does repentance apply to me if I haven't done anything that bad?*

Sometimes we may think that we are pretty good and that because we aren't major sinners that we do not need repentance as much as other people. This is not true for two reasons. First, everybody needs to repent because everyone commits sin (see Romans 3:23). Everyone needs to be covered and cleansed by Christ, no matter how serious the sin, because nobody is perfect (see Matthew 5:48). The good news is that as we repent and come unto Christ, he will perfect us and free us from all our sins, whether large or small. Second, if we keep in mind that repentance means to change and become more like God[17] then, as Elder Marvin J. Ashton pointed out, "daily repentance is needed for progress."[18] Every improvement we make, every time we conquer a bad habit, every good attribute we develop is a type of repentance. Elder Neal A. Maxwell said, "Repentance . . . is available to the gross sinner as well as to the already-good individual striving for incremental improvement."[19] We not only need the Atonement to cover and cleanse us from sin, but the atoning grace of Jesus Christ will strengthen us to do good works as we try to become better each day through repentance.

THERE IS A DIFFERENCE BETWEEN AN HONEST MISTAKE AND COMMITTING A SIN

Have you ever done something wrong that you didn't really know was wrong? For example, imagine that there is a commandment that you shouldn't look at pictures of dogs dressed up like cheerleaders. Ah, man! Most of us just broke a commandment and didn't mean to! (Please note: there is no such commandment, just to be clear. ☺)

There is a difference between *sinning* and making an honest or ignorant mistake. The scriptures tell us that a *sin* is when we know a commandment and we purposefully choose not to follow it out of willful rebellion (see 3 Nephi 6:18; Mosiah 2:36-37; 16:5). On the other hand, an honest mistake or error—although it still violates a commandment—usually does not require the same type of repentance as a willful sin. Notice how the Lord expresses the difference between error and sin in these verses: "And inasmuch as they erred it might be made known; . . . And inasmuch as they sinned they might be chastened, that they might repent" (D&C 1:25-27).

Remember, the Savior is so good, kind, and merciful that he doesn't hold people accountable who don't know or really understand that they are violating his commandments (see 2 Nephi 9:25; Moroni 8:22). It is when we willfully rebel and do things we know we shouldn't be doing that we sin and therefore need to repent.

Live Righteously

President Spencer W. Kimball taught, "Repentance must involve an all-out, total surrender to the program of the Lord. That transgressor is not fully repentant who neglects his tithing, misses his meetings, breaks the Sabbath, fails in his family prayers, does not sustain the authorities of the Church, breaks the Word of Wisdom, does not love the Lord nor his fellowmen. A reforming adulterer who drinks or curses is not repentant. The repenting burglar who [is immoral] is not ready for forgiveness. God cannot forgive unless the transgressor shows a true repentance which spreads to all areas of his life."[20] Elder Richard G. Scott taught that true repentance "includes things you might not initially consider part of repentance, such as attending meetings, paying tithing, giving service, and forgiving others."[21]

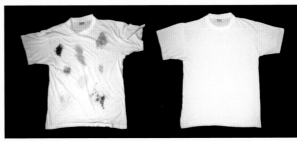

Through real repentance, the stains of sin can be cleansed and we can be pure again.

The great news of the gospel is that as we exercise our faith in Jesus Christ and implement these elements of repentance, "though [our] sins be as scarlet, they shall be as white as snow" (Isaiah 1:18). The Lord has promised, "He who has repented of his sins, the same is forgiven, and I, the Lord, remember them no more" (D&C 58:42). Repentance is a great blessing in our lives. We testify that through the atonement of Jesus Christ and our real repentance, we truly can be forgiven.

TELL ME ONE MORE TIME!

How Can I Really Repent?

- **Exercise faith in Heavenly Father and Jesus Christ**
- **Feel godly sorrow for sin**
- **Confess sin**
- **Abandon sin**
- **Make restitution**
- **Live righteously**

How Can I Know When I've Been Forgiven?

What do a pile of stones and tearing a roof apart have to do with each other?

Both of them are connected to one of the greatest miracles Jesus performed in his lifetime—and still performs today: *the miracle of forgiveness.*

To a woman about to be stoned for her sins, the Lord rebuked her accusers and told the woman, "Hath no man condemned thee? . . . Neither do I condemn thee: go, and sin no more" (John 8:10–11). On another occasion, Jesus was in a house and the friends of a sick man broke up the roof in order to get their friend to him, and "when Jesus saw their faith, he said unto the sick of the palsy, Son, thy sins be forgiven thee" (Mark 2:5).

One of the greatest blessings in the entire gospel is that through the Atonement of Jesus Christ we too can be forgiven of the sins and mistakes in our lives. Doctrine and Covenants 58:42 states, "Behold, he who has repented of his sins, the same is forgiven, and I, the Lord, remember them no more."

However, even after we have truly repented (see chapter 3), sometimes we are left wondering: "Have I actually been forgiven?" Here are a few principles that teach us how we can know when the miracle of forgiveness has taken place in our lives, just as it did for those in Jesus' time.

We Have Peace of Mind

Elder F. Burton Howard of the First Quorum of the Seventy counseled with a young man through the repentance process. The young man asked, "'How can I ever know the Lord has really forgiven me?'

"'That is the easy part,' [Elder Howard] replied. 'When you have fully repented, *you feel an inner peace.* You know somehow you are forgiven because the burden you have carried for so long, all of a sudden isn't there anymore. It is *gone* and *you know* it is gone. . . .

"'I wouldn't be surprised,' [Elder Howard] said, 'if when you leave this room, you discover that you have left much of your concern in here. If you have fully repented, the relief and the peace you feel will be so noticeable that it will be a witness to you that the Lord has forgiven you.'"[1]

Another form of this peace of mind is peace of conscience. *For the Strength of Youth* puts it this way: "When you do what is necessary to receive forgiveness, . . . [y]ou will feel the peace of the Lord Jesus Christ."[2]

HOW can I enjoy the blessings of forgiveness if I still remember my sins?

Some mistakenly think that just because they can still remember their sins, they haven't been forgiven. This isn't true. Elder Jeffrey R. Holland had this to say about remembering our sins: "You can remember just enough to avoid repeating the mistake."[3] The scriptures say that the Lord will remember our sins no more (D&C 58:42), not that we won't!

WORLD PEACE? FIND INNER PEACE FIRST

It is a cliché that pageant contestants say they want world peace for our society. However, as the Dalai Lama said, "We can never obtain peace in the world if we neglect the inner world and don't make peace with ourselves. World peace must develop out of inner peace."[4]

Finding inner peace through repentance and forgiveness can be the first step we all can take toward establishing world peace.

World peace!

The Sin Has Lost Its Appeal

One key to knowing if we have been forgiven is that we have lost the desire to commit the sin we have repented of. We may still be *tempted* to commit that sin, but now we don't *want* to commit that sin—we don't desire it anymore. When King Benjamin's people were moved to repentance they said, "we have no more disposition to do evil, but to do good continually" (Mosiah 5:2). They had lost their *desire* to sin. Alma taught, "Now they, after being sanctified by the Holy Ghost, having their garments made white, being pure and spotless before God, *could not look upon sin save it were with abhorrence"* (Alma 13:12; emphasis added). When the sin begins to lose its appeal, we begin to find forgiveness.

abhorrence (ab-hor-rence): to loathe or hate.

DOES THIS LOOK APPEALING TO YOU?

When we begin to lose the desire for our sins on the same level that we don't desire a fly in our soup, then we can know we are on the path to being forgiven.

We Enjoy the Gift of the Holy Ghost and Fruits of the Spirit

One of the roles of the Holy Ghost is to sanctify, or purify, us of sin. Christ taught the Nephites that we are "sanctified by the reception of the Holy Ghost" (3 Nephi 27:20). If we are enjoying the gifts of the Holy Ghost, then we generally are enjoying the gift of forgiveness as well because the Holy Ghost cleanses, sanctifies, and purifies us. Similarly, President Henry B.

WATER ON YOUR BACK

Imagine that you are on your hands and knees with several cups of water on your back and legs. How could you stand up without getting wet? The answer is, you probably can't—on your own. When it comes to being forgiven we must understand that it is a gift from Jesus Christ. Symbolically speaking, he will take away those cups of water and give us the strength to stand on our feet.

Eyring taught, "Reception of the Holy Ghost is the cleansing agent as the Atonement purifies you. . . . That is a fact you can act on with confidence. . . . And when he is your companion, you can have confidence that the Atonement is working in your life."[5]

DO TRY THIS AT HOME!

Do you think we have been commanded to forgive others for *their* benefit? Think again. This activity might help you see why: Pick up a large, heavy object like a book (or a chair if you are feeling really tough!). Carry it around with you for a while. Try to do some simple tasks while holding on to it, like tying your shoe. You can't set down the object at any time, or rest it on anything. You need to hold on to it and carry it all the time!

Do you want to set it down yet? We thought so.

Now read Doctrine and Covenants 64:9–11 and ask yourself: Why does the Lord command us to forgive others? It is usually not until we "let go," forgive, and "put down" our grudges that we can move on with our lives. The commandment to forgive is just as much for our benefit as it is for others. When we forgive, we let go of a burden and feel greater peace.

"Your Sins Are Forgiven You"

Over and over in the scriptures, the Lord tells people, "Your sins are forgiven you" (see D&C 36:1). As a matter of fact, the phrase "sins are forgiven" appears in the scriptures *fifteen different times*. Truly, the Lord is willing and able "to make you holy, and your sins are forgiven you" (D&C 60:7).

We Are Willing to Forgive Others

Another key to knowing if we have truly enjoyed the gift of forgiveness is that we are willing to extend forgiveness to others. The Savior stated on multiple occasions "for if ye forgive men their trespasses, your heavenly Father will also forgive you" (Matthew 6:14; see also D&C 64:9–10; Ephesians 4:32). To be forgiven, we must forgive.

HOW can I forgive others if they aren't sorry for what they've done?

Our willingness to forgive others should not depend on whether or not they forgive us. President Gordon B. Hinckley shared the story of a woman who was driving her car when a young man threw a frozen turkey that smashed into her windshield. As a result, the woman had to undergo hours of surgery and learned that it would take years of physical therapy to return to normal. But she frankly forgave the young man who had injured her and worked to reduce the penalties he would face.[6] One lesson we can gain from this story is that we can forgive others—even if they have done terrible things to us. Whether or not they are sorry does not really matter.

Invitation to Act

Read the parable of the unmerciful servant in Matthew 18:23–35. After reading that parable, if there is someone that you are holding a grudge against or if you are withholding forgiveness for some reason, speak to the Lord or speak to the person about it and begin to forgive them.

HOW FORGIVING AM I?

Forgiving others means more than just accepting an apology or saying, "It's okay." Here are a few questions to ask ourselves to see how forgiving we might be:

1. Do I ever say, "I will forgive, but never forget?"

2. Am I ever secretly happy when something unfortunate happens to someone I don't like?

3. Do I try to "get even" with people for something they have done to me?

4. Is there anyone with whom I refuse to speak?

5. In arguments, do I bring up things that others have done in the past?

6. When I disagree or get angry with someone, do I sulk and pout and take a few days to get over it?

7. Do I talk unkindly to others about someone who has hurt or offended me?

8. Do I ever justify my grudges by rationalizing, "If they would say they are sorry, then I would forgive them"?

9. When someone does apologize to me, do I ever think or say, "It'll take more than just words to make it right"?

10. When I hear a certain person's name, do I still feel bitterness or anger inside?

Our Priesthood Leader Says We Are Worthy to Participate in Gospel Ordinances

For the Strength of Youth points to the critical role bishops play in knowing when we are forgiven: "Talk with your bishop. He will help you obtain the forgiveness available to those who truly repent."[7] To be clear, bishops do not forgive us. Only the Lord can forgive sins. However, the bishop acts as the Lord's agent and as a judge in Israel. Specifically, he has the authority to judge when we are worthy to participate in gospel ordinances. When a bishop judges us worthy to participate in gospel ordinances after we have repented, we can know that the Lord has freed us from the guilt of our sin. Elder Richard G. Scott said, "I testify that when a bishop or stake president has confirmed that your repentance is sufficient, know that your obedience has allowed the Atonement of Jesus Christ to satisfy the demands of justice for the laws you have broken. Therefore you are now free. Please believe it."[8]

We Are Willing to Keep *All* the Commandments

The scriptures teach us that another indicator that we have been forgiven of a particular sin is that we are willing to keep *all* the commandments, not just the one we have broken: "Nevertheless, he that repents and *does the commandments* [note the plural] of the Lord shall be forgiven" (D&C 1:32; emphasis added; see also Mosiah 5:5). When President Henry B. Eyring was a bishop, a young man asked him how he could know if he had been fully forgiven. Bishop Eyring later saw Elder Spencer W. Kimball (who was then a member of the Quorum of the Twelve), and asked him how the young man could receive revelation to let him know if he had been forgiven. The following transcript is President Henry B. Eyring's account of what transpired:

"I thought Elder Kimball would talk to me about fasting or prayer or listening for the still small voice. But he surprised me. Instead he said, 'Tell me something about the young man.'

"I said, 'What would you like to know?'

"And then he began a series of the most simple questions. Some of the ones I remember were:

"'Does he come to his priesthood meetings?'

"I said, after a moment's thought, 'Yes.'

"'Does he come early?'

"'Yes.'

"'Does he sit down front?'

"I thought for a moment and then realized, to my amazement, that he did.

"'Does he home teach?'

"'Yes.'

"'Does he go early in the month?'

"'Yes, he does.'

"'Does he go more than once?'

"'Yes.'

"I can't remember the other questions. But they were all like that—little things, simple acts of obedience, of submission. And for each question I was surprised that my answer was always yes. Yes, he wasn't just at all his meetings: he was early; he was smiling; he was there not only with his whole heart, but the broken heart of a little child, as he was every time the Lord asked anything of him. And after I had said yes to each of his questions, Elder Kimball looked at me, paused, and then very quietly said, 'There is your revelation.'"[9]

If we are alive with an all-around righteous life, then the guilt of a specific sin may be dying.

As we see these principles of forgiveness working in our lives, they will become indicators that we have been forgiven. We can experience what Enos felt when he said, "And there came a voice unto me, saying: Enos, thy sins are forgiven thee, and thou shalt be blessed. And I, Enos, knew that God could not lie; wherefore, my guilt was swept away" (Enos 1:5–6).

TELL ME ONE MORE TIME!

How Can I Know When I've Been Forgiven?

- **We have peace of mind.**
- **The sin has lost its appeal.**
- **We enjoy the gift of the Holy Ghost and fruits of the Spirit.**
- **We are willing to forgive others.**
- **Our priesthood leader says we are worthy to participate in gospel ordinances.**
- **We are willing to keep *all* the commandments.**

How Can I Make the Temple a More Important Part of My Life?

Sister Anne C. Pingree shared the following story that illustrates how strongly some Latter-day Saints felt about the temple. She said:

"I will never forget a sauna-hot day in the lush rain forest of south-eastern Nigeria. My husband and I had traveled to one of the most remote locations in our mission so

Guess that **TEMPLE!**

London, England

he could conduct temple recommend interviews with members in the Ikot Eyo district. Some in this growing district had been Church members less than two years. All the members lived 3,000 miles away from the nearest temple in Johannesburg, South Africa. None had received their temple endowment.

"These members knew the appointed day each month we would come to their district, but even we didn't know the exact hour we would arrive; nor could we call, for telephones were rare in that part of West Africa. So these committed African Saints gathered early in the morning to wait all day if necessary for their temple recommend interviews . . .

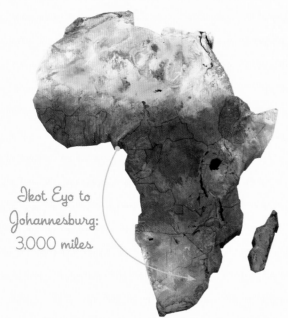

Ikot Eyo to Johannesburg: 3,000 miles

"Many hours later, after all the interviews were completed, as my husband and I drove back along that sandy jungle trail, we were stunned when we saw . . . two sisters still walking. We realized they had trekked from their village—a distance of eighteen miles round-trip—just to obtain a temple recommend they knew they would never have the privilege of using."[1]

It is clear that those two women felt strongly about the importance of the temple. Even though they probably knew they would never have the opportunity to use their temple recommend, they wanted to be worthy of it. How can we be more like these Saints and have the temple become a more important part of our lives?

DO TRY THIS AT HOME!

What does this address mean?

800 East 7400 South
Midvale, Utah

If you were in downtown Salt Lake City, and you told me your address was 800 East and 7400 South, what are you 8 blocks east and 74 blocks south of?

Read Mosiah 2:5-6 or Numbers 2 to figure it out.

Answer: Most addresses in the Salt Lake Valley are based on their location relative to the Salt Lake Temple. In other words, the address above is 8 blocks east and 74 blocks south of the Salt Lake Temple. Every time someone writes a Salt Lake City address it shows the temple is the center of the city!

Guess that TEMPLE!

Montréal, Québec

Be Worthy of a Temple Recommend

One of the first things we can do to make the temple more important in our lives is to be worthy of a temple recommend. President Howard W. Hunter said, "It would be the deepest desire of my heart to have every member of the Church temple worthy. I would hope that every adult member would be worthy of—and carry—a current temple recommend, even if proximity to a temple does not allow immediate or frequent use of it."[2]

What Does It Take to Be Worthy of a Temple Recommend?

The *Gospel Principles* manual says we are asked questions like the following in an interview for a temple recommend:

"1. Do you have faith in and a testimony of God the Eternal Father; His Son Jesus Christ; and the Holy Ghost? Do you have a firm testimony of the restored gospel?

"2. Do you sustain the President of The Church of Jesus Christ of Latter-day Saints as the prophet, seer, and revelator? Do you recognize him as the only person on earth authorized to exercise all priesthood keys?

"3. Do you live the law of chastity?

"4. Are you a full-tithe payer?

"5. Do you keep the Word of Wisdom?

"6. Are you honest in your dealings with others?

"7. Do you strive to keep the covenants you have made, to attend your sacrament and priesthood meetings, and to keep your life in harmony with the laws and commandments of the gospel?"[3]

In addition, President Dieter F. Uchtdorf has pointed out, "The standards set by the Lord in the temple recommend questions are very similar to the standards found in *For the Strength of Youth*."[4]

If the temple is an important part of our lives, we should be worthy to be there. President Howard W. Hunter also taught, "The things that we must do and not do to be worthy of a temple recommend are the very things that ensure we will be happy as individuals and as families."[5]

SET THE PRISONERS FREE!

Joseph Smith taught, "Every man that has been baptized and belongs to the kingdom has a right to be baptized for those who have gone before; and *as soon as the law of the Gospel is obeyed here by their friends who act as proxy for them, the Lord has administrators there to set them free.*"[11] When you go to the temple to perform temple ordinances for the dead you may be literally setting people free from bondage.

HOW can the temple give me increased power?

Here are a few ways the temple can endow (or give) us power:

1. "The power of enlightenment, of testimony, and of understanding."[6]
2. "Power [to] thwart the forces of evil."[7]
3. "Power which enables us to use our gifts and capabilities with greater intelligence and increased effectiveness."[8]
4. "Power to overcome the sins of the world and 'stand in holy places' (D&C 45:32)."[9]
5. "Greater powers that [we] might be better qualified to teach."[10]
6. "Power with which to strengthen [our] earthly families."[12]
7. "The promised personal revelation that may bless [our] life with power, knowledge, light, beauty, and truth from on high."[13]

Go to the Temple More Often

One of the most obvious things we can do to make the temple a more important part of our lives is to go to the temple. President Howard W. Hunter said, "We should hasten to the temple as frequently, yet prudently, as our personal circumstances allow."[14]

On March 11, 2003, the First Presidency issued a letter saying, "Where time and circumstances permit, members are encouraged to replace some leisure activities with temple service. . . . We particularly encourage newer members and youth of the Church who are 12 years of age and older to live worthy to assist in this great work by serving as proxies for baptisms and confirmations."[15]

Guess that TEMPLE!

Ciudad Juárez, Mexico

John Says:

I grew up in Seattle and lived about twenty minutes from the Seattle Temple. I went to the temple on trips with my ward, but never went by myself. Honestly, the idea never even occurred to me. When I started teaching seminary in Spanish Fork, Utah (about twenty minutes from the Provo Utah Temple), I was really surprised when some of my students told me that they had gone to the temple early that morning. "Did you have a ward temple trip?" I asked.

"No," they told me. "We just go to the temple before school sometimes." I was so impressed with their dedication, and I realized that I could have gone to the temple more frequently as a youth.

Not all temples allow you to just walk in and do baptisms for the dead any time you want. But the temple closest to you might. Ask your parents or church leaders what the rules of your closest temple are. It's almost certain they will let you schedule a personal or family appointment to do baptisms for the dead if you bring the names of your own ancestors! (Keep reading to learn more about that.)

Our actions speak louder than our words. When we sacrifice some of our casual or free entertainment time to go to the temple, we are showing the Lord how important the temple is in our lives. After Abraham showed the Lord through his actions that God was the most important thing in his life, even above the life of his own precious son Isaac, the Lord said, "Now I know that thou fearest God, seeing thou hast not withheld thy son, thine only son from me" (Genesis 22:12). Similarly, if we give of some more of our free time to attend the temple, we will show the Lord through our actions that we love his holy house more than other things.

MAKE A TEMPLE GROUP WITH YOUR FRIENDS

Many youth are part of a temple group that attends the temple on a set day each week or month. This picture is from a group of teenagers who gather together after school each Wednesday to go do baptisms for the dead.

These youth said that having a temple group to go with has made the temple more important in their lives because they go more often: "It's easier to go when you have a group and everyone's there encouraging you to go."

Guess that TEMPLE!

St. George, Utah

Search Out Your Ancestors and Perform Temple Work for Them

President Howard W. Hunter wrote, "The dead are anxiously waiting for the Latter-day Saints to search out their names and then go into the temples to officiate in their behalf, that they may be liberated from their prison house in the spirit world. *All* of us should find joy in this magnificent labor of love."[16]

Notice the word *all* in that quote. Sometimes we think that doing family history is a work for old people—but it is a work for everyone. Especially now that the Church has created http://new.familysearch.org it may be that family history becomes a work for tech-savvy teenagers. This website allows you to more easily figure out who your ancestors are, and which ones need to have their baptisms performed by proxy (that's you!).

Invitation to Act

Log on to

http://new.familysearch.org. You'll need your membership number—it's on your patriachal blessing, or you can get it from your ward clerk. Spend some time studying who your ancestors were. How far back does your history go? Find out if any of your ancestors need temple work done. If so, use the website to prepare their names for the temple. If you need help, ask a family history consultant in your ward!

"Let us prepare every missionary to go to the temple worthily and to make that experience an even greater highlight than receiving the mission call."—President Howard W. Hunter[17]

Learn All You Can about Temples

One factor to increasing our desire to attend the temple is to better understand its meaning and purposes. We highly recommend reading a short booklet printed by the Church entitled *Preparing to Enter the Holy Temple*.[18] Also, study the promises made about temple worship in Doctrine and Covenants 109.

PREPARING TO ENTER THE HOLY TEMPLE

HOW can attending the temple help me receive answers to my problems?

President Ezra Taft Benson taught, "In the peace of these lovely temples, sometimes we find solutions to the serious problems of life. Under the influence of the Spirit, sometimes pure knowledge flows to us there. Temples are places of personal revelation.

When I have been weighed down by a problem or a difficulty, I have gone to the house of the Lord with a prayer in my heart for answers. These answers have come in clear and unmistakable ways."[19] Go to the temple with questions—you will find answers.

CASTLES AND TEMPLES

Have you ever noticed that some of the early temples look like castles? The Salt Lake Temple even has "battlements" on its roof (the place where archers would hide behind to shoot their bows and arrows). Now, why would they design it like that? Did Brigham Young really intend for archers to sit on top of the temple and shoot arrows? Probably not. Think of all the possible meanings about how a temple is similar to a castle:

_____

_____

_____

Here are a few of many possible analogies to temples and castles:
• They both are places of protection
• Inside them are found royalty—future kings and queens

When You Are in the Temple, Focus on the Work You Are Doing

We can do small things while in the temple that will help us focus and gain more from the experience, and thus make the temple a more important part of our lives.

For example, as you are being baptized or confirmed for another person, try to imagine that this person was a close friend. Don't just go through the motions of being baptized for a bunch of people—consider each one as an individual child of God with infinite worth—for that is who they are. If possible, learn the names of the people for whom you are being baptized. Take the time to look at the year in which they lived and where they are from. Getting to know these people as best you can will make the temple experience more powerful. As Elder Richard G.

Scott suggested, "Be mindful of the individual for whom you are performing the vicarious ordinance. At times pray that he or she will recognize the vital importance of the ordinances and be worthy or prepare to be worthy to benefit from them."[20]

Consider this—when the person baptizing you states the name of the person you are being baptized for, it might be the first time in hundreds of years that that person's name has been said out loud on the earth. It is a sacred moment for that person, who may, in fact, be present for the ordinance. Do everything you can to make it sacred for him or her.

WATCH YOUR WATCH

Follow Elder Richard G. Scott's counsel to "remove your watch when you enter a house of the Lord."[21] Doing so can help you stay focused on the temple ordinances and forget the world a little more.

REMEMBER: THOSE IN THE SPIRIT WORLD ARE ALIVE!

Elder W. Grant Bangerter of the Seventy said, "May we always remember that we perform the temple ordinances for people and not for names. Those we call 'the dead' are alive in the spirit and are present in the temple."[22]

Won't it be neat to perhaps meet the people we performed temple ordinances for in the next life?

Put the Temple Where You Can See It!

A great way to have the temple be a more important part of your life is to look at temples more often. You could put a picture of the temple in your bedroom, car, or locker—even on your cell phone!

Guess that TEMPLE!

Mesa, Arizona

At the beginning of this chapter we shared an experience from Sister Pingree that illustrated the dedication some African Saints had to the temple. We conclude with an account of Elder Jeffrey R. Holland where he describes how some faithful Saints in South America showed their dedication to the temple. He said,

"The Punta Arenas Chile Stake is the Church's southernmost stake anywhere on this planet, its outermost borders stretching toward Antarctica. Any stake farther south would have to be staffed by penguins. For the Punta Arenas Saints it is a 4,200-mile round-trip bus ride to the Santiago temple. For a husband and wife it can take up to 20 percent of an annual local income just for the transportation alone. Only 50 people can be accommodated on the bus, but for every excursion 250 others come out to hold a brief service with them the morning of their departure.

"Pause for a minute and ask yourself when was the last time you stood on a cold, windswept parking lot adjacent to the Strait of Magellan just to sing with, pray for, and cheer on their way those who were going to the temple, hoping your savings would allow you to go next time? One hundred ten hours, 70 of those on dusty, bumpy, unfinished roads looping out through Argentina's wild Patagonia."[23]

We may not need to walk eighteen miles to get a temple recommend, or take a 110-hour bus ride to get to the temple—but the Lord still expects us to give the temple the high importance that it deserves. May we follow the counsel of President Howard W. Hunter and make the temple "our ultimate earthly goal and the supreme mortal experience."[24]

TELL ME ONE MORE TIME!

How Can I Make the Temple a More Important Part of My Life?

- **Be worthy of a temple recommend.**
- **Go to the temple more often.**
- **Search out your ancestors and perform temple work for them.**
- **When you are in the temple, focus on the work you are doing.**

How Can I Prepare for an Eternal Marriage?

If you had to marry somebody right now, and you had to choose one of the following three people, whom would you choose to marry?

A. Somebody who is physically attractive, but only semi-active in the Church

B. Somebody who is rich, but totally inactive in Church

C. Somebody who is worthy of a temple recommend

We hope this wasn't a difficult question to answer. If you care a lot about wealth, you probably picked B. If you're the kind of person who wants to get married in the temple, you probably picked C. The principle this scenario illustrates is that *we are generally attracted to, and attract the same kind of person that we are.* Notice that principle in the following verse:

"For intelligence cleaveth unto intelligence; wisdom receiveth wisdom; truth embraceth truth; virtue loveth virtue; light cleaveth unto light; mercy hath compassion on mercy and claimeth her own; justice continueth its course and claimeth its own" (D&C 88:40).

Intelligence cleaveth unto (sticks to) intelligence: If you love books and learning you probably will be attracted to someone who values education. Truth embraces truth: A lover of truth will probably be interested in an honest individual. Virtue (goodness) loves virtue: If you are a virtuous person, you

Kids' thoughts on love and why it happens between two particular people:

- "No one is sure why it happens, but I heard it has something to do with how you smell. That's why perfume and deodorant are so popular." (Jan, age 9)

- "I think you're supposed to get shot with an arrow or something, but the rest of it isn't supposed to be so painful." (Harlen, age 8)[1]

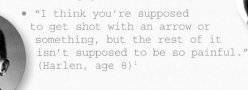

likely desire to marry someone who is morally clean and lives a virtuous life. *Like attracts like.* This truth leads us to one of the first principles in preparing for an eternal marriage.

DO TRY THIS AT HOME!

Pretend that there has just been some catastrophic disaster and that the only people who have survived on earth are your period 1 class at school. If the human race is to continue, you must marry someone in this class! Without saying a word, think whom you would marry if you had to. Now that you have someone in mind, or have rejected everyone in the entire class and decided the solitary life is better than anyone in period 1, ask yourself this question: what were the criteria or standards you used to make your marriage decision? What made you say, "no . . . no . . . hmm . . . maybe . . . definitely no . . ." etc.? Were you choosing based on looks? Hygiene? Money? Righteousness? Humor? Mentally evaluate what your criteria were, as it usually reveals what you are truly prioritizing as most important in a future spouse, and therefore what you are as a person (light cleaves to light, remember?).

Be the Kind of Person You Want to Marry

Please don't misunderstand this first principle. It is not saying that a person has to marry somebody who is *exactly* the same as they are. If Marie likes to watch movies and Nathan prefers to read, they can still have a happy marriage. However, most likely we will marry somebody who has the same *qualities of character* and the same priorities that we have. Therefore, if we usually attract somebody who has the same character we have, *we must make sure that we have the right attributes that will lead to a successful eternal marriage.*

Elder David A. Bednar said that he is frequently asked by young adults what characteristics they should look for in a future spouse. It seems as though these youth are creating lists of all the attributes they hope to find in a future spouse.

He said that he responds to these questions by saying, "If there are three primary characteristics that I hope to find in an eternal companion then those are the three things I ought to be working to become. Then it will be attractive to someone who has those things. So my advice is: you're not on a shopping spree looking for the greatest value with a series of characteristics. You become what you hope your spouse will be, and you'll have a greater likelihood of finding that person."[3]

If we want to marry somebody who puts a high

Kids' thoughts on what people do on dates:

- "Dates are for having fun, and people should use them to get to know each other. Even boys have something to say if you listen long enough." (Lynette, age 8)

- "On the first date, they just tell each other lies, and that usually gets them interested enough to go for a second date." (Mike, age 10)[2]

priority on daily scripture study, then we need to have a high priority on scripture study. If we want to marry somebody who loves children, then *we* need to love children. If we want to marry somebody who puts family first, we need to put family first.

The beauty of this principle is that it gives us something to focus on that is in our control. Young women may not be able to control how many guys ask them out on dates, but they do determine the kind of person they become. A young man can't make a certain young woman like him, but he does control the type of person he is. We can prepare for an eternal marriage by becoming today the kind of person we want to marry in the future.

HOW can I know if the person I like is my "soul mate"?

We hate to break it to all of you hopeless romantics, but the idea of a "soul mate" (one person and one person only on this earth you are destined to marry) is misleading. President Kimball taught, "'Soul-mates' are fiction and an illusion."[4]

President Dieter F. Uchtdorf said, "I know this may be a disappointment for some of you, but I don't believe there is only one right person for you. I think I fell in love with my wife, Harriet, from the first moment I saw her. Nevertheless, had she decided to marry someone else, I believe I would have met and fallen in love with someone else. I am eternally grateful that this didn't happen, but I don't believe she was my one chance at happiness in this life, nor was I hers."[5]

President Boyd K. Packer said: "While I am sure some young couples have some special guidance in getting together, I do not believe in predestined love. If you desire the inspiration of the Lord in this crucial decision, you must live the standards of the Church, and you must pray constantly for the wisdom to recognize those qualities upon which a successful union may be based. You must do the choosing, rather than to seek for some one-and-only so-called soul mate, chosen for you by someone else and waiting for you. You are to do the choosing."[6]

PREPARE FOR ETERNAL MARRIAGE BY GRADUATING FROM SEMINARY AND INSTITUTE!

"The percent of temple marriages among the graduates of seminaries and institutes is *more than double* the Church average. . . . Do you need any better endorsement than that?"
—President Boyd K. Packer[7]

Learn to Be Selfless

The greatest factor in a happy marriage is . . .

So your sister wants to borrow your favorite shirt? If you want a happy marriage in the future, maybe you should let her. What? Don't think sharing shirts and preparing for an eternal marriage are related? Think again. President Gordon B. Hinckley observed, "I have long felt that the greatest factor in a happy marriage is an anxious concern for the comfort and well-being of one's companion. In most cases selfishness is the leading factor that causes argument, separation, divorce, and broken hearts."[8]

One of the greatest things we can do right now to prepare for a successful future marriage is to learn how to be more selfless—how to place the needs of others above our own. Practicing this in our current family will help us create a successful future family.

Anthony Answers: WHAT IS LOVE?

One of the *many* things that attracted me to my wife was a conversation we had right when we began dating. Like all romantics, I asked her what she felt her definition of "love" was. Without hesitation, she answered, "sacrifice." It reminded me of the Savior's definition of true love: "Greater love hath no man than this, that a man lay down his life for his friends" (John 15:13). I attribute much of the happiness in our marriage to the fact that my wife had learned—in her youth—that true love was placing the needs of others above our own.

Stay Morally Clean

Another way we can prepare for an eternal marriage is to stay morally clean. President Ezra Taft Benson promised, "When we . . . keep ourselves morally clean, we will experience the blessings of increased love and peace, greater trust and respect for our marital partners, deeper commitment to each other, and therefore a deep and significant sense of joy and happiness."[9]

For example, James faced temptations as a young man to violate the law of chastity. Instead he trusted in the counsel and promise of Church leaders that staying morally clean would strengthen his future marriage. After he was married he said, "I am so grateful that both my wife and I waited to share sexual relations only with each other. I can see how I would have weakened our marriage if I had shared these intimate relationships with others."

HOW *can I know when I'm ready to be married?*

President James E. Faust taught that "there are a few simple, relevant questions which each person, whether married or contemplating marriage, should honestly ask in an effort to become 'one flesh.' They are:

"First, am I able to think of the interest of my marriage and partner first before I think of my own desires?

"Second, how deep is my commitment to my companion, aside from any other interests?

"Third, is he or she my best friend?

"Fourth, do I have respect for the dignity of my partner as a person of worth and value?

"Fifth, do we quarrel over money? Money itself seems neither to make a couple happy, nor the lack of it, necessarily, to make them unhappy, but money is often a symbol of selfishness.

"Sixth, is there a spiritually sanctifying bond between us?"[10]

For the Strength of Youth teaches, "When you obey God's commandment to be sexually pure, you prepare yourself to . . . build a strong marriage and to bring children into the world as part of a loving family."[11] Most importantly, being morally clean prepares us to be worthy to enter the holy temple and make sacred covenants leading to an eternal marriage.

HOW *can I know when I'm in love?*

President David O. McKay answered this question by saying, "Years ago at the University of Utah, a fellow student and I considered that query one night as we walked together. . . .

"In answer to my question, 'How can we know when we are in love?' [He] replied: 'My mother once said that if you meet a girl in whose presence you feel a desire to achieve, who inspires you to do your best, and to make the most of yourself, such a young woman is worthy of your love and is awakening love in your heart'"[13]

LIVING TOGETHER BEFORE MARRIAGE HURTS MARRIAGE

"Couples who live together before they are engaged have a higher chance of getting divorced than those who wait until they are married to live together. . . . In addition, couples who lived together . . . and then married, reported a lower satisfaction in their marriages."[12]

Higher Chance of Divorce

Lower Satisfaction

Love Your Future Spouse Now

A powerful verse that can help strengthen our future marriage is D&C 42:22, which says, "Thou shalt love thy wife with all thy heart, and shalt cleave unto her and none else." One young woman said, "That verse applies to me because I'm going to get married some day, and I can show love for my future spouse by making right choices today."

What a great insight! We don't have to wait until our wedding day to show love to our future spouse. As a matter of fact, we don't even need to wait until we meet them to show love to them. We can show love for our future spouse by all the choices we make today. This goes beyond staying morally clean. For example, a young man could choose to serve a mission, knowing that this preparation would prepare him to be a better spiritual leader with his future companion.

Elder M. Russell Ballard said, "The most important decision you will make in this life is the decision to marry the right [person] in the temple!"[15] We can and should prepare early for this important decision!

Kids' thoughts on what falling in love is like:

- "Like an avalanche where you have to run for your life." (Roger, age 9)
- "If falling in love is anything like learning how to spell, I don't want to do it. It takes too long." (Leo, age 7)[14]

HOW can I want to start a family when the world today seems like such a terrible place?

President Howard W. Hunter addressed this question by saying, "There have always been some difficulties in mortal life and there always will be. . . . Here are some actual comments that have been made and passed on to me in recent months. This comes from a fine returned missionary: 'Why should I date and get serious with a girl? I am not sure I even want to marry and bring a family into this kind of a world. I am not very sure about my own future. How can I take the responsibility for the future of others whom I would love and care about and want to be happy?'. . .

"And this from a recent college graduate: 'I am doing the best I can, but I wonder if there is much reason to even plan for the future, let alone retirement. The world probably won't last that long anyway.'

"Well, isn't that a fine view of things? Sounds like we all ought to go and eat a big plate of worms.

"I want to say to all . . . that you have every reason in this world to be happy and to be optimistic and to be confident."[16]

Do not be discouraged as you look to the future. Know that God will bless you and your family. Go forward with faith!

Think of an attribute that you hope your future spouse will have. Begin today to more fully develop that quality in your own life so that kind of person will be attracted to you.

Invitation to Act

TELL ME ONE MORE TIME!

How Can I Prepare for an Eternal Marriage?

- **Be the kind of person you want to marry.**
- **Learn to be selfless.**
- **Stay morally clean.**
- **Love your future spouse now.**

How Can I Strengthen My Testimony?

What is it that causes a young man or woman to get up hours before school starts each day to go to seminary and learn the scriptures? What is it that leads missionaries to voluntarily give up eighteen to twenty-four months of their lives to go to foreign lands and preach the gospel, and pay their own way? What is it that motivates Latter-day Saints to freely give 10 percent of their income to the Church?

President Hinckley gives the answer: "This thing which we call testimony is the great strength of the Church. It is the wellspring of faith and activity. . . . [It] is the element which motivates the membership to forsake all in the service of the Lord. . . . This testimony . . . is of the very essence of this work. It is what is moving the work of the Lord forward across the world."[2]

Since testimony is the critical element to activity and faithfulness in the Church, the question becomes: *How* can we gain or strengthen our testimony?

"HOW DO WE KNOW WHAT REALLY IS TRUE?"

Elder Robert D. Hales taught the following points:

"Cultivate a diligent desire to know that God lives.

"This desire leads us to ponder on the things of heaven—to let the evidence of God all around us touch our hearts.

"With softened hearts we are prepared to heed the Savior's call to 'search the scriptures' and to humbly learn from them.

"We are then ready to ask our Heavenly Father sincerely, in the name of our Savior, Jesus Christ, if the things we have learned are true."[3]

Study the Book of Mormon

President Ezra Taft Benson called the Book of Mormon the "keystone of testimony."[4] That means that if we can gain a testimony of the truthfulness of the Book of Mormon it will be the key to obtaining the rest of our testimony. If we know the Book of Mormon is true, then we will know that Jesus is the Christ, for it testifies of his divinity. If we gain a testimony of the Book of Mormon, then we'll have a testimony of Joseph Smith—because he translated it—and a testimony of the Church he founded, The Church of Jesus Christ of Latter-day Saints. Having a testimony of the Book of Mormon helps everything else fall into place.

IF THE BOOK OF MORMON IS TRUE . . .

Having a testimony of the Book of Mormon helps everything else fall into place.

1. If the Book of Mormon is true,

then Joseph Smith was a prophet.

2. If Joseph Smith was a prophet,

then The Church of Jesus Christ of Latter-day Saints is the true church.

3. If The Church of Jesus Christ of Latter-day Saints is the true church,

then it is led by a true prophet today.

PROVE IT TO ME!

Have you ever had people say to you something like: "Well, I want proof that there is a God" or "Show me some real evidence that Joseph Smith was a prophet, then I'll believe." Have you ever wished that there was some sort of proof, some sort of real, touchable thing that could prove that Jesus is the Christ, that Joseph did see God, and that Joseph was a prophet? Oh, wait, God already gave us something!

President Benson said: "I testify that through the Book of Mormon God has provided for our day *tangible evidence* that Jesus is the Christ and that Joseph Smith is His prophet."[5]

If someone doubts your testimony or asks for proof, hand them a copy of the Book of Mormon and say, "There's your proof! It's either true, or it's not. I testify it is."

Since the Book of Mormon is the keystone of our testimony we need to know how to gain a testimony of the Book of Mormon. At the end of the book, Moroni gives us a promise: "And when ye shall receive these things, I would exhort you that ye would ask God, the Eternal Father, in the name of Christ, if these things are not true; and if ye shall ask with a sincere heart, with real intent, having faith in Christ, he will manifest the truth of it unto you, by the power of the Holy Ghost" (Moroni 10:4).

If we read the Book of Mormon and pray about it with a sincere heart, with real intent to obey its teachings, having faith in Christ, the Spirit will tell us through our mind and heart that the Book of Mormon is true (see chapter 8). Each of us can have this divine and sacred experience! President Hinckley said, "Without reservation I promise you that if you will prayerfully read the Book of Mormon, regardless of how many times you previously have read it, there will come . . . a stronger testimony of the living reality of the Son of God."[6] Obtaining a testimony comes through prayer and scripture study, but particularly through a study of the Book of Mormon.

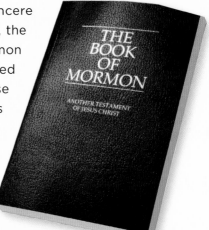

WHAT WOULD IT TAKE TO MAKE UP THE BOOK OF MORMON? . . . HOW 'BOUT YOU START WRITING ABOUT OUTER MONGOLIA?

Those who claim that the Book of Mormon is not true are by default claiming that the book was made up—fabricated by Joseph Smith, his friends, or someone else and pulled off as one of the great hoaxes of this world. Here is roughly what it would take to make up the Book of Mormon:

- You must write the religious, social, and political history of some ancient people, like the Mongols or people from Greenland.

- You must write the book off the top of your head, using no reference material—no Google in Joseph's day!

- You must complete the whole book in 65 to 75 working days.

- You must invent over 280 new names the world has never heard, and they must be properly derived from your ancient people's language, a language which you don't know. Have fun with that one.

- Your book must include the fullness of the gospel of Jesus Christ, including sermons that are so inspiring that people willingly read them again and again and again.

- Your book must be over 500 pages long and 300,000 words.

- Your first draft must stand forever (other than minor grammatical changes).

- You must be willing to give your life, and the life of a family member, for the book you write.[7]

Our testimony to the world is that the Book of Mormon was not made up by Joseph Smith. As Elder Jeffrey R. Holland's grandfather President George Q. Cannon said, "No wicked man could write such a book as this; and no good man would write it, unless it were true and he were commanded of God to do so."[8] Logic tells most rational people the book is true, but the Spirit provides an even more powerful witness: The book is of God.

Live What We Learn; Live the Gospel

The Savior taught, "If any man will *do* his will, he shall *know* of the doctrine" (John 7:17; emphasis added). In other words if we want to *know* if a gospel principle is true, we need to *live* that principle (*do* the things we are supposed to do).

PROPHETIC TESTIMONY

"I know that my redeemer liveth, and that he shall stand at the latter day upon the earth."

JOB (Job 19:25)

For example, a young woman we know said that she never read her scriptures. She didn't think they would help in her life. Then she starting having some problems and began to read the scriptures on a daily basis. As she read the scriptures every day, she felt different. She felt better and though she still had problems she was able to work through them. She bore her testimony of the value of scripture study. She gained her testimony of scripture reading by reading the scriptures.

HOW can I know if something I learn in school is true or false?

Most of the things you will learn in your formal education will be true, but—unfortunately—sometimes the theories, philosophies, and values of the world are mixed in and presented as facts or absolute truths, when they are not. There are two primary ways to be able to discern what is and is not true.

Study the Book of Mormon: President Ezra Taft Benson said: "God, with his infinite foreknowledge, so molded the Book of Mormon that we might see the error and know how to combat false educational, political, religious, and philosophical concepts of our time."[9] Match what you hear and learn against the standards and truths taught in the Book of Mormon, the holy scriptures, and with what the current prophets are teaching. If the ideas and values you learn in school contradict what the scriptures and prophets plainly teach, then stick with the scriptures and prophets.

Listen to the Holy Ghost: The Savior taught: "Howbeit when he, the Spirit of truth, is come, he will guide you into all truth" (John 16:13). Pay attention to how you *feel* when learning something. If it doesn't feel right, it probably isn't.

Example of step #4.

DO TRY THIS AT HOME!

There are many levels of testimony:

I hope it's true . . .
I think it's true . . .
I believe it's true . . .
I know it's true . . .

What if we told you that your ring finger is less flexible than your other fingers? Do you hope, think, believe, or know that is true? What is the only way to move from "hope" to "know"? Experiment and test it out! Do the following:

1. Put your hands together, palm to palm.

2. Keeping your palms together, see if you can separate your pointer fingers. Can you do it? Good, now keeping your palms together, fold your pointer fingers over.

3. With your palms together and pointer fingers folded over, try to separate your pinky fingers. Can you do it? Good. Now fold those over.

4. What about your thumbs, and your middle finger? Good. Fold those over.

5. Now with your palms firmly pressed together and all your fingers folded over *except your ring fingers*, try to separate your ring fingers from each other. Interesting, isn't it?

So how many of you now "know" your ring finger is less flexible than your others? Gaining a witness of spiritual things is much the same: When we first experiment and act in obedience, then the testimony comes.

President Howard W. Hunter taught, "Action is one of the chief foundations of personal testimony. The surest witness is that which comes firsthand out of personal experience.

". . . This, then, is the finest source of personal testimony. One knows because he has experienced."[10]

Notice that we must act in faith first, then the witness comes (see chapter 1). It is not the other way around. There are some who say, "When God gives me a testimony of tithing, then I'll pay it." However, that simply is not the way the Lord works. We first act, then our testimonies will grow.

HOW come I can't try the bad stuff (sin) to learn if it's bad and gain my testimony that way?

Some think they can gain a testimony of the Word of Wisdom by drinking alcohol or doing drugs to see how bad it is, or gain a testimony of the need to be chaste and morally clean by being immoral. Remember, the Savior taught, "If any man will *do* [God's] will, he shall know" (John 7:17; emphasis added). The Holy Ghost will only testify to us that something is true if we are obedient and live what God teaches. The Spirit can't testify that something is true when we are rebelling against God and being disobedient.

Share What You Know and Believe with Others

John Says:

I can still remember the first time I bore my testimony. I was about ten years old and was in our Primary room. I was wearing a dirty coat and didn't want to bear my testimony. But everyone else was doing it, so I got up and said (and this is about how I said it), "I'dliketobearmytestimonythatIknowthischurchistrue, I'm thankfulformyfamilyinthenameofJesusChristAmen."

Have you ever shared or heard a testimony like that?

I remember the second time I bore my testimony. I was twelve years old and it was at the end of a ward youth conference. I was a deacon at the time, and every other deacon in my quorum had already borne his testimony. All the older deacons were saying, "John, go bear your testimony!" I didn't want to, but I did because of the peer pressure. That testimony was about as meaningful as my first.

I can also clearly remember the third time I shared my testimony. I was fifteen at the time and was at EFY. Going into the testimony meeting, I really didn't plan on bearing my testimony, but as the meeting went on, I really started to feel the Spirit. Finally, I got up and began to explain the feelings I had in my heart for the gospel. A feeling of warmth came over me as I shared my testimony, and I felt the Spirit like I never had before. My testimony got stronger because I bore it. When I sat down, I felt so good. I learned for myself that a testimony was found in the bearing of it.

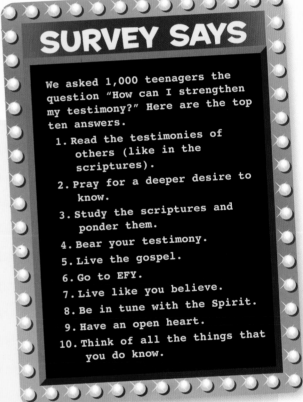

SURVEY SAYS

We asked 1,000 teenagers the question "How can I strengthen my testimony?" Here are the top ten answers.

1. Read the testimonies of others (like in the scriptures).
2. Pray for a deeper desire to know.
3. Study the scriptures and ponder them.
4. Bear your testimony.
5. Live the gospel.
6. Go to EFY.
7. Live like you believe.
8. Be in tune with the Spirit.
9. Have an open heart.
10. Think of all the things that you do know.

When Brigham Young called a new leader over the young men of the Church, he told him, "At your meetings you should begin at the top of the roll and call upon as many members as there is time for to bear their testimonies and at the next meeting begin where you left off and call upon others, so that all shall take part and get into the practice of standing up and saying something. Many may think they haven't any testimony to bear, but get them to stand up and they will find the Lord will give them utterance to many truths they had not thought of before. More people have obtained a testimony while standing up trying to bear it than down on their knees praying for it."[11]

We can bear our testimonies at any time, not just in testimony meetings. We can share our knowledge of truth in conversations with friends, at home with our families, and using technology. We don't have to wait for fast and testimony meeting to bear a testimony.

Invitation to Act

How is your

testimony? Answer these questions posed by Elder Richard G. Scott. He said, "Honestly evaluate your personal life. How strong is your own testimony? Is it truly a sustaining power in your life, or is it more a hope that what you have learned is true? . . . Does your testimony guide you to correct decisions?"[12]

Take a moment and answer his questions. How is *your* testimony?

"I'd like to bear my testimony. My dad knows this church is true. My mom has read the Book of Mormon . . ."

You've got to find out for yourself. Share what you know and you'll know it as you share.

A Testimony Is Like Spinning a Basketball

How do people spin a basketball on their finger for a long time? The key is in not letting the ball slow down, but to keeping it spinning on your finger by tapping it. If we don't tap the ball, it will eventually slow down, lose its momentum, and fall. Our testimonies are similar: once we get them up and going, we keep them going by "tapping" them on a consistent basis through daily scripture study, prayer, living the gospel, and sharing our testimony with others. If we don't do those things, our testimonies can eventually get spiritually weak, lose momentum, and perhaps fall apart altogether.

For most, receiving a testimony takes time—it doesn't come overnight. We might be doing all the right things and still feel like we don't have a testimony or that our testimony is not strong enough. Don't get discouraged. Someone who is six-foot four didn't become that height overnight, nor do talented piano players play Bach's *Minuet in G* their first day. Remember that sometimes when we are seeking our testimonies, it's not that we're not doing the right things—we just haven't done the right things long enough.

Alma the Younger said, "I have fasted and prayed *many days* that I might know these things of myself" (Alma 5:46; emphasis added). This teaches us that not only can fasting help us gain a testimony, but perhaps more importantly that it may take *many days,* or weeks, or months, or years.

We know that as we gain a testimony of the Book of Mormon, live the gospel, and share what we know with others our testimonies will slowly grow and strengthen into a powerful witness of the truths of the gospel.

TELL ME ONE MORE TIME!

How Can I Strengthen My Testimony?

- **Study the Book of Mormon.**
- **Live what we learn; live the gospel.**
- **Share what you know and believe with others.**

How Can I Know When the Holy Ghost Is Speaking to Me?

ch 8

Please sincerely answer the following question in your mind: When was the last time you remember really feeling the Spirit or having been influenced by the Holy Ghost?

Got your answer?

So when was it? How long ago was the event that you immediately thought of? What was the event? We have asked this question to many youth over the years, and we hear common answers such as: "It was at our testimony meeting at camp" or "When I received my patriarchal blessing" or "I really felt the Spirit at EFY." However, it's less common for a youth to answer this question by saying, "I really felt the Spirit this morning when I prayed," or "About ten minutes ago when we sang the opening hymn and I felt peace," or "Just this morning when I received a subtle impression to say 'hi' to a person without many friends." Why is that so?

Each week when we partake of the sacrament we are promised to "always have [God's] Spirit to be with [us]" (Moroni 4:3). Notice the word *always.* The promise is not that we will have the Holy Ghost with us *sometimes,* or just in Church buildings, or during major life events. No, we are promised that the Spirit will be with us *always*—at school, at practice, in our home, with our friends, at work, and at play. Always. So why then do we at times have to search back months or years into the deep recesses of our memories to recall the last time we think the Spirit influenced us?

Elder David A. Bednar said, "Sometimes as Latter-day Saints we talk and act as though recognizing the influence of the Holy Ghost in our lives is the rare or exceptional event" when the reality is that "the Holy Ghost can tarry with us much, if not most, of the time—and certainly the Spirit can be with us more than it is not with us."[1]

Perhaps the problem is not that we aren't being influenced by the Holy Ghost in our daily lives, but simply that we don't recognize it and are overlooking it.

Looking for a SPECTACULAR SPIRITUAL EXPERIENCE?

You might be missing something . . .

President Kimball taught, "Expecting the spectacular, one may not be fully alerted to the constant flow of revealed communication from the Holy Ghost."[2]

HOW *long will it take for an answer to come or for me to receive the revelation I need?*

The answer to this question depends on the situation, and on the Lord's divine timing (see D&C 88:68). Elder Richard G. Scott gave a great insight to receiving answers from the Spirit through prayer when he taught: "Often when we pray for help with a significant matter, Heavenly Father will give us gentle promptings that require us to think, exercise faith, work, at times struggle, then act. It is a step-by-step process that enables us to discern inspired answers. . . . Seldom will you receive a complete response all at once. It will come a piece at a time, in packets, so that you will grow in capacity. As each piece is followed in faith, you will be led to other portions until you have the whole answer."[3] Revelation often comes in pieces—a little at a time (see 2 Nephi 28:30).

Perhaps we are even like the Lamanites who "were baptized with fire and with the Holy Ghost, *and they knew it not*" (3 Nephi 9:20; emphasis added). If we are missing the subtle daily guidance of the Spirit because we are looking for something more incredible, we might even mistakenly think that we aren't feeling the Holy Ghost at all! So how can we know and recognize when the Holy Ghost is speaking to us? We will use D&C 8:2 as our foundational scripture to answer this question. It says, "Yea, behold, I will tell you in your *mind* and in your *heart,* by the Holy Ghost" (emphasis added). The Holy Ghost will speak to our minds through our *thoughts,* and to our *hearts* through our feelings.

Let's look at how that can happen.

The Holy Ghost Will Give Us Instructions in Our Mind

Have you ever had a thought pop into your mind to *do* something? Maybe you saw your mom clear off the dinner table and thought, "I should help her," or perhaps you came home from school and were ready to sit down and watch some TV but thought, "I should get my homework done first so I don't get behind." Maybe you've had a clear warning voice of instruction in your mind, such as, "This show isn't good . . . turn it off" or "Don't do that" or "I should get out of this situation now." The Lord taught us, "As often as thou hast inquired thou *hast received instruction of my Spirit*" (D&C 6:14; emphasis added). These instructions in our mind often come in the form of "Do this . . ." "Don't do that . . ." "Go here . . ." "Don't go there . . ." "Look into this . . ."

Elder Richard G. Scott testified that "sometimes the direction [from the Holy Ghost] comes so clearly and so unmistakably that it can be written down like spiritual dictation."[4] The spiritual instructions that come to our minds will lead us to follow Christ, obey his gospel, and draw closer to him. If we receive an instruction in our mind to do something we know is wrong, we can know it is not of God (see chapter 9).

The Holy Ghost Will Enlighten Our Mind

To enlighten means "to give spiritual or intellectual insight to."[5] When Oliver Cowdery wanted to have a clearer knowledge and understanding of Joseph Smith's work on the Book of Mormon, the Lord said, *"I did enlighten thy mind;* and now I tell thee these things that thou mayest know that thou hast been *enlightened by the Spirit of truth"* (D&C 6:15, emphasis added). An easy way to notice when this is happening is when we have those "Aha!" moments. Those moments when we understand something more clearly, or more deeply. It is often noticed in statements such as "That makes sense" or "I get it now" or "I understand that better." For example, if you are reading a book about how the Holy Ghost enlightens our mind, and you think "That makes sense," then you were just enlightened by the Spirit! The Holy Ghost enlightened you about how he can enlighten you. Pretty cool.

The Holy Ghost can not only enlighten your mind regarding gospel principles, but also regarding any truth. Our Savior taught, "Howbeit when he, the Spirit of truth, is come, he will guide you into all truth" (John 16:13). That includes truths in math, truths in science, truths in sociology. *All truth.* If you understand a truth more clearly, you are being influenced by the Holy Ghost.

The Holy Ghost Will Help Reassure Our Mind

Have you ever been going through a difficult time or having a bad day and then as you studied the scriptures, or prayed, or heard a gospel talk or lesson the thought came to you, "I'm going to be okay," or "Everything will work out," or "Stay positive," or "God is aware of you and your situation. He loves you and will help you." Reassuring thoughts similar to those are another way the Lord speaks to our mind through the Holy Ghost.

> ### PAY ATTENTION TO WHEN YOU DON'T HAVE THE SPIRIT WITH YOU
>
> Elder David A. Bednar shared an important key that can be helpful for us as we try to always have the Spirit with us. He said, "Precisely because the promised blessing is *that we may always have His Spirit to be with us,* we should attend to and learn from the choices and influences that separate us from the Holy Spirit. The standard is clear. If something we think, see, hear, or do distances us from the Holy Ghost, then we should stop thinking, seeing, hearing, or doing that thing."[6]

Once again, to Oliver Cowdery, the Lord said, "Verily, verily, I say unto you, if you desire a further witness, *cast your mind upon the night* that you cried unto me. . . . Did I not *speak peace to your mind* concerning the matter? What greater witness can you have than from God?" (D&C 6:22–23; emphasis added). If we will pay attention to these different ways the Holy Ghost speaks to our mind (enlighten, instruction, reassurance) we can say with the prophet Enos, "The voice of the Lord came into my mind again, saying . . ." (Enos 1:10).

❓ **HOW** *do desire and worthiness affect my ability to receive revelation on a daily basis?*

Our desire to receive instruction and personal worthiness will affect the revelation we receive. President Spencer W. Kimball said: "The Lord will not force himself upon people; and if they do not believe, they will receive no visitation. If they are content to depend upon their own limited calculations and interpretations, then, of course, the Lord will leave them to their chosen fate. . . . If there be eyes to see, there will be visions to inspire. If there be ears to hear, there will be revelations to experience. . . . Revelation can come to every good, faithful [person]. . . . The Lord will give you answer to your questions and to your prayers if you are listening. . . . [A]ll people, if they are worthy enough and close enough to the Lord, can have revelations."[8]

♥ The Holy Ghost Gives Us Divine Feelings

When some people are asked what it is like to *feel* the Holy Ghost they say, "I get a burning in my bosom!" This comes from D&C 9:8: "If it is right I will cause that your bosom shall burn within you; therefore, you shall feel that it is right." Does this mean your chest is on fire? Like heartburn? Maybe. But probably not. Remember, the Spirit often works through the quiet, the subtle, the delicate, and not usually through the intense or dramatic. Elder Dallin H. Oaks explained the burning in the bosom this way: "Surely, the word 'burning' in this scripture signifies a feeling of (comfort) and (serenity)."[7]

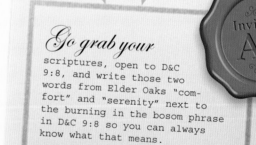

Go grab your scriptures, open to D&C 9:8, and write those two words from Elder Oaks "comfort" and "serenity" next to the burning in the bosom phrase in D&C 9:8 so you can always know what that means.

Invitation to Act

IS *HOMEWARD BOUND* TRUE?

Just because we feel *emotion* doesn't mean we are feeling the Holy Ghost. Just because we might cry when Shadow comes over the hill in *Homeward Bound* doesn't mean that *Homeward Bound* is true. President Howard W. Hunter explained: "I get concerned when it appears that strong emotion or free-flowing tears are equated with the presence of the Spirit. Certainly the Spirit of the Lord can bring strong emotional feelings, including tears, but that outward manifestation ought not to be confused with the presence of the Spirit itself."[9]

If we don't understand this principle we might mistakenly bear our testimony that we know something is true, just because we shed a tear.

One of the great gifts of God is divine feelings. Feelings such as love, peace, joy, hope, faith, humility, gentleness, gratitude, comfort, and serenity. These feelings can only come from God, and cannot come through wickedness, rebellion, or from the adversary. If we are experiencing those divine feelings, they come through the Holy Ghost and we are being influenced by him. This is a burning in the bosom! If we are looking for fire, we might miss the divine.

DO TRY THIS AT HOME!

To do this activity you must purchase an "Air Zooka" (you can find them online or at major retail stores in their toy section), or you can simply use a powerful fan. The Air Zooka is a large bucket-looking gun that compacts and shoots balls of air across the room. The ball of air is powerful enough to turn pages of scripture, shake the leaves of a tree, or send someone's hair flying. Shoot a few things with it. Shoot it past some family members and friends and let them feel it and hear it. After playing with it, answer this question: How is the air or wind like the Spirit? Read John 3:7–8 where the Savior compares the Spirit to the wind. Just because we can't see or touch something, doesn't mean it isn't real!

Here are some answers we thought of: You can't see it but you can feel it. You can hear it. It can be soothing or powerful. You can't touch it but you can see its effect on things.

♥ The Holy Ghost Gives Us Feelings of Warning

It is important to know that God is not the author of fear, doubt, and discouragement (see 2 Timothy 1:7). But sometimes we are about to head in the wrong direction, and God knows it. So in his love, he warns us through our feelings by the power of the Holy Ghost. The scriptures simply put it this way, "If it be not right you shall have no such feelings [of comfort and serenity], but you shall have a stupor of thought" (D&C 9:9). Elder Franklin D. Richards said the stupor of thought is "a questionable feeling."[10] President Boyd K. Packer taught: "If ever you receive a prompting to do something that makes *you feel* uneasy . . . do not respond to it!"[11] Remember, these feelings of uneasiness usually come when we are about to head in a direction that leads us into spiritual or physical danger. They are usually accompanied by thoughts of instruction to stop or to leave. If we are feeling uncomfortable with a situation, it may be a stupor of thought, with the Holy Ghost telling us not to proceed.

DON'T LET A JALAPEÑO OVERPOWER YOUR GRAPE

"The inspiring influence of the Holy Spirit can be overcome or masked by strong emotions, such as anger, hate, passion, fear, or pride. When such influences are present, it is like trying to savor the delicate flavor of a grape while eating a jalapeño pepper. Both flavors are present, but one completely overpowers the other. In like manner, strong emotions overcome the delicate promptings of the Holy Spirit."—Elder Richard G. Scott[12]

We have been promised that the Holy Ghost can be with us *always*—each day of our lives, not just each major event in our lives. We testify that this is true, and that we all can be spiritually influenced and led each day—multiple times each day. The next time somebody asks, "When was the last time you felt the Spirit?" you want to be able to respond by saying, "Well, what time is it?"

TELL ME ONE MORE TIME!

How Can I Know When the Holy Ghost Is Speaking to Me?

- **The Holy Ghost will give us instructions in our mind.**
- **The Holy Ghost will enlighten our mind.**
- **The Holy Ghost will help reassure our mind.**
- **The Holy Ghost gives us divine feelings.**
- **The Holy Ghost gives us feelings of warning.**

How Can I Avoid Being Deceived When Receiving Revelation?

Consider the following scenario: Katie and David were both good LDS kids. David was eighteen years old and Katie was seventeen when they met. They quickly developed feelings for each other and began to date each other exclusively. One day Katie's mom approached her and said, "Katie, I'm concerned that you and David are spending so much time together. You know the prophet has told us not to get involved in steady dating in high school before a young man's mission call. Can you and David talk it over and pray about it individually to see how you should handle the situation?"

Katie talked with David. They both reasoned that their relationship was a good thing. David said that Katie was helping him by motivating him to want to marry her in the temple, which is more important than serving a mission anyway. Katie said she didn't think that

DO TRY THIS AT HOME!

Get an empty two-liter bottle and place it on the edge of a countertop. On top of the two-liter bottle place a ping-pong ball. Create a walkway where you (or others) can walk from one end of the room to the other where the two-liter bottle is located. The purpose of this activity is to try to flick the ping-pong ball off the two-liter bottle as you walk past it. There are three rules: 1) you must flick it as you walk past it in full stride; you cannot slow down when you get close to the bottle, 2) you must flick it with your middle finger and 3) your arm must be fully extended and you must be standing up straight, no leaning over. No bent elbows or being hunched over! Give it a try a number of times with some friends or classmates!

How did it turn out? If you did it right, most of you probably missed the ball by aiming too high, meaning you flicked above the ball. The reason we miss the ball is because our depth perception gets thrown off as we aim down our fully extended arm (like a rifle) and try and flick the ball. Also, our hand gets in the way just at the moment we are getting ready to flick, blocking our view of the ball and causing us to miss. How does the adversary do the same to us? How does he throw off our spiritual depth perception? How does he shorten our vision? How do our own emotions and thoughts "get in the way" of real revelation and direction from the Lord?

all of these feelings of love for each other could be from the adversary. Although they hadn't gone "all the way" yet with their physical affection, they had come close on a number of occasions. They said that they helped each other to stop. They felt their relationship was right and that their closeness would only lead to good things. "Revelation comes to the mind and heart," they reasoned. David said he had prayed about it and told Katie they should stay together. Katie took all these factors as her answer and told her mom she would keep seeing David.

The scriptures warn us that Satan seeks "that all men might be miserable like unto himself" (2 Nephi 2:27). The adversary wants "to deceive and to blind men, and to lead them captive at his will" (Moses 4:4), and one of the ways Satan tries to deceive the children of God and members of Christ's Church is through false revelation. President Boyd K. Packer warned, "Know this: There are counterfeit revelations which, we are warned, 'if possible . . . shall deceive the very elect, who are the elect according to the covenant' (JS–M 1:22)."[1] The adversary knows that faithful Latter-day Saints are looking for promptings from the Holy Ghost to give them direction (see chapter 8). Therefore, Satan tries to use inspiration against us by giving false or counterfeit revelations. So how can we avoid being deceived by these false revelations? Let's look at three revelation tests to help us out.

Use the Edification Test

Doctrine and Covenants 50:23 says "and that which doth not edify is not of God, and is darkness." To edify means to uplift or build up—in this context to uplift or build us up spiritually. If the results of our thoughts, feelings, and desires do not edify our lives, then we know the prompting is not from God but is "darkness." If it is a good prompting then we will feel fruits of the Spirit like "love, joy, peace, longsuffering, gentleness, goodness, faith" (Galatians 5:22). The fruit, or result, of a false prompting is just the opposite: rebellion, hatred, guilt, defensiveness, anger, doubt, etc. A good question to ask ourselves is: What will be the result of this action I am feeling prompted to take? Will it lift me up spiritually or tear me down?

HOW can I be sure if something is "edifying" or right? What if I'm not sure?

This is an important question. Because of our behavior, sometimes we can become desensitized to what is right and what is wrong. Nephi told his brothers, "[God] hath spoken unto you in a still small voice, but ye were past feeling, that ye could not feel his words" (1 Nephi 17:45). At times, talking with a parent or trusted leader or spiritually sensitive friend can be helpful. It takes a lot of humility, but they usually can see what we have become blinded or desensitized to. For example, you could approach such a person and say, "I'm really not sure if this music is edifying. It makes me feel good, but I'm not sure if it's a 'spiritual' good. Could you listen to the song and let me know what you think?"

President Boyd K. Packer was being interviewed for a PBS documentary and was asked the question, "How do you test the promptings and know whether they come from God or from yourself?" President Packer responded, "It's a very fine line to determine whether the impression or prompting is *revelation* or just a personal thought. *One of the tests is to ask yourself: Is it good? Does it make you happy? Or is it destructive? You can test.*"[2]

HOW can I tell the difference between my own thoughts and the Holy Ghost?

A short answer to this question is this: if you have a feeling to do something (and it doesn't violate one of the tests mentioned in this chapter), do it. If you have a thought to do something that is clearly good (like text a friend to invite them to church), do it! If you are walking down the street and feel like you should turn right, do it. Don't worry if it's you or the Spirit—just follow what you feel you should do.

If you want to read a longer answer (and we recommend that you do), we've read several talks that directly address this question. You can link to a couple of our favorites at http://ldswhy.com.[3]

For example, a football player once said that he likes to listen to music that pumps him up before a football game—that it gets his emotions going. He said, "It just pumps me up so bad that it makes me want to kill someone! Is that the Spirit?" You might laugh, but this was a real situation. He was confusing his emotions with the Holy Ghost. Think about the "fruit" of his feelings: It makes him want to kill someone!

YOU'VE BEEN DECEIVED

Read the following scenario and determine which one of the three revelation "tests" the following situation may be violating:

"You know, everybody says that when you feel the Spirit you feel good. Well, I feel really good when my friends and I egg people's houses. It is such a rush!! Holy cow, I get goose bumps and chills up my spine when we are running away from the police and the homeowners. It is so exciting! It makes my heart beat really fast when I'm hiding in the bushes from my crimes. I think I need to bear my testimony about this next month in sacrament meeting. Sweet!"

Answer: The edification test.

WHICH IS LONGER?

Take a look at the two horizontal lines below. Which one is longer? (see page 68).

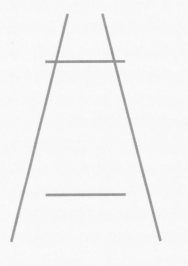

Use the Stewardship Test

Stewardship is responsibility over something. For example, we are all stewards of our physical bodies. A newly ordained teachers quorum president can receive inspiration regarding how to govern his quorum and help its members. Parents can receive inspiration regarding how to direct their family. We cannot receive revelation for something or someone we do not have stewardship over or responsibility for. For example, we can't receive a revelation telling the bishop how to run the ward, or who to call to a calling, unless we are given responsibility to direct the bishop in a higher calling (such as the stake president). Elder Russell M. Nelson said that this "principle precludes receiving revelation for anyone outside one's defined circle of responsibility."[4] False revelation in this category might come through thoughts such as, "My Young Women president doesn't know what she is doing," or "I don't think I should have gotten my mission call to Boise, Idaho. I'm not sure if that call was inspired." In our example of Katie and David, David can't tell Katie what to do because he has no stewardship over her. The overriding principle is this: Is this prompting/revelation I am receiving outside of my line of steward-ship or responsibility?

YOU'VE BEEN DECEIVED

Read the following scenario and determine which one of the three revelation tests the following situation may be violating:

Rufus approaches Sha-nay-nay after their first date and says, "You know Nay-Nay, after our date last night I prayed to the Lord to find out if you were the right one for me, and the Spirit told me that you were. So you need to marry me. If you choose not to marry me, then you are denying the Spirit, and you will go to outer darkness. It doesn't matter that you have only known me for a week, or that I am hideously unattractive to you—the Spirit has told me this so you must obey."

Answer: The stewardship test.

SPOT THE FAKE

Can you figure out which bill is the fake? How could you learn how to tell the difference? Elder David E. Sorenson said, "There was a man who worked for the United States Treasury Department. . . . One evening at a press conference following his breaking up of a major counterfeit ring, one of the reporters directed this statement to him: 'You must spend a lot of time studying counterfeit bills to recognize them so easily.' His reply to this was, 'No, I don't ever study counterfeit bills. I spend my time studying genuine bills; then the imperfection is easy to recognize.'"[5] The lesson for us should be obvious. If we want to avoid false revelation, we should immerse ourselves in true revelations (like scripture and teachings from general conference). The more time we spend with real revelation, the easier false revelation will be to detect.

Read the following scenario and determine which of the three revelation tests the following situation may be violating:

A bishop asks a young man if he is planning on serving a mission. The young man says, "I have been praying about it a lot, and I don't feel like serving a mission is right for me. When I think about it, there are just too many reasons why the Lord has set me up to stay: I have a great job, a fantastic college scholarship, and I have this sweet righteous girlfriend named Dorcas. It just doesn't make sense for me to go. I am a little scared to go, too. So, when I think about it these are the thoughts that come to my mind, and I really think that the Lord is telling me not to go on a mission and to keep going in the direction I am going. I love the Lord though!"

Answer: The edification test (leads away from keeping the command to serve a mission) and the stewardship test (the young man does not have the authority to judge whether he should or should not be excused from serving a mission. His bishop, stake president, and the General Authorities determine that).

In early Church history, a member named Hiram Page found what he thought was a seer stone. He believed this stone was giving him revelations (see section heading of D&C 28). Some of what Hiram Page was teaching through his false revelations was different than what Joseph Smith was teaching. The Lord told Joseph, "Thou shalt take thy brother, Hiram Page, between him and thee alone, and tell him that those things which he hath written from that stone are not of me and that Satan deceiveth him; For, behold, these things have not been appointed unto him, neither shall anything be appointed unto any of this church *contrary to the church covenants*" (D&C 28:11–12; emphasis added).

In other words, we cannot receive revelation telling us to do or believe something different from the living prophets of God. A young man and woman can't receive a "feeling" telling them that it is okay to become sexually active with each other because they plan to get married anyway if "God has commanded that sexual intimacy be reserved for marriage."[6] Another form of being contrary to the living prophets is thinking that you know more than the leaders about a certain topic that the Church has an official position on. Thoughts like, "The prophets don't know as much about this as I do. The Church's position on this issue is wrong. They need to adjust their thinking!" simply reveal that we are the ones that need to adjust our thinking. Nephi said, "When they are learned they think they are wise, and they hearken not unto the counsel of God, for they set it aside, supposing they know of themselves, wherefore, their wisdom is foolishness and it profiteth them not. And they shall perish" (2 Nephi 9:28). We must ask ourselves: Is what I am being prompted to think, believe, or do contrary to what the current living prophets are teaching?

If we think we are wiser than the prophets, we need to think again.

HOW should I act if I feel I haven't received an impression or an answer at all?

"We are expected to assume accountability by acting on a decision that is consistent with His teachings without prior confirmation. We are not to sit passively waiting or to murmur because the Lord has not spoken. We are to act.

"Most often what we have chosen to do is right. He will confirm the correctness of our choices His way. That confirmation generally comes through packets of help found along the way. . . . If, in trust, we begin something which is not right, He will let us know before we have gone too far. We sense that help by recognizing troubled or uneasy feelings."

—Elder Richard G. Scott[7]

YOU'VE BEEN DECEIVED

Read the following scenario and determine which of the three revelation tests the following situation may be violating:

"I know that the Prophet tells us that we need to get married in the temple . . . but Hans is so amazing! He is not a member of the Church, but he is a really good guy! We just get along so well and can talk about anything. He makes a hundred million dollars a year, he is a supermodel for the magazine *GQ*, and he runs a charity for orphaned chimpanzees in Africa. He is soooooooo WONDERFUL! I just don't think the Lord would send a man like Hans my way and then expect me to not marry him. I feel like marrying him is the right thing to do. I mean, there are no great LDS guys like this who I can truly love . . . they were all killed in the war in heaven! So I guess temple marriage will just have to wait until later. The Lord will understand."

Answer: This fails at least two tests because it leads away from the temple, which violates both the edification test and the Brethren test.

Let's conclude with where we began. How does Katie and David's situation measure up to the three tests? It violates the edification test because it is leading to immorality and disobedience to parents. It violates the stewardship test because neither David nor Katie have made any covenants with one another and therefore have no stewardship or authority to tell each other how to act and what to do. Last, it violates the Brethren test because they are steady dating contrary to specific counsel to not steady date in high school, and David is thinking of not serving a mission, which the prophet has commanded him to do. As the First Presidency said in 1913: "Be not led by any spirit or influence that discredits established authority, contradicts true scientific principles and discoveries, or leads away from the direct revelations of God for the government of the Church. The Holy Ghost does not contradict its own revealings. Truth is always harmonious with itself. . . . Therefore, O! ye Latter-day Saints, profit by these words of warning."[8] If we know and follow these principles, we will not be deceived when receiving revelation.

Here is the answer to "Which is Longer?" on page 65: Although the horizontal line up top may appear to be longer, the lines are actually the same length. We get deceived by the tilted lines surrounding the top line. Similarly, some get deceived by their surroundings, situations, thoughts, and feelings. Hope you weren't deceived!

We invite you to weigh any decisions you are making against the three tests outlined in this chapter. Do any of your decisions violate the tests? If so, we invite you to reconsider the decision and reconfirm with the Lord what direction he would have you take.

Invitation to Act

TELL ME ONE MORE TIME!

How Can I Avoid Being Deceived When Receiving Revelation?

- **Use the edification test: Does the revelation build you up spiritually?**
- **Use the stewardship test: Is the revelation coming from one with proper stewardship?**
- **Use the Brethren test: Is the revelation in harmony with the teachings of living prophets?**

How Can I Recognize and Develop Spiritual Gifts?

In a revelation to the early Saints, the Lord said, "Seek ye earnestly the best gifts" (D&C 46:8). By this he didn't mean the best Christmas or birthday gifts, but the best spiritual gifts. Spiritual gifts are heavenly abilities that come from God that he gives us to help us build up his kingdom on the earth and serve others. The great thing is that the Lord has given at least one of these spiritual gifts to all of us: "To *every man* is given a gift by the Spirit of God" (D&C 46:11; emphasis added). The Apostle Paul and the prophet Moroni both taught that we can receive several spiritual gifts if we seek them (see 1 Corinthians 12:11; Moroni 10:17). Since everyone has spiritual gifts, the question is: How can we recognize and develop the spiritual gifts we each have or desire? This is an important question to answer because, as Elder Marvin J. Ashton taught, "It is up to each of us to search for and build upon the gifts which God has given. . . . It is our right and responsibility to accept our gifts and to share them."[1]

"We know too little about spiritual gifts. This is evident in our communications, and it is also evident in our failure to seek after and use spiritual gifts."—Dallin H. Oaks[2]

Learn About Spiritual Gifts

One of the first keys to recognizing spiritual gifts is to learn about them. Three separate scriptures provide extensive lists of spiritual gifts. We can find these lists in 1 Corinthians 12:8–11, 28–30; Moroni 10:8–19; and D&C 46:8–29. If we are serious about developing our spiritual gifts, we should read each of these chapters carefully to be able to identify our gifts more fully and understand their purpose. In addition, it's important to know that there are many more spiritual gifts than are listed in those verses.

Elder Marvin J. Ashton taught that there are many spiritual gifts that we overlook. He said, "Let us review some of these less-conspicuous gifts: the gift of asking; the gift of listening; the gift of hearing and using a still, small voice; the gift of being able to weep; the gift of avoiding contention; the gift of being agreeable; the gift of avoiding vain repetition; the gift of seeking that which is righteous; the gift of not passing judgment; the gift of looking to God for guidance; the gift of being a disciple; the gift of caring for others; the gift of being able to ponder; the gift of offering prayer; the gift of bearing a mighty testimony; and the gift of receiving the Holy Ghost."[3]

DO TRY THIS AT HOME!

Get two friends to help you with this one. Each of you read one of the three chapters that talks about spiritual gifts: 1 Corinthians 12:8-11, 28-30; Moroni 10:8-19; and D&C 46:8-29. As each of you read, make a list of spiritual gifts you find. Compare what you learn with each other.

SPIRITUAL GIFTS ARE A LOT LIKE THE GOLDEN PLATES

When Joseph Smith was told about the golden plates, Moroni warned him that Satan would tempt him "to get the plates for the purpose of getting rich. This he forbade me, saying that I must have no other object in view in getting the plates but to glorify God, and must not be influenced by any other motive than that of building his kingdom; otherwise I could not get them" (Joseph Smith—History 1:46). Our own spiritual gifts from heaven are similar: If we want to use them for selfish purposes, we might lose them. Remember the Lord said that "all these [spiritual] gifts come from God, *for the benefit of the children of God*" (D&C 46:26; emphasis added).

THE SPIRITUAL GIFT OF PROPHECY

As a young boy, Reed Smoot heard Brigham Young prophesy that "the day would come when the human voice could be heard from New York to San Francisco." Reed did not believe it and told his mother, "'Now that's a big lie. That's absolutely impossible. It couldn't be.'

"His mother, who was woman of very great faith, told her son, 'Yes, you'll live to see the fulfillment of what the President has said today.'"

Many years passed, and Reed Smoot became a United States senator. During this time, "a broadcasting system was built so you could speak from New York City to San Francisco. One of his colleagues in the Senate . . . [was in charge of this system and] invited Senator Smoot to come to New York City and be the first man to speak over the completed network, which he did, and his voice was heard clearly and distinctly across the continent." Brigham Young's prophecy was fulfilled.[4]

Desire and Pray for Spiritual Gifts

After listing several spiritual gifts, Moroni says, "And all these gifts come by the Spirit of Christ; and they come unto every man severally, according as he will" (Moroni 10:17).

President Boyd K. Packer taught, "I have thought that the last phrase, 'every man severally, according as he will,' refers to the man himself. If a man wills that the gift should come to him, and he desires it, the gift shall be his."[5]

That is a powerful promise. If we really desire spiritual gifts, we must show the Lord by our desires and actions. Elder Robert D. Hales taught, "To find the gifts we have been given, we must pray and fast."[6] There may be spiritual gifts that the Lord wants to give us that he is simply waiting for us to ask for.

WHICH SHOES ARE BEST?

Are basketball shoes better than hiking boots? Well, it depends on whether we are playing basketball or hiking. One isn't better than the other, they are just different. Spiritual gifts are similar; we shouldn't get caught up in wondering if the gifts we have are better than other gifts. All spiritual gifts are important—that is why there is a variety of gifts given to a variety of individuals, just like a variety of shoes.

President George Q. Cannon taught, "If any of us are imperfect, it is our duty to pray for the gift that will make us perfect. Have I imperfections? I am full of them. What is my duty? To pray to God to give me the gifts that will correct these imperfections. If I am an angry man, it is my duty to pray for charity, which suffereth long and is kind. . . . No man ought to say, 'Oh, I cannot help this; it is my nature.' He is not justified in it, for the reason that God has promised to give strength to correct these things, and to give gifts that will eradicate them."[8]

Girls and Spiritual Gifts

Sometimes we read the list of spiritual gifts in the scriptures, such as healings, prophecy, visions, and revelations, and we think they only apply to men or the priesthood. That simply is not true! Spiritual gifts are gifts of the Spirit—gifts that apply equally to men and women.

So can a girl have a vision? You better believe it! The prophet Joel tells us that in the last days "your sons *and your daughters* shall prophesy . . . and upon the *handmaids* in those days will I pour out my spirit" (Joel 2:28-29; emphasis added). For example, Eliza R. Snow wrote the lyrics to the hymn "O My Father."[7] Speaking about that hymn, Wilford Woodruff said, "That hymn is a revelation. . . . There are a great many sisters who have the spirit of revelation. There is no reason why they should not be inspired."[9]

When was the last time we specifically prayed for a spiritual gift? We have been instructed to pray "with all the energy of heart" for the spiritual gift of charity—have we done that for that gift, or for the other gifts we are seeking to develop (see Moroni 7:48)?

SPIRITUAL GIFTS QUIZ

Match the statements below with the gift being described.

1. "[It is] a gift which is not much thought of by many and probably seldom prayed for; yet it is a gift that is of exceeding value and one that should be enjoyed by every Latter-day Saint."

2. Without this gift you are "nothing."

3. "As members of the Church, we are given two spiritual gifts: the Light of Christ given to all men at birth and _____."

4. "Many Latter-day Saints have this gift."

A. The gift of the Holy Ghost

B. The gift of testimony

C. The gift of charity

D. The gift of discernment

1. D. George Q. Cannon, *Gospel Truth: Discourses and Writings of President George Q. Cannon*, comp. Jerreld L. Newquist, 2 vols. (Salt Lake City: Deseret Book, 1974), 1:198. 2. C. See Moroni 7:46. 3. A. Carol B. Thomas, "Developing Our Talent for Spirituality," *Ensign*, May 2001, 88. 4. B. Dallin H. Oaks, "Spiritual Gifts," *Ensign*, September 1986, 68.

Study Your Patriarchal Blessing

One way we can find spiritual gifts we have is to carefully read our patriarchal blessing. Elder Robert D. Hales said, "Often patriarchal blessings tell us the gifts we have received and declare the promise of gifts we can receive if we seek after them."[10] As we study our blessing, remember that there are many kinds of spiritual gifts. For example, our patriarchal blessing may not specifically use the word "gift" but might say, "You have the ability to communicate well with others." That could be a spiritual gift of communication.

"Read [your patriarchal blessing] frequently. Study it carefully. Be guided by its cautions. Live to merit its promises. If you have not yet received your patriarchal blessing, plan for the time when you will receive it, and then cherish it."—President Thomas S. Monson[11]

Invitation to Act

If you have received your patriarchal blessing, read it carefully and look to see if it talks about any spiritual gifts you might have. Pray and ask the Lord to help you know what spiritual gifts you have and how you can develop them.

? HOW *can I* know if I should get my patriarchal blessing?

One way you can tell that you are getting ready to receive your patriarchal blessing is when you start thinking about it more frequently. An article in *The New Era* said, "The best time for you to receive a blessing is when you are ready. Being 'ready' means being emotionally as well as spiritually prepared. This will probably be during your teenage years. This is when you start to become independent and begin to wonder about life and what will happen to you."[12]

We recommend that you pray and talk with God directly about your patriarchal blessing. As you seek his counsel, we know he will give you guidance. Seek counsel also from your bishop and your parents.

The Gift of Tongues

Elder John H. Groberg recorded how the gift of tongues blessed him on his mission to Tonga. As he was teaching some investigators he found that he was able to use words and phrases that he had never used before. This same gift is experienced by thousands of missionaries every day.[14]

Pay Attention to That Which Comes Naturally

Remember that some of our spiritual gifts are talents and abilities that we already developed in the pre-mortal life. Joseph Fielding Smith taught, "The spirits of men were created with different dispositions and likes and talents. Some evidently were mechanically inclined, from them have come our inventors. Some loved music, and hence they have become great musicians. We evidently brought to this world some if not all of the inclinations and talents that we had there."[13] If we find that we are naturally drawn to books and reading, perhaps we developed the gift of knowledge before we came to earth. If we find ourselves inclined to creative pursuits, perhaps we learned a little about creation from the Greatest Creator before we came to earth. Paying attention to the positive abilities that come naturally to us is another form of recognizing our spiritual gifts.

President Thomas S. Monson answered this question saying, "My counsel . . . to each young person is that you should study and prepare for your life's work in a field that you enjoy, because you are going to spend a good share of your life in that field. I believe it should be a field that will challenge your intellect and a field that will make maximum utilization of your talents and capabilities; and finally, I think it should be a field that will provide you sufficient remuneration to provide adequately for a companion and children. Such is a big order; but I bear testimony that these criteria are very important in choosing one's life's work."[15]

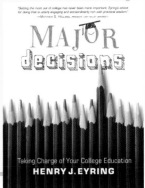

"Getting the most out of college has never been more important. Eyring's advice for doing that is utterly engaging and extraordinarily rich with practical wisdom."
—MATTHEW S. HOLLAND, PRESIDENT, UTAH VALLEY UNIVERSITY

MAJOR decisions

Taking Charge of Your College Education
HENRY J. EYRING

Serve Others

LOST & FOUND

Jesus Christ taught a profound truth in finding ourselves and developing our gifts: "He that findeth his life shall lose it: and he that loseth his life for my sake shall find it" (Matthew 10:39). Service is not only a spiritual gift itself, but a gift that leads to the development of other spiritual gifts. *For the Strength of Youth* teaches this connection between service and developing our gifts: "As you devote yourself to serving others, you will draw closer to Heavenly Father. Your heart will be filled with love. *Your capacities will increase.*"[16] We may find that spiritual gifts come to us or are developed as we accept Church callings or work to serve others.

As we seek for and develop our spiritual gifts, remember that they do not always all appear at once. Joseph Smith taught that some spiritual gifts do not appear until they are needed. He said that "it would require time and circumstances to call these gifts into operation."[17]

God has given each of us spiritual gifts. "As we develop and share our God-given gifts and benefit from the gifts of those around us, the world can be a better place and God's work will move forward at a more rapid pace."[18]

TELL ME ONE MORE TiME!

How Can I Recognize and Develop Spiritual Gifts?

- Learn about spiritual gifts.
- Desire and pray for spiritual gifts.
- Study your patriarchal blessing.
- Pay attention to that which comes naturally.
- Serve others.

How Can I Tell the Difference Between Right and Wrong?

"Should I be kind to my little sister, or should I kick a kitten?" Sometimes it's easy to tell what the right decision is. (Hint: DON'T kick the kitten.)

The Lord has clearly defined many things for us in the gospel: loving your neighbor: right; immorality: wrong. Taking the sacrament worthily: right; taking the sacrament unworthily: wrong. Going to the temple: right; going to a party where drugs and alcohol are offered: wrong. But sometimes it is a little harder to tell the difference between what is right and what is wrong.

For example: Is it okay to watch football on Sunday night? Is it wrong to skip a school class if there is a substitute who won't care if I'm there? What kind of bathing suit is modest, and when does it become immodest? When is it all right to kiss someone? How can we make sure we are always on the Lord's side?

WHICH DRAWING IS CORRECT?

These drawings each represent a way of looking at life. The first drawing suggests that some things are right and some things are wrong and there is a "gray" zone in the middle. The second drawing illustrates that the choices we make are black or white, either right or wrong. So which is correct?

President George Albert Smith quoted his grandfather (who was also an Apostle) as saying, "'There is a line of demarcation well defined between the Lord's territory and the devil's territory. If you will remain on the Lord's side of the line, the adversary cannot come there to tempt you. You are perfectly safe as long as you stay on the Lord's side of the line. But . . . if you cross onto the devil's side of the line, you are in his territory, and you are in his power, and he will work on you to get you just as far from that line as he possibly can, knowing that he can only succeed in destroying you by keeping you away from the place where there is safety.'"[1] For most situations, if we are in tune with the Spirit of the Lord we can find out what the Lord's side is and how we personally should act, even in circumstances when what should or shouldn't be done hasn't been plainly stated in scriptures or by the prophets.

But how can we do that? Keep reading . . .

Search the Scriptures and the Words of the Prophets to Know Where Right and Wrong Have Clearly Been Stated

The more we understand the scriptures and the words of the prophets, the more clearly we will know right from wrong. We have often heard teenagers debate whether it is "okay" to do a certain thing, not realizing that the answer to their question was clearly stated in *For the Strength of Youth* or another official Church publication. Don't fall into the mistake of not knowing what to do when, indeed, the Lord or his prophets have clearly defined right from wrong on a particular matter.

Search for True Principles to Guide You When Commandments Haven't Been Given

Elder Richard G. Scott taught a deep and important truth that can be applied to this question of knowing right and wrong under confusing circumstances. He said that one of the keys is to know the *principles* of the gospel because "principles are concentrated truth, packaged for application to a wide variety of circumstances. A true principle makes decisions clear even under the most confusing and compelling circumstances."[2]

For example, suppose a young man is asked by his friends to ride down the street in a garbage can strapped on top of a skateboard (this may seem like an unrealistic example, but one of our students really asked us if it was wrong). Now, there is no commandment we know of that says, "Thou shalt not attempt high-risk stunts"—(though who knows, maybe there is in the lost 116 pages ☺)—but how can the following principle help him know whether it is right or wrong in this area? *Principle: Our bodies are sacred creations in the image of God. Our bodies are the tabernacle of our spirit, and we are stewards to Christ over them.*

What if a young woman wants to know if it is okay to study pictures of the human body in her anatomy class textbook to learn her material? How could the same principle help her in making her decision?

President Boyd K. Packer said, "A principle is an enduring truth, a law, a rule you can adopt to guide you in making decisions. Generally principles are not spelled out in detail. That leaves you free to find your way with an enduring truth, a principle, as your anchor."[3]

As we come to know, understand, and believe true principles of the gospel of Jesus Christ, they will effectively guide our way in the areas that seem unclear or confusing.

HOW *can I tell what media are appropriate?*

The Church will probably never come out with a list of songs or bands that are approved and a list of those that are not approved. Same with television shows, and most movies. Instead, the prophets generally teach us the correct principles and let us govern ourselves in our media selections. *For the Strength of Youth* teaches us to "pay attention to how you feel when you are listening [to music]. Don't listen to music that drives away the Spirit, encourages immorality, glorifies violence, uses foul or offensive language, or promotes Satanism or other evil practices."[4] It also says, "Do not attend, view, or participate in entertainment that is vulgar, immoral, violent, or pornographic in any way. Do not participate in entertainment that in any way presents immorality or violent behavior as acceptable."[5] Using those principles as your guidelines, go through your music and movie collection and determine which ones are or are not appropriate, and act accordingly by getting rid of the bad ones.

DO TRY THIS AT HOME!

Do You Have a Blind Spot?

"Close your left eye and stare at the cross mark in the diagram with your right eye. Off to the right you should be able to see the spot. Don't LOOK at it; just notice that it is there off to the right (if it's not, move farther away). . . . Now slowly move toward the book. Keep looking at the cross mark while you move. At a particular distance . . . the spot will disappear."[6] In a similar way we may have "blind spots" when it comes to making right choices. Maybe we have some "favorite" sins that we just don't want to let go of. Honestly evaluate your life—do you have any blind spots? Since we usually can't see our blind spots, a good practice is to ask a loving and trusted family member or friend what they think.

Ask: Where Does It Lead?

The prophet Mormon warned, "Wherefore, take heed . . . that ye do not judge that which is evil to be of God, or that which is good and of God to be of the devil" (Moroni 7:14). Mormon then taught us how to do this. He said, "I show unto you the way to judge; for every thing which inviteth to do good, and to persuade to believe in Christ, is sent forth by the power and gift of Christ; wherefore ye may know with a perfect knowledge it is of God. But whatsoever thing persuadeth men to do evil, and believe not in Christ, and deny him, and serve not God, then ye may know with a perfect knowledge it is of the devil; for after this manner doth the devil work, for he persuadeth no man to do good, no, not one; neither do his angels; neither do they who subject themselves unto him" (Moroni 7:16–17).

This question—Does it lead me to do good and believe in Christ?—helps confusing decisions between right and wrong be less difficult. If we wonder to ourselves, "Is X okay?" then we simply need to ask ourselves a few questions: Does this thing bring me closer to Christ? Does this invite me to do good? Does it help me more fully live the gospel? Does X persuade me to do evil? Does X persuade me to not serve God, or does it affect my belief in Christ? If so, it's not okay.

One of the principles

in this chapter to knowing good from evil is evaluating what something leads to. Go through the lyrics of several of your favorite songs. Honestly ask yourself, "Do these songs point me toward Jesus Christ?" If you find that your music isn't as good as it should be, delete it!

WHERE DOES YOUR PATH LEAD?

Christ taught, "No man can serve two masters" (Matthew 6:24). We cannot serve God and the devil. Many of our choices bring us closer to one or the other. Our choices can lead us down different paths. When we have to make a choice, we can ask ourselves, "Is this choice leading me down a path that leads toward God or the devil?"

"SEARCH . . . IN THE LIGHT OF CHRIST"

Mormon taught that we "should search diligently in the light of Christ that [we] may know good from evil" (Moroni 7:19). That phrase "search . . . in the light of Christ" is an important one. When we're trying to figure out the difference between right and wrong, we need to have the light of Christ with us. Here's an example. If I have been involved in inappropriate activities, I may become desensitized and have less of the light of Christ with me. In this state it will be more difficult to discern the difference between right and wrong. But if I am living right, I will have more of the light of Christ, and it will be easier to know what is right.

Ask: How Will My Actions Affect Others?

Another key to distinguishing between right and wrong is to honestly ask ourselves how our actions affect others. A great example of this principle is taught in the New Testament. The Apostle Paul was asked a question about whether or not it was okay to eat meat that had been offered to idols. In ancient times, some people would sacrifice an animal to an idol, and then later sell or eat the meat that had come from that animal. People asked Paul, "Is that okay?"

Paul said, "Meat commendeth us not to God: for neither, if we eat, are we the better; neither, if we eat not, are we the worse" (1 Corinthians 8:8). In other words, the answer was, "It doesn't really matter if you eat that meat or not." "But," Paul says, "take heed lest by any means this liberty of yours become a stumbling-block to them that are weak. For if any man see thee which hast knowledge sit at meat in the idol's temple, shall not the conscience of him which is weak be emboldened to eat those things which are offered to idols" (1 Corinthians 8:9–10).

So even though it doesn't really matter if you eat meat or not, you still need to be careful because what you do might affect what others do. Some people might see you (a person with knowledge) eating meat offered to idols and take it one step further and say, "It's okay for me to worship idols."

Therefore, Paul tells us, "If meat make my brother to offend, I will eat no flesh while the world standeth, lest I make my brother to offend" (1 Corinthians 8:13). In other words, Paul says, "If eating meat will have a negative effect on others, I will never eat meat."

Jesus taught this same principle when he was asked to pay taxes. Although he didn't have to pay taxes, he said to his disciples, "Notwithstanding, lest we should offend them, . . . give unto [the tax collectors] for me and thee" (Matthew 17:27). Our Lord was ever aware of how his actions affected others, and he acted accordingly. We should be too.

THE SPIRIT OF THE LAW

Sometimes people justify making wrong decisions because they say, "I'm following the spirit of the law." Elder M. Russell Ballard said that it is Satan who tries to persuade us that we can "live the spirit of the law even if we are in violation of its letter."[7]

Elder David A. Bednar said, "The small things really do matter when it comes to personal worthiness and inviting the Holy Ghost into our lives."[8]

WHICH IS MORE DANGEROUS?

Quick quiz—which of these two animals is most likely to kill you?

Although it might seem surprising, you are actually 300 times more likely to be killed by a deer (by crashing into it with your car) than you are by a shark.[9]

Some people might think that "big" sins like doing drugs are going to get us in trouble while "little sins" aren't such a big deal. Let's not fall into the trap of thinking something isn't wrong just because it is small or seemingly insignificant. Just like a deer, it can be deadly.

Remember That in Some Cases, "It Mattereth Not" unto the Lord

Of course, not everything comes down to a question of right or wrong. For example, "Should I have corn flakes or toasted O's for breakfast?" might not warrant a commandment or direction from the Lord (unless perhaps, the toasted O's were poisoned, in which case you might get a prompting, but back to reality . . .). The Lord sometimes says, "You choose. It's up to you. Either way, you're fine." This might be true for many circumstances we find ourselves in when making decisions. In the Doctrine and Covenants the Lord repeatedly used the phrase, "It mattereth not" (see D&C 60:5; 62:5; 80:3). We have been given the gift of agency, and the Lord wants us to use it. We don't need to be "compelled in all things" (D&C 58:26), especially in the things that don't really have a right or wrong.

Listen to the Holy Ghost

Ultimately, knowing the difference between right and wrong can be boiled down to this: What is the Holy Ghost telling me to do? (see chapter 8). After Joseph Smith died, he appeared to President Brigham Young in a dream. In this dream, Joseph told Brigham Young, "Tell the [Saints] to be humble and faithful, and be sure *to keep the spirit of the Lord and it will lead them right.* Be careful and not turn away the small still voice; it will teach them what to do and where to go; it will yield the fruits of the Kingdom."[10] Like Nephi of old, we can be "led by the Spirit" (1 Nephi 4:6) even if we aren't quite sure what we should do (see Conclusion).

Why Does My Foot Fall Asleep?

What makes your foot fall asleep? When you sit on your foot you block the flow of blood to your foot. You also squish the nerves in that area. So when you stand up, you feel that prickly feeling like you're walking on pins. But in a way that feeling is good. It signals to your body that you need to stop sitting on your foot—that something needs to change.[11] In a similar way, when we feel the Spirit leave it should be a signal to us that what we are doing is not right.

WOULD YOU EAT THIS?

Most would not want to eat this toast. But suppose by the time you got to the toast that the cockroaches weren't there. If you hadn't seen the cockroaches crawling all over the toast, but still knew they had been there, would you eat the toast? Of course not! In a similar way, there are some things that we might not see as wrong, but prophets have warned us against them. Just like you wouldn't eat cockroach-infested toast (even if you hadn't seen the bugs), we shouldn't do things that we don't see as wrong if prophets have warned us against them.

TELL ME ONE MORE TIME!

How Can I Tell the Difference Between Right and Wrong?

- **Search the scriptures and the words of the prophets to know where right and wrong have clearly been stated.**
- **Search for true principles to guide you when commandments haven't been given.**
- **Ask: Where does it lead?**
- **Ask: How will my actions affect others?**
- **Remember that in some cases, "It mattereth not" unto the Lord.**
- **Listen to the Holy Ghost.**

How Can I Set Standards That Will Keep Me Spiritually Safe?

WHAT WOULD YOU DO FOR 10 MILLION DOLLARS?

President Monson reported on a survey that asked people what they would do for 10 million dollars. Let's see what YOU would do for that amount of cash.

"For ten million dollars in cash, would you leave your family permanently?

"Would you marry someone you didn't love?

"Would you give up all your friends permanently?

"Would you serve a year's jail term on a framed charge?

"Would you take off your clothes in public?

"Would you take a dangerous job in which you had a 1-in-10 chance of losing your life?

"Would you become a beggar for a year?

"Of the people polled, 1 percent would leave their families, 10 percent would marry lovelessly, 11 percent would give up friends, 12 percent would undress in public, 13 percent would go to jail for a year, 14 percent would take the risky job, and 21 percent would beg for a year."[1]

From the example above, obviously money cannot be the driving force in the standards that we keep. In order to set firm standards we need to base them on the truths found in the doctrines of the gospel. Elder Richard G. Scott said, "Firmly establish personal standards. Choose a time of deep spiritual reflection, when there is no pressure on you, and you can confirm your decisions by sacred impressions. Decide then what you will do and what you will not do. . . . The Spirit will guide you. Then do not vary from those decisions no matter how right it may seem when the temptation comes. . . . The realization of your dreams depends upon your determination to never betray your standards."[2]

Let's look at three keys from this statement that give counsel on how we can set standards that will keep us spiritually safe.

"Choose a Time of Deep Spiritual Reflection, When There Is No Pressure on You"

An important part of setting standards is to make them in a spiritual setting. For example, we might be more able to set a powerful spiritual goal in a quiet room, in the temple, or in nature, rather than somewhere noisy or distracting. We could find a private place where we could have the scriptures, *For the Strength of Youth*, and a paper and pen to write down impressions we feel as we pray about our standards. It is also important to have enough time set aside that we can wait for impressions to come. Perhaps approaching such a setting with a fast would be appropriate.

Is there a commandment that you have not yet set a firm standard to keep? If so, take some time to ponder, and prayerfully set a standard in this area that you will never deviate from.

Invitation to Act

It is also wise to make sure there is no pressure on us at the time we set our standards. The time to decide whether or not we will view pornography is before our friend says, "Look at this picture." The time to decide whether or not you are going to kiss is before somebody gives you "the kiss look." President Spencer W. Kimball said, "Right decisions are easiest to make when we make them well in advance. . . . The time to decide on a mission is long before it becomes a matter of choosing between a mission and an athletic scholarship. The time to decide on temple marriage is before one has become attached to a boyfriend or girlfriend who does not share that objective."[3]

"Confirm Decisions by Sacred Impressions . . . the Spirit Will Guide You"

There is power that comes when the Holy Ghost gives us direction. Suppose a young man goes to Sunday School and hears the teacher say, "You shouldn't watch R-rated movies." Compare this with a young man who prays about his standards and feels the Holy Ghost tell him that he shouldn't watch R-rated movies. Which will leave a more powerful impression upon the young man's mind and heart?

Speaking of the youth of the Church, President Henry B. Eyring said, "They must choose obedience to the Lord's commandments in the face of greater temptations and trials. They must do it out of faith in Jesus Christ. *And that faith can only come through the witness of the Spirit.*"[4] Elder Richard G. Scott has repeatedly told of a sacred experience he had receiving inspiration during a Church meeting. Of the process he said, "I received further impressions, and the process of writing down the impressions, pondering, and *praying for confirmation* was repeated."[5] The Spirit confirmed revelation to Elder Scott, and it can impress the standards we should commit to live in our minds more powerfully than anything else.

HOW can I set a standard I will keep for the rest of my life?

Maybe right now you don't need to set a standard that you will keep for the rest of your life. For example, think about the law of chastity. You don't need to say "I will never kiss anybody in my life" (because someday you'll kiss your future spouse, we hope!), but you may be inspired to set a personal standard like, "I will not engage in passionate kissing before marriage. And I am not going to kiss anybody until I am in a meaningful relationship that could lead to marriage."

As another example, you could say, "Between now and the time I am sixteen, I will never watch a PG-13 movie." When you turn sixteen, you could seek inspiration about whether or not you should continue with that standard.

DO TRY THIS AT HOME!

Take a look at the picture below. How tall would you say this person is?

Now, guess how tall the person is, but this time guess in "spans."

Don't know what a span is? It's the distance between the end of the thumb to the end of the little finger when your fingers are extended.

Why was it easier to guess "feet and inches" compared to spans? Because we all know and accept the standard of feet and inches. When a standard is defined and accepted, it becomes easy to judge whether you are on or off. Spans differ depending on the size of a person's hand (my span might be bigger than your span), so there is inconsistency and error. Additionally, some people don't know what a span means, so they don't know the standard to judge from.

The standards of the Church are more like measuring in feet and inches than measuring in spans. The measurements are clear. The more we are familiar with those standards and accept them, the easier it is to know if our lives are on the mark. However, if we use the world's ever-shifting standards, it is much like a span . . . you never really know if you are truly correct!

"Do Not Vary from Those Decisions No Matter How Right It May Seem When the Temptation Comes"

There is always a temptation to vary from our standards. Let's look at two stories from the scriptures and compare what Lehonti and Nehemiah did as they were faced with continual temptation.

Lehonti led a group of Lamanites who didn't want to fight Nephites. The Lamanite king wanted to fight the Nephites and sent an evil man named Amalickiah to make Lehonti and his group go to war. Lehonti and his men were safe on a mountain. Now notice what happens.

"And it came to pass that when it was night [Amalickiah] sent a secret embassy into the mount Antipas, desiring that the leader of those who were upon the mount, whose name was Lehonti, that *he should come down to the foot of the mount,* for he desired to speak with him. And it came to pass that when Lehonti received the message he durst not go down to the foot of the mount. And it came to pass that *Amalickiah sent again the second time,* desiring him to come down. And it came to pass that Lehonti would not; and *he sent again the third time.* And it came to pass that when Amalickiah found that he could not get Lehonti to come down off from the mount, *he went up into the mount, nearly to Lehonti's camp;* and *he sent again the fourth time his message unto Lehonti,* desiring that he would come down, and that he would bring his guards with him. And it came to pass that . . . Lehonti [came] down with his guards to Amalickiah" (Alma 47:10–13; emphasis added).

So the first three times Lehonti refused to come down from his place of safety. But on the fourth time, Amalickiah went up, almost to where Lehonti was, and said, "Just come down a little bit—and bring your guards." That might be like Satan tempting us today saying, "It's not that big of a deal. As long as you're with your friends, it won't hurt you to do this."

On the fourth time, Lehonti gave in. Within a short period of time, he had been murdered, and Amalickiah was in command of the army.

Compare that account with that of Nehemiah. Nehemiah was in charge of rebuilding a wall around Jerusalem. His enemies, Sanballat, Tobiah, and Geshem, wanted to stop the wall from being built and devised a plan to harm Nehemiah. They asked him to come to the plains of (Ono) and "thought to do [him] mischief" (Nehemiah 6:2).

OH NO!

Nehemiah's enemies wanted to meet him in the plain of "Ono." If you're asked to go somewhere or do something that would make your parents say, "Oh no!"—don't do it!

Nehemiah refused to go to Ono. He said, "I sent messengers unto them, saying, I am doing a great work, so that I cannot come down: why should the work cease, whilst I leave it, and come down to you?" (Nehemiah 6:3).

Notice what happens next. He said, "They sent unto me *four times* after this sort; and I answered them after the same manner" (Nehemiah 6:4).

Amalickiah tried to get Lehonti to "come down" from the mountain and he succeeded on his fourth try. Sanballat tried to get Nehemiah to "come down" from his wall. But Nehemiah refused. Not just once or twice or three times, but on the fourth time as well.

Elder Richard G. Scott said, "Do not vary from [your decision] no matter how right it may seem when the temptation comes."[6] The difference between Lehonti and Nehemiah is what they did "the fourth time." In life, our standards will be challenged repeatedly. We must decide now that on the fourth, fifth, and every time we will hold fast to our standards.

DON'T LET DOWN!

In the 2006 Winter Olympics, Lindsey Jacobellis competed in the Women's Snowboard Cross event. She was in the lead and clearly going to win the gold medal. But on the last jump she was showing off and attempted a method grab. She didn't land it, and as a result, she lost the gold medal, settling for silver. She had been in the lead the whole time, but a small mistake at the end cost her. When it comes to your standards, don't ever let your guard down. Keep strong to the end![7]

Set a Standard That Will Help Keep You from Ever Getting Close to the Line

Another important part of setting firm standards is that we set a standard that will help us keep from ever getting close to the line of sin. For example, when it comes to the law of chastity, *For the Strength of Youth* says, "Do not participate in passionate kissing."[8] The question isn't, "How long can I kiss before it's passionate?" but "What standard can I set to keep far away from passionate kissing?" What matters isn't how close can we get to the line, but rather, how we can avoid even getting close.

The question "How far can I go and not sin?" is *not* the important question. President Henry B. Eyring, when he was a member of the Quorum of the Twelve, taught, "The question that really matters is this: 'How can I learn to sense even the beginning of sin and so repent early?'"[9]

As we set standards for ourselves we must make sure that they are standards that will help keep us *far away* from the line of sin, not right next to it.

HOW strict should I be when I set a standard for myself?

Perhaps it's less important that you be super-strict with yourself, and more important that you try hard to receive personal revelation for what your standards should be. You could get really strict and say, "I'm setting a standard to never watch a movie" (and maybe some people would feel inspired to set that standard). But instead of focusing on being strict (or on trying to get away with as much as you can), try to focus on what you think your Father in Heaven would have you do to stay far away from the line of sin.

So don't set a standard to go right up to the line of sin. For example, when it comes to the law of chastity, the line might look like this:

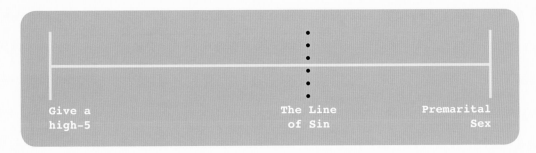

Instead, set a standard that will keep you from even getting close to the line of sin.

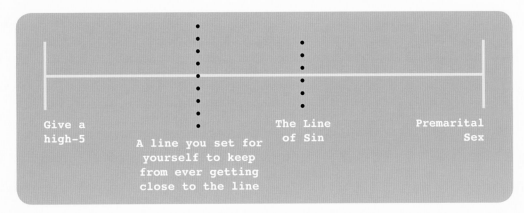

The same principle applies to other standards.

TELL ME ONE MORE TIME!

How Can I Set Standards That Will Keep Me Spiritually Safe?

- "Choose a time of deep spiritual reflection, when there is no pressure on you."
- "Confirm decisions by sacred impressions . . . the Spirit will guide you."
- "Do not vary from those decisions no matter how right it may seem when the temptation comes."
- Set a standard that will help keep you from ever getting close to the line.

How Can I Stay Morally Clean?

President Gordon B. Hinckley said that staying morally clean was "the most common and most difficult of all problems for . . . young men and young women to handle."[1] Alma taught his son Corianton that immorality is one of the "most abominable" of all sins (see Alma 39:3–5). Because of the seriousness of this commandment, and the difficulty for some in keeping it, it is vital that we understand how we can stay morally clean.

Learn from a Proverb

There's a powerful story from the book of Proverbs that provides several suggestions as to how we can stay morally clean. We're going to quote this story, and as you read it, you'll see comments we've made to go along with it (Proverbs 7:6–27).

6. For at the window of my house I looked through my casement, ...

> This can be seen as a metaphor that God is watching us and our actions. This young man's actions were being watched. Immorality is usually a sin that is done in the dark or in a secluded place, where others don't see. But one person always sees. We cannot hide our actions from our loving Heavenly Father.

7. And beheld among the simple ones, I discerned among the youths, a young man void of understanding, . . .

> In other words, this young man doesn't get it. He either doesn't know how serious immorality is, or how to avoid becoming involved in it. Either way, we must "learn wisdom in [our] youth" (Alma 37:35) and become Saints who understand how serious immorality is and how to avoid it.

8. Passing through the street near her corner; . . . . . and he went the way to her house,

> Notice that the young man is walking in a bad area. One way that we can stay morally clean is to stay out of places where temptation will be lurking, such as being alone in a bedroom with someone, or laying down with him or her, or being alone in the house or a far basement corner.

9. In the twilight, in the evening, in the . . . . . black and dark night:

> Being out too late often leads to trouble. At night we often are more tired, which causes us to not think as clearly and to relax our inhibitions.

10. And, behold, there met him a woman with the attire of an harlot, and subtil of heart. . . . .

> The way the person was dressed should have been a tip-off that they weren't going to make it easier to live the law of chastity. We're not suggesting that you judge people based on the clothes they wear; but at the same time, we can sometimes tell from other's clothes what their values might be.

11. (She is loud and stubborn; her feet abide not in her house:

12. Now is she without, now in the streets, and lieth in wait at every corner.) · · · ·

It's important to realize that temptation is everywhere. This kind of situation can happen "at every corner."

13. So she caught him, and kissed him, · · and with an impudent face said unto him,

Although kissing has its time and place, remember that the prophets tell us to avoid "passionate kissing" before marriage. Many things start with a couple getting "caught" up in passionate kissing that soon leads to further violations of the law of chastity.

14. I have peace offerings with me; this day have I payed my vows. · · · · · · · · · ·

The woman is trying to sound like she is righteous. Sometimes people will use their "righteousness" (or the fact that they are a member of the Church) to get us to do things that are wrong. Don't fall for that trap!

15. Therefore came I forth to meet thee, diligently to seek thy face, and I have found thee.

16. I have decked my bed with coverings of tapestry, with carved works, with fine linen of Egypt.

17. I have perfumed my bed · · · · · with myrrh, aloes, and cinnamon.

She's trying to make it seem like everything will be great if they are immoral together. The sweet scents, the feelings. Satan wants us to get caught up in the moment and to not think about consequences.

18. Come, let us take our fill of love until the morning: let us solace ourselves with loves. · · · · · · · · · ·

Notice how she is using the word "love" here to seduce him. Love is not shown through immorality. This word should be replaced with "lust." Love is of God, and these feelings are not of God.

19. For the goodman is not · · · at home, he is gone a long journey . . . :

The word "goodman" can also mean "husband." She's saying, "Don't worry. My husband isn't home, nobody will find out." If we're tempted to do something because "nobody will know" it's a sure sign that we shouldn't be doing it.

21. With her much fair · · · speech she caused him to yield, with the flattering of her lips she forced him.

People are going to use "much fair speech" to persuade us to make wrong choices. Don't listen to the flattering words of others. If they are trying to persuade us to do something we know is wrong, it is a sign we should end the conversation and get out of there.

22. He goeth after her straightway, as an ox goeth to the slaughter, or as a fool to the correction of the stocks; . . .

25. Let not thine heart decline to her ways, go not astray in her paths.

26. For she hath cast down many wounded: yea, many strong men have been slain by her. ·

While we are free to choose, we are not free to choose our consequences. Immorality will always result in the "slaughter" of our peace of mind, and leave us bound in "stocks" or chains of guilt, shame, and remorse.

In order to stay morally clean we must realize that we can fall. If we think, "Well I can push the line a little bit, I'm strong enough to stop later," that is a sure sign of serious danger. The scripture says that "many strong men" have fallen into the trap of immorality. None of us are above it.

The law of chastity is serious stuff! Doctrine and Covenants 76 tells us that unrepentant people guilty of immorality will not inherit the celestial kingdom.

27. Her house is the way to hell, · · · · going down to the chambers of death.

Let's summarize some of the lessons we can learn from this account.

- Don't put ourselves in dangerous situations by being alone with a member of the opposite sex whom you feel a strong attraction for.
- Don't be out too late. An all-night prom party might sound fun, but it's a recipe for disaster.
- Only date those with high moral standards.
- Always be on guard. Moral temptation can come at us at 12:00 noon as well as at 12:00 midnight, on a first date or a fifth date.
- Beware of justifications such as "We didn't go all the way," or "It's not a big deal," or "We're in love." Also, don't think that "nobody will know." Two people always know: you and God. We should ask ourselves, "Is this something I feel like I need to hide from my parents or from God?" If the answer is yes, don't do it!
- Even if we think we are strong, we still need to be careful.

President Spencer W. Kimball taught that when faced with temptation long enough, "the best boy and the best girl will finally succumb and fall."[2]

HOW *can I avoid morally compromising situations?*

Sister Susan W. Tanner gave some valuable advice that can help us avoid morally compromising situations. She said, "Avoid the dangers of the dark. Stay in well-lit places—literally and figuratively. . . . Beware the hazard of the horizontal. Don't lie down together with a date. Just don't do it—not to watch a movie or to read a book or to rest at a picnic. . . .

Remember the perils of privacy. Find public places to be alone. Learn to have your intimate talks where others are. There is great safety in being together where you can easily be interrupted. . . . Modesty is a must. Everything about your appearance, your speech, and your demeanor should bespeak that you are a literal spirit son or daughter of Heavenly Father."[3]

GET A PARK BENCH

If you really need to be alone with someone you are attracted to in order to talk, go to a public place where there are a lot of people around.

DO TRY THIS AT HOME!

Sit down and play the piano, but just press random keys and bang on it. Sounds ugly, right? Now, if you know how to play, play a piece of music or listen to someone play a beautiful piano piece. Notice the difference? It is nice. Isn't it interesting that it is the same instrument that is producing the ugly sound and the beautiful one? Physical intimacy with someone is very much the same as a piano: If done at the right time and right place and right order and timing—in marriage—it is "beautiful and sacred."[4] If played out of order and without the right timing, it turns ugly.

President Gordon B. Hinckley said, "Nothing really good happens after 11 o'clock at night."[5] If you have a curfew, keep it. If you don't have one, create one for yourself and keep it.

We're not sure we'd go this far . . .

KISS THE POST!

One young man said, "Kissing doesn't affect me." Elder Gene R. Cook responded to this young man by saying, "When you take your girlfriend home tonight, why don't you shake hands with her at the door and then kiss the post in front of her house?" The young man could tell that it wouldn't be the same, and realized that kissing did affect him.[6]

Speaking of kissing, President Spencer W. Kimball taught, "To kiss in casual dating is asking for trouble. What do kisses mean when given out like pretzels or robbed of sacredness? . . . Even if timely courtship justifies the kiss, it should be a clean, decent, sexless one."[7]

? **HOW** *can I respond if somebody is trying to kiss me and I don't want them to?*

Give them a karate chop to the nose. Or say, "Hey, look, an eagle," and when your date looks up in the sky, run inside. Or you could simply say, "Well, it's too bad that I just got mono. I'm really contagious." Just kidding. There are actually some pretty cool maneuvers you can do like pulling your head to the side, or leaning to the side to give a quick friendly hug. One girl we know follows the rule to simply never make eye contact at the doorstep. Probably the best approach is to be clear and direct and tell the person firmly, "I do not want to kiss you." If that doesn't work, then maybe a karate chop will be okay after all! ☺

Learn from Joseph

Most of us are familiar with the story of Joseph in Egypt, who was sold into slavery by his brothers. While Joseph was working for a man named Potiphar, Potiphar's wife wanted him to be sexually immoral with her. Let's take a look at that account (Genesis 39:1, 7–12).

7. And it came to pass after [Joseph had been put in charge of Potiphar's affairs], that [Potiphar's] wife cast her eyes upon Joseph; and she said, Lie with me.

8. But he refused, and said unto his master's wife, Behold, my master wotteth not what is with me in the house, and he hath committed all that he hath to my hand;

9. There is none greater in this house than I; neither hath he kept back any thing from me but thee, because thou art his wife: how then can I do this great wickedness, and sin against God?

10. And it came to pass, as she spake to Joseph day by day, that he hearkened not unto her, to lie by her, or to be with her.

11. And it came to pass about this time, that Joseph went into the house to do his business; and there was none of the men of the house there within.

12. And she caught him by his garment, saying, Lie with me: and he left his garment in her hand, and fled, and got him out.

What a powerful three-word phrase: "But he refused." When others tempt us to be immoral, we can do likewise and refuse.

Part of what gave Joseph the courage to resist sexual temptation was the understanding that it was "great wickedness" and a "sin against God" to be immoral.

Note that Joseph avoided temptation by steering clear of Potiphar's wife.

Trouble came when Joseph was alone with Potiphar's wife.

When push comes to shove, it's better to just run away and get out of a bad situation.

This scriptural account teaches us a powerful principle that will help us stay morally clean: Avoid being alone with someone you are attracted to. Logic tells us that adhering to this one principle alone would alleviate much of the temptation to violate the law of chastity with those we date. It was when they were alone that Potiphar's wife tried to seduce Joseph. Perhaps this is why Elder David E. Sorensen said, "When you're on a date, plan to be in groups and *avoid being alone.*"[8]

For the Strength of Youth says plainly, "When you begin dating, go in groups or on double dates."[9] Notice that when Joseph saw he was alone with Potiphar's wife and she tried to seduce him, he "fled, and got him out" (Genesis 39:12). Paul tells us to "flee fornication" (1 Corinthians 6:18). If you find yourself alone with the person you are attracted to, there is no shame in showing some good legs and getting out of there.

Consider a modern-day Joseph

A young woman named Marie refused to give in to sexual temptation. Marie had made friends with a guy named Tom at her school. She didn't know him very well, but one weekend he asked her on a date. It was a group date and so she

said yes. There were a bunch of guys and girls together, but she did not know any of them. When she asked where they were going, her date said, "Downtown." They drove to a hotel and then all the guys got out of the car and said, "We'll be right back." When they came back to the car, Marie could tell the boys were hiding something inside their coats. The boys said, "We've got a bunch of beer and we've rented a hotel room. We're going to have a great time!"

Marie looked at the other girls and could tell that they felt uncomfortable. She definitely did. She had never been tempted to break the Word of Wisdom before, but she didn't know what to do. Her date pulled her aside and said, "C'mon, Marie, we'll get drunk and have the time of our lives. You won't even remember it if you don't want to."

Marie refused. "I'm not doing this and you girls aren't either," Marie said to the other young women. Marie called her mother and all but one of the girls came home with them. When faced with temptation, Marie refused, and then like Joseph, "fled" and got out.

The #1 Road to Immorality: Early Steady Dating (Avoid it!)

In addition to the great principles taught from Proverbs 7 and Genesis 39, we'd like to discuss a few other specific principles that will help us stay morally clean.

President Spencer W. Kimball taught, "A vicious, destructive, social pattern of early steady dating must be changed. . . . The change of this one pattern of social activities of our youth would immediately eliminate a majority of the sins of our young folks."[10]

If we want to avoid immorality we should avoid having a steady boyfriend or girlfriend until we're ready to be married. This would be after a young man has returned from his mission. (So, guys, don't steady date until after your mission,

Invitation to Act

If you are currently involved in an exclusive steady dating relationship prior to the time of a young man's mission call, call your girlfriend/boyfriend and discuss with them your desire to follow prophetic teachings to avoid steady dating too early in a relationship.

and girls, don't steady date a young man before his mission.) One study showed that more than 80 percent of LDS teens who steady dated had gone beyond the boundary described in *For the Strength of Youth.*[11] President Gordon B. Hinckley taught, "Steady dating at an early age leads so often to [moral] tragedy. . . . Have a wonderful time, but *stay away from familiarity.*"[12]

"But wait!" you might say. "Everyone at my high school has a boyfriend or a girlfriend. It can't be *that* bad." Maybe a fashion analogy can help.

Do these clothes look cool? They used to be 100 percent in fashion. But now, most kids wouldn't be caught dead in them. Believe it or not, if we "wanted to do what everyone else was doing" back in the day, we would have worn these clothes. That's the danger with doing things "because everybody else is doing it." The fads and trends of the world change. And when we follow those trends, sorrow is often the result.

Are you obsessed with following fads and trends?

A scriptural example of this can be seen in 1 Samuel 8. The Lord had told the Israelites to have a system of judges, but instead the Israelites wanted a king. They said, "Make us a king to judge us *like all the nations*" (1 Samuel 8:5; emphasis added). The prophet tried to help them see that having a king was a bad idea, but still the people said, "We will have a king over us; that we also may be *like all the nations*" (1 Samuel 8:19–20; emphasis added). Like some of us, the Israelites wanted to be like everybody else.

The Israelites *were* given a king, and within a short space of time they were brought into bondage. Just because it seems that many people at our school steady date doesn't mean we should. Avoid the number one source of immorality and decide today not to steady date until the young man in the relationship is a returned missionary.

STAY MORALLY CLEAN: AVOID PORNOGRAPHY AT ALL COSTS

For the Strength of Youth specifically states that "pornography . . . can lead you to sexual transgression."[13] This is because what we see affects what we think, what we think affects what we desire, and what we desire determines our actions (see chapter 14).

Dress Modestly

Remember that what we wear isn't just cute, it also sends a message about us. "Your dress and grooming send messages about you to others."[14] If we are consistently revealing our bodies, then people get the message that we must not think our body is too important or sacred and will treat us that way.[15]

MORAL PURITY AND YOUR BRAIN

Recent research has shown that when people have intimate physical contact with multiple people it actually changes the chemicals in their brains, making it more difficult to develop deep relationships. Just one more reason why it is so important to stay morally clean.[16]

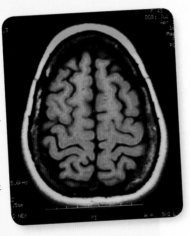

HEY GIRLS! WHAT TYPE OF BOY DO YOU WANT TO ATTRACT?

Anthony Says:

I had a young woman come into my office one day, crying. She was cute and kind and popular, but she also had a tendency to dress very immodestly. I asked her what was wrong, and she said, "I can't understand why the only kind of guys who want to date me are the ones who want to do bad things. No matter what, I only seem to attract bad guys. I don't get it."

I asked her if I could be honest and open with her, to which she consented. I said to her in as kind, yet straightforward way as possible, "Immoral boys are attracted to immodest girls. Moral boys are attracted to modest girls. The way you are dressing is sending a message to these boys that your body isn't that sacred to you, and that you are using your body to get their attention."

She looked at me surprised, not at what I had said, but at the idea that the way she was dressing was affecting the *type* of boy she was attracting. I don't think she had ever connected those two ideas before.

? HOW *does moral purity apply to those who have been victims of sexual abuse?*

For the Strength of Youth says, "Victims of rape, incest, or other sexual abuse are not guilty of sin. If you have been a victim of any of these crimes, know that you are innocent and that God loves you. Seek your bishop's counsel immediately so he can help guide you through the process of emotional healing."[17]

When it comes to staying morally clean, it is *so* important that we hold to clear standards and never deviate from them. In fact, this principle is so important that we've devoted a whole separate chapter to it—go read it! (See chapter 12.)

We testify that if we will follow the scriptural and prophetic principles outlined in this chapter, we can all live a morally clean life from this day forward.

TELL ME ONE MORE TiME!

How Can I Stay Morally Clean?

- **Remember the lessons from Proverbs 7:**
  1. Don't be alone with a member of the opposite sex whom you feel a strong attraction for.
  2. Don't be out too late.
  3. Only date those with high moral standards.
  4. Always be on guard.
  5. Beware of justifications such as "We didn't go all the way," or "It's not a big deal," or "We're in love," or "Nobody will know."
  6. Even if you think you are strong, you still need to be careful.

- **Follow the lessons learned from Joseph:**
  1. Understand the serious nature of immorality.
  2. Avoid situations of moral temptation and leave immediately when those situations arise.

- **Do not steady date before the young man in the relationship is a returned missionary.**
- **Dress modestly.**

14 ch How Can I Resist and Overcome Pornography?

Pornography. It is "one of the most damning influences on earth."[1] We could list a bunch of statistics about the prevalence of pornography, but we won't. They are too depressing and too obvious. Whether it is through the Internet, television shows, movies, advertisements, magazine covers, lyrics and music, filthy books, crude jokes, or simply by the dress and behavior of those around us, "we are exposed to [pornography] daily."[2] Pornography comes in many forms, but its purpose is always the same: to stimulate unwholesome sexual feelings. The question for this generation is not "*Will* I see pornography?" but "What will I do *when* I see pornography?" We need a generation who is keenly aware of the evil of pornography and who has the knowledge, resources, and spiritual strength to withstand it.

So how can we resist and overcome pornography?

THIS CHAPTER ISN'T JUST FOR BOYS!

Sister Julie B. Beck warned, "The new target audience for those who create pornography is young women."[3]

? HOW are young women being targeted by pornography?

Although we don't know exactly how the pornography industry is targeting young women, one potential source is through books that are sexually explicit or create sexual feelings. An article in the *Ensign* described a woman's perspective on this issue from someone who had struggled with addiction to such books: "Often when we hear about the evils of pornography, we think of pornographic magazines, movies, and Web sites. Because men are more visually oriented, such material seems to appeal primarily to them. Yet the sexually explicit literature targeted at women, who are more verbally oriented, can be damaging as well. Like visual pornography, such literature presents a warped view of sexuality and is arousing and addictive. It dulls our spiritual senses, which distances us from God, and it can impair our ability to have healthy, lasting relationships."[5]

Flu Virus

WHICH IS DEADLIER?

Did you know that more Americans died from the 1918 flu than died in World War I, World War II, the Korean War, and the Vietnam War combined?[4] Although we might have thought the wars were much more dangerous than the flu, we would have been wrong. In a similar way we may underestimate how deadly a disease pornography is.

Know That We Have the Divine Ability and Strength to Resist Pornography

The Prophet Joseph Smith taught an empowering truth that we can relate to pornography: "The devil has no power over us only as we permit him."[6] In other words, we have our agency, and we can choose our behavior. Lehi taught us that we were created by God with power "to act" and not just "to be acted upon" by outside influences, like pornography (see 2 Nephi 2:13–14). We can "do many things of [our] own free will, and bring to pass much righteousness; for the power is in [us]" (D&C 58:27–28). We can choose how we will respond when we are confronted with pornography. We have the power to "turn away from [pornography] immediately."[7] The adversary cannot control our eyes, our minds, or our mouse!

John Says: SPIT IT OUT!

On a trip to the Universal Orlando Resort theme park, I was chosen to participate in a game based on the television show *Fear Factor*. My job was to drink a terrible drink that included sour milk, chicken, and bugs (seriously). It was so nasty that as soon as I started drinking it, I had to spit it out.

Pornography is just as nasty. As soon as you encounter it, spit it out!

Have a Spiritual Understanding of the Sacredness of the Human Body and the Divine Power of Procreation

Two main false ideas contribute to the problem of pornography. The first is the false message that the human body is just an object, and the second is that sexual intimacy exists for selfish purposes. Both of these statements are deceptions used by the adversary to have God's children misuse their bodies and procreative power. God's prophets have taught us that our bodies are "the temple of God" (1 Corinthians 3:16) and that our physical body is directly linked with our very soul (see D&C 88:15).

Elder Jeffrey R. Holland has taught that "one who uses the God-given body of another without divine sanction abuses the very soul of that individual."[8] Using another's body through pornography abuses his or her soul. If we understand the sacredness of the human body, we will be less tempted to treat it as a common object or misuse it. We will want to reject anything that is inconsistent with the message of the sacredness of the human body, such as pornography.

In Moses' time, the ark of the covenant was a chest that was placed in the center of the holy of holies in the tabernacle or temple. On the lid of the ark was the mercy seat, where the Lord told Moses, "I will meet with thee, and I will commune with thee from above the mercy seat" (Exodus 25:22). Sacred items, such as the tables of the law, were held inside the ark. It was considered to be the "most sacred of the religious symbols of the Israelites" and "it was treated with the greatest reverence."[9] It was so sacred that only authorized Israelites could touch the ark when it needed to be moved—the unauthorized would die (see 2 Samuel 6:6-7). It was covered with the veil of the temple and a cloth of skins (see Numbers 4:5-6).

Would the Israelites have treated the ark differently if Moses had told them it was simply a nice piece of furniture? (That's right, boys, just throw it in the moving van with the rocking chair!) Without the knowledge of its sacredness, the Israelites would probably have misused and abused the ark. However, having knowledge of the sacredness of the ark shaped the Israelites' behavior so they treated it as a special item. The same can be true for us. We can honor the sacredness of our bodies and our procreative power in order to avoid pornography. Accepting the sacred aids in rejecting the profane.

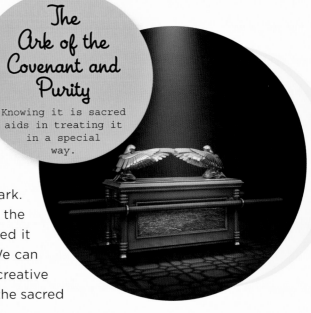

The Ark of the Covenant and Purity

Knowing it is sacred aids in treating it in a special way.

DO TRY THIS AT HOME!

WHAT DO YOU SEE IN THIS PERSON?

If you tilt your head sideways, you'll see that he is a liar (it spells liar in cursive). Now, the interesting thing is this: try *not* to see him as a liar. Can you? Or has viewing the word liar changed the way you see him? How is this like pornography?

For the Strength of Youth says, "Pornography is a poison that . . . changes the way you see others."[10] If we become involved in pornography, instead of seeing a young woman as an intelligent, creative, fun, humorous, athletic, kind, daughter of God, we may only see her as a physical object to be used for lustful desires. We can lose the ability to see her for who she really is, and we miss out on her true beauty. This change in how we view others partially fulfills President Gordon B. Hinckley's warning that pornography "will rob you of a sense of the beauties of life."[11]

Know and Think About the Short- and Long-Term Consequences of Pornography

One of the tools of the adversary is to tell us to not think about the consequences of our actions, but to be selfish and enjoy the moment, to "eat, drink, and be merry" (2 Nephi 28:7). But there are consequences for viewing pornography—they are real, and they are devastating. Here are some consequences that have been mentioned by the modern prophets:[12]

- Loss of the Holy Ghost
- Loss of priesthood power
- Loss of feeling for the beauties of life
- Unworthiness to participate in the ordinances of the gospel (such as baptism, the sacrament, and the temple)
- Negative changes about how others are viewed
- Weakened self-control
- Destructively powerful addiction that takes control of life
- Loss of energy, time, and dedication to productive things
- Distorted views about the purpose and nature of physical intimacy, including an inability to have a normal relationship with future or current spouse
- Feelings of shame, guilt, and remorse
- Loss of trust by others
- Emotional damage to loved ones
- Immoral thoughts
- Crude language or behavior
- Criminal behavior due to deviant sexual desires
- Immorality and adultery
- Destruction of marriage and family life through infidelity
- Loss of eternal salvation and exaltation

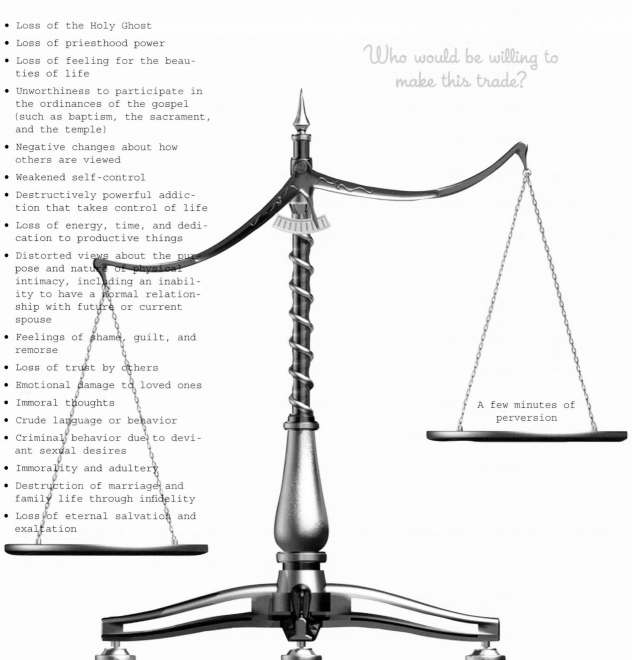

Who would be willing to make this trade?

A few minutes of perversion

THE INCREDIBLE SHRINKING BRAIN

Want another negative consequence? Research indicates that viewing pornography shrinks the size of your brain![13]

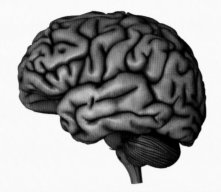

What a heavy price to pay for viewing filthy images! Do not be deceived by Satan's lies. The seemingly momentary pleasure is not worth the negative consequences that will follow in the days, months, years, and perhaps lifetime that follows. If we can remember the destructive consequences of pornography, we will have increased power to resist it.

PORNOGRAPHY AND THE BARK BEETLE

This tiny bark beetle has been responsible for taking down entire forests by infecting large trees with Dutch Elm disease. Using this small but deadly beetle as an analogy, President Thomas S. Monson said, "The beetle of pornography is doing his deadly task—undercutting our will, destroying our immunity, and stifling that upward reach within each of us."[14]

Remember That There Are No "Private" Sins

The adversary tells many lies about pornography: that it is a "private" sin, that it doesn't hurt anybody, that it is just you and the filthy image, and that nobody else knows so it's no big deal. They are all *lies!* Don't fall into the trap described by Elder Richard G. Scott. He said, "I've heard some men argue that it isn't that bad to look at things that are inappropriate on the screen because they are not hurting anyone. They are damaging their own spiritual strength and they certainly are creating harmful influences in their sacred relationship as husband and wife."[15]

If we take another look at the potential consequences of pornography on page 103 and ask, "Which of these consequences has a public consequence?" we will find that most all of them do. When we understand that there is no such thing as a private sin, it will help us overcome pornography. When the temptation to view pornography arises, imagine your father, mother, sister, brother, or current or future spouse sitting there, and ask yourself if your "private" decision will publicly and negatively affect those you love.

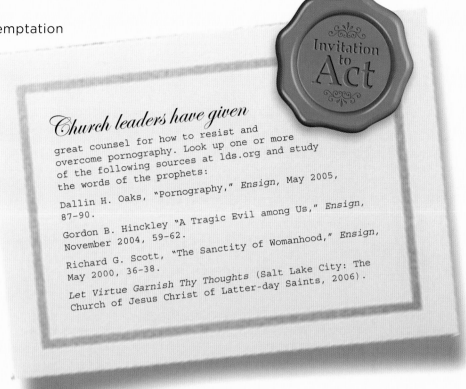

Church leaders have given great counsel for how to resist and overcome pornography. Look up one or more of the following sources at lds.org and study the words of the prophets:

Dallin H. Oaks, "Pornography," *Ensign*, May 2005, 87–90.

Gordon B. Hinckley "A Tragic Evil among Us," *Ensign*, November 2004, 59–62.

Richard G. Scott, "The Sanctity of Womanhood," *Ensign*, May 2000, 36–38.

Let Virtue Garnish Thy Thoughts (Salt Lake City: The Church of Jesus Christ of Latter-day Saints, 2006).

Fill Our Lives with Light and Truth

The Lord said, "Light and truth forsake that evil one" (D&C 93:37). As we fill our lives with more and more light and truth, we will "chase darkness from among [us]" (D&C 50:25). In other words, the closer we come to the Light of the World—Jesus Christ—the further away from us the darkness of sin will go. As we fill our lives with light and truth we will receive increased power to refuse and reject pornographic images.

THE HOUSE OF LIGHT HELPS CHASE AWAY DARKNESS

President Gordon B. Hinckley said, "Make a habit of going to the house of the Lord. There is no better way to ensure proper living than temple attendance. It will crowd out the evils of pornography."[16]

Practice the Proactive and the Practical

Captain Moroni provides us a great example of the principles related to proactive self-defense. Even during a time of peace, "Moroni did not stop making preparations for war, or to defend his people against the Lamanites" (Alma 50:1). He had his people build towers, walls, and pickets, and establish mounds of earth to protect their cities (see Alma 50:1–4). His actions prepared his people and helped them defeat their enemies. Similarly, we can take practical and proactive measures to help defend ourselves against the enemy of pornography. The following are a few defensive suggestions:

- Install filters on each computer you use in order to block offensive and pornographic content. Some Internet filtering software will provide reports of websites visited, or keywords used to search, or sites that were blocked, etc. These reports of Internet activity can be valuable to both parents and youth.

- Put computers where everyone can see what you're doing. Elder M. Russell Ballard said, "Move your computer into a room where there is always the possibility of someone walking in on you. Make sure the monitor faces the room so that others can see what it is you are doing on the screen at any time. . . . Take action when you are strong so that if you are tempted you will have armed yourself and it will be much more difficult to fall."[17]

- Don't surf the Internet aimlessly. Have a specific reason for being online. We could change the proverbial saying and state that "An idle mouse is the devil's playground." The Church publication *Let Virtue Garnish Thy Thoughts* specifically states, "Limit the time you spend watching TV, playing video games, and using computers for entertainment. Set standards for your participation in these activities, such as restricting Internet use to specific purposes."[18]

- Place a picture of your family, the temple, or the Savior next to televisions, personal computers, cell phones, and media players to remind you what is important. A wise bishop once gave advice to a young father and said that each time he goes on a business trip he carries a framed picture of his wife and children and places it next to the television in his hotel room. That way, as he watches television when he is alone, he is strengthened by the image of his family and is given increased power to avoid the potential filth available to him.

Always remember Him . . . Especially on the Internet

Elder Dallin H. Oaks said, "Young women, please understand that if you dress immodestly, you are magnifying this problem by becoming pornography to some of the men who see you."[19] Most young women would never participate in the pornography industry. However, we must understand that we can inadvertently participate in pornography through the way we dress.

If Involved in Pornography, Immediately Seek the Help of Priesthood Leaders and Professionals

If you have been in contact with pornography, immediately seek help from your parents and bishop. Pornography is a dark sin, and Satan often wants us to stay in the dark. He knows the longer we stay in the dark, the harder it will be to make it back to the light. Remember that because of the atonement of Jesus Christ, we all can repent and change. What great hope! Jesus Christ will cleanse you and give you the strength to go forward. Have the courage to talk to your bishop. He will help in the process of repentance and can provide wise counsel and, if necessary, recommend professional resources in overcoming the sin of pornography.

GET HELP!

Elder Joseph B. Wirthin gave this analogy: "Pornography is much like quicksand. You can become so easily trapped and overcome as soon as you step into it that you do not realize the severe danger. Most likely you will need assistance to get out of the quicksand of pornography."[20]

We testify that through the Lord's atoning grace and power, and through the direction of his servants, the sin of pornography can be forgiven, erased, resisted, and overcome!

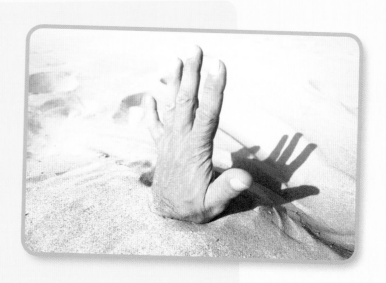

Seek Shelter from the Storm of Pornography

Although the temptation of pornography is everywhere in our day, we do not need to be a part of it. We have the strength to resist and overcome it. President Gordon B. Hinckley said, "The excuse is given that it is hard to avoid, that it is right at our fingertips and there is no escape. Suppose a storm is raging and the winds howl and the snow swirls about you. You find yourself unable to stop it. But you can dress properly and seek shelter, and the storm will have no effect upon you. Likewise, even though the Internet is saturated with sleazy material, you do not have to watch it. You can retreat to the shelter of the gospel and its teaching of cleanliness and virtue and purity of life."[21]

TELL ME ONE MORE TIME!

How Can I Resist and Overcome Pornography?

- **Know that we have the divine ability and strength to resist pornography.**
- **Have a spiritual understanding of the sacredness of the human body and the divine power of procreation.**
- **Know and think about the short- and long-term consequences of pornography.**
- **Remember that there are no "private" sins.**
- **Fill your life with light and truth.**
- **Practice the proactive and the practical.**
- **If involved in pornography, immediately seek the help of priesthood leaders and professionals.**

15^{ch} How Can I Honor My Parents?

A student approached his seminary teacher with this difficult situation: "My dad is not a member of the Church. What should I do if he asks me to do things that are not against his standards, like going boating or hunting with him on Sunday, but they are against the Church's standards? If I honor my father and obey him, I'm breaking commandments, and if I don't obey him I'm breaking the commandment to honor him. What do I do?"

On another occasion, a student said, "I love my parents very much and am so grateful for them. But sometimes I totally disagree with my mom about some things because she is being unreasonable or just doesn't understand the full situation. If I'm right, do I still have to honor her wishes just because she's my mom?"

We should all desire to honor our parents, but sometimes it is not clear how to do this. In order to know how to truly *honor* our father and mother we need to understand what the word "honor" means. Let's look at different meanings of the word "honor."

Honor Means High Respect

Every year on Memorial Day in the United States, we honor those we love who have died. We usually visit their graves and show our love to them by placing flowers by the headstones, talking respectfully about their lives and accomplishments, and acting with reverence in the cemetery. The honor we pay is reflected in the respect we show in our words and actions on that day. There are special days set aside in most countries to pay honor and respect to ancestors.

Similarly, we can honor our parents by showing respect to them in how we talk and act in their presence. This is as simple as not raising our voices at them, not calling them names, and not talking bad behind their backs. We can also be respectful by saying "please" and "thank you." Even as we honor our Heavenly Father by speaking to him in respectful words such as "thee" and "thine," we can honor our parents by speaking to and treating them with respect, even if we might disagree with them.

"You do not have the right ever to be disrespectful to your mother or your father. Period."
—Elder M. Russell Ballard[1]

What is the punishment for a "stubborn and rebellious son, which will not obey the voice of his father, or the voice of his mother"? Read Deuteronomy 21:18–21 to find out how serious the Lord is about us obeying our parents. Ouch!

Honor Means Creating a Good Name

Another way we can honor our parents is by living an *honorable* life. Whatever we decide to do with our lives reflects on our parents' names and their reputation. For example, think of what Osama, Adolf, and Joseph have done to the family names of Bin Laden, Hitler, or Stalin since they came along? On the other hand, think of what Albert, William, Rosa, Winston, or Gordon have done to honor the family names of Einstein, Shakespeare, Parks, Churchill, and Hinckley. Helaman told his sons Nephi and Lehi—who were named after the original Nephi and Lehi—"Behold, I have given unto you the names of our first parents who came out of the land of Jerusalem; and this I have done that when you remember your names ye may remember them; and when ye remember them ye may remember their works; and when ye remember their works ye may know how that it is said, and also written, that they were good. Therefore, my sons, I would that ye should do that which is good, that it may be said of you, and also written, even as it has been said and written of them" (Helaman 5:6–7). We can honor our father and mother by bringing honor to our family names through the caliber and quality of our lives.

Honor Means Giving Dignity to Parents' Position as the Heads of the Family

Another definition for "honor" has to do with honoring a station or a position. That is why when we go to court we call the judge "your honor." We can fulfill the command to honor our parents by honoring their position as the leaders of our family. By divine design, parents have been put in charge of presiding over, nurturing, and caring for their children. One way we can honor our parents' position is by seeking their advice and counseling with them on matters in our lives. Elder M. Russell Ballard taught, "Ask your father for advice. . . . Nothing shows respect for another person as much as asking for his advice, because what you are really saying when you ask for advice is, 'I appreciate what you know and the experiences you have had, and I value your ideas and suggestions.' Those are nice things for a father to hear from his son."[2]

Which of these deserves to be called "your honor" when you talk with them about your speeding ticket?

President Ezra Taft Benson said, "Receive your mother's counsel as she loves and instructs you in righteousness. And honor and obey your father as he stands as the head of the home."[3] We owe honor to our parents because of our parents' divine position as the leaders of our family.

? HOW can I respond to my parents if I don't agree with what they want me to do?

Maybe you have strong feelings about a certain subject, and your parents do too. It can be hard to have a calm discussion when emotions are running high. Elder M. Russell Ballard gave great counsel as far as what to do if you are having a hard time agreeing with your parents. He said, "Young people, you do have the right to be heard. If you are having difficulty getting your mother and your father to listen to you, in a calm manner just ask: 'Mom and Dad, I've got a different feeling about a matter. Can we set a time to talk about it?'"[4]

SURVEY SAYS

We asked 1,000 teenagers the question "How can I honor my parents?" Here are the top ten answers.

1. Have patience and long suffering.
2. Talk to them—they can be your best friends.
3. Tell them you love them.
4. Listen to them.
5. Thank them.
6. Show them that you love them.
7. Obey them.
8. Respect them.
9. Don't complain.
10. Do things before you're asked.

GO THE EXTRA MILE

Want a fun way to honor your parents? Try this one! The next time your mom or dad asks you to do the dishes say, "Sure, and I'll sweep the floor, too." Then do it! One young woman tried this and reported, "My mom flipped when I went and got the broom." Try it out, and see if your parents do a flip!

Honor Means Remembering and Recognizing Your Parents

If you were to be honored at a banquet this Saturday, you would probably expect to be recognized or remembered for something. Similarly, we can honor our parents by trying to be mindful of them, their needs, their service, their lives, and their accomplishments.

We can honor our parents simply by carrying or posting pictures of them, by remembering their birthdays, by talking about them positively with our friends, by reading their life history, by writing about them in our journal, by asking them about their accomplishments and successes, by praying for them, by giving them a quick call or text or e-mail to say "hi," and by being mindful of all they have done for us. The same principle applies to us and our parents as when Nephi scolded his brothers, "Yea, and how is it that ye have forgotten what great things the Lord hath done for us?" (1 Nephi 7:11). We could rephrase that by saying, "How is it that we have forgotten what great things our parents have done for us?" Let us honor our parents by remembering and recognizing them.

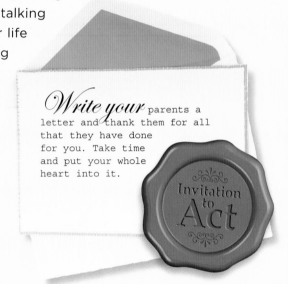

Write your parents a letter and thank them for all that they have done for you. Take time and put your whole heart into it.

Invitation to **Act**

Honor Means Being Honest with Your Parents

The statement "I'll honor that promise" implies that there is more of a connection between honesty and honor than the first three letters of each word. One way we can honor our parents

HOW *can I initiate a heart-to-heart conversation with my parents?*

Sister Ardeth G. Kapp, a former general Young Women president, tells a story about a young woman who was struggling with her mom. "I love my mom," the young woman said. "And I want to talk to her, but she never listens to me!" Later Sister Kapp was talking with the young woman's mother. The mother said, "I love my daughter so much. And I want to talk to her, but she never listens to me!" Sister Kapp observed that sometimes there is just miscommunication between parents and children who really want to talk to each other.[5]

You might try saying to your parents, "Mom, Dad, I'd really like to talk with you. Do you have some time we could talk?" If that doesn't work, consider talking with a bishop or trusted leader for advice specific to your situation.

is by being completely honest with them. President Thomas S. Monson said, "How do you honor your parents? . . . Be honest with your mother and your father."[6] It is disrespectful to hide things from our parents, to deceive them, or to lie to them. It shows a lack of loyalty and trust on our part. On the plus side, it is actually a form of honoring them when we are totally honest with our parents—even when we have made mistakes. Our honesty shows respect, loyalty, and trust. Let us honor our parents by being completely honest with them.

Above all, we can "honor [our] parents by showing love and respect for them and by being obedient."[7] We should rarely find occasion to not obey our parents, but even if we are faced with the rare situation when we do—like the young man at the beginning of this chapter—we can still honor them in many other ways.

Dad, let me honor you: I chopped down the cherry tree.

TELL ME ONE MORE TIME!

How Can I Honor My Parents?

- **Show high respect to them.**
- **Make sure you hold your family name in high regard. Do nothing to shame your family name or your parents.**
- **Show dignity to your parents for their position as the heads of the family.**
- **Remember and recognize your parents.**
- **Be completely honest with your parents.**

How Can I Have a Fun and Clean Date?

You've been looking forward to this day for years and now it finally has arrived—sweet sixteen. Let the dating games begin! As we begin dating, most of us want to simply enjoy ourselves and our friends and have the opportunity to meet and be with different people in social settings. We want to have good, clean, enjoyable dates. So how can we make sure we do that as we begin dating? *For the Strength of Youth* gives us some great ideas: "When you begin dating, go in groups or on double dates. Avoid going on frequent dates with the same person. Make sure your parents meet those you date. You may want to invite your dates to activities with your family. Plan dating activities that are positive and inexpensive and that will help you get to know each other. Do things that will help you and your companions maintain your self-respect and remain close to the Spirit of the Lord."[1]

Let's take a closer look at this prophetic counsel and see how it can help us have fun on dates.

GROUP DATES AND GROUP GAMES

Think about how many games require more than two people to play—whether they are board games or sporting games. Two people playing dodgeball gets lame pretty fast. Being on a group date opens up the possibility to do many other enjoyable things that a single couple otherwise wouldn't be able to do. Group dating lets the dating games begin!

When You Begin Dating, Go in Groups or on Double Dates

Group dates are when multiple couples participate in a date together. Dating with a group gives us more people to talk to, be with, and enjoy. When we go out with more people there is usually less pressure on us individually, and we can relax a little more. Perhaps most importantly, we minimize some of the moral temptations that come from being alone for extended periods of time with members of the opposite sex to whom we are attracted (see chapter 13).

President Gordon B. Hinckley said that youth should "kneel alone in prayer before they leave home on a date that they may remain in control of themselves."[2]

Brainstorm a list of super fun dates.

E-mail us your best ideas at answers@ldswhy.com

FIVE GREAT GROUP DATES

- Go with a group on a moonlight hike.
- Play a classic playground game such as Capture the Flag.
  - Have a watercolor painting contest (your date chooses what you paint).
  - International dinner: Each couple brings food from a different country and gives some background on the culture. Rent a film with subtitles to watch together.
  - Have a car wash and wash each others' cars (or maybe even other people's cars or the cars of your date's parents). That will impress them!

? HOW can I appropriately tell my date that I'm not comfortable with the activity we are doing?

A girl was out on a group date and the boys in the group were trying to get the girls to participate in an activity they didn't feel good about. The girl simply said, "I don't want to do this," and her date backed down. You might need to be firm with your date and let him or her know that you do not feel good about what you are doing.

Avoid Going on Frequent Dates with the Same Person

This standard obviously applies to young men before their mission calls and young women who are not ready to be married. We might phrase this standard this way: "Avoid steady dating, or having a boyfriend/girlfriend in high school."

So how can we avoid going on frequent dates with the same person? Perhaps the most important thing we can do is to follow the principle of being honest with our dates about our standards and expectations. We can tell those we date of our desire to avoid getting involved in a serious relationship and that we are striving to follow the prophetic counsel of not going on frequent dates with the same person. If we communicate early our desire to simply date and have fun in our teenage years and not get involved in a steady dating relationship, then our date probably won't take it personally. They will see it as a commitment to a standard, not as a slap to their ego or a rejection of them as an individual.

Make Sure Your Parents Meet Those You Date

It is interesting to note that in the Book of Mormon when Lehi said "his sons should take daughters to wife" (1 Nephi 7:1), that Nephi recorded, "We went up unto the house of Ishmael, and we *did gain favor in the sight of Ishmael,* insomuch that we did speak unto him the words of the Lord" (1 Nephi 7:4; emphasis added). Nephi and his brothers didn't just go to Ishmael's daughters and try to win them over, but they went to the girls' father. Nephi knew that the Lord had placed Ishmael in charge of his family, and he understood the importance of gaining the approval of the parents.

When we get to know our date's parents it will help us see that we are being given a stewardship of trust for an evening with the parents' daughter/son. It also allows us to make clear to the parents what our plans for the night will be—where their daughter/son will be, what we will be doing, and who we are going with—as well as establish what time the parents expect their daughter/son to be home. (Want some bonus points? Ask the parents what time they want their daughter home, then return her home a half an hour earlier. Nice work, Mr. Smooth!)

Making the effort to meet the parents is a good, solid sign of respect for your date and your date's parents. We could expand the commandment and say: Honor thy *date's* father and thy *date's* mother that thy days may be long in the land!

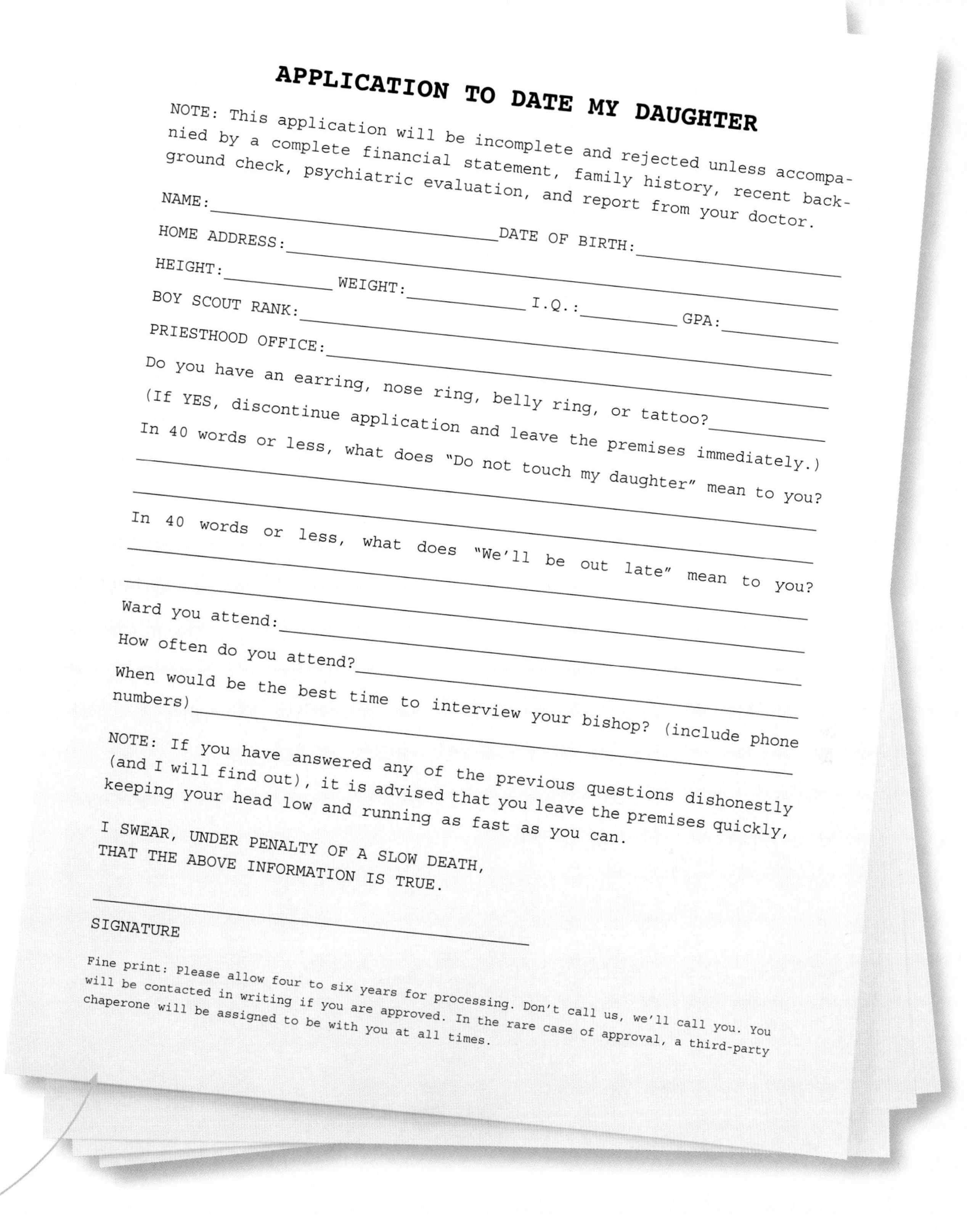

APPLICATION TO DATE MY DAUGHTER

NOTE: This application will be incomplete and rejected unless accompanied by a complete financial statement, family history, recent background check, psychiatric evaluation, and report from your doctor.

NAME: _____

HOME ADDRESS: _____ DATE OF BIRTH: _____

HEIGHT: _____ WEIGHT: _____

BOY SCOUT RANK: _____ I.Q.: _____ GPA: _____

PRIESTHOOD OFFICE: _____

Do you have an earring, nose ring, belly ring, or tattoo? _____
(If YES, discontinue application and leave the premises immediately.)

In 40 words or less, what does "Do not touch my daughter" mean to you?
_____
_____

In 40 words or less, what does "We'll be out late" mean to you?
_____
_____

Ward you attend: _____

How often do you attend? _____

When would be the best time to interview your bishop? (include phone numbers) _____
_____

NOTE: If you have answered any of the previous questions dishonestly (and I will find out), it is advised that you leave the premises quickly, keeping your head low and running as fast as you can.

I SWEAR, UNDER PENALTY OF A SLOW DEATH, THAT THE ABOVE INFORMATION IS TRUE.

_____
SIGNATURE

Fine print: Please allow four to six years for processing. Don't call us, we'll call you. You will be contacted in writing if you are approved. In the rare case of approval, a third-party chaperone will be assigned to be with you at all times.

FIVE GREAT DATES TO DO WITH YOUR FAMILY

- Waffle Party. Make waffles for younger siblings.
- Have a baseball or basketball game (avoid football . . . you won't get very far tackling your date's dad).
- Visit your date's grandparents and ask them to tell you about dating when they were growing up.
- Go on a family outing (like to the zoo).
- Help your parents with a home repair project. ("Hey, Dad, can my date and I double with you and Mom to weed the garden?" Sounds corny, we know, but maybe Dad will take you all to dinner afterward!)

Plan Dating Activities

A major obstacle to having fun in dating is *not going on dates!* Why do people not go on dates? We have talked to many young people who say, "There is nothing to do where I live." It doesn't matter if we live in a small farm town or a big city, some people still think "there is nothing to do," while others get creative and can almost always find something constructive to do. *For the Strength of Youth* tells us to "plan" dates.[3] That usually requires a little advance thinking on our part, particularly with the people we are going to group date with. But it's amazing how many creative ideas you can come up with for a good, clean, fun date when a group of people get together to plan a night's activities—and the actual planning can be a lot of fun, too!

Wow, I am really getting to know this person well by seeing him quietly stare at a large screen in the dark. This is awesome.

For the Strength of Youth tells us that part of planning a clean and fun date is to "plan dating activities . . . that will help you get to know each other."[4] This can happen in a variety of ways—practically with almost any social activity—so we won't mention those here (see all the dating ideas listed in this chapter). But we will call some negative attention to the one date that seems to be the default when creativity is lacking—going to a movie! While quietly staring at a screen may be safe and easy, it makes it difficult to really get to know someone. It is better to plan an activity where people can talk, engage socially, express themselves, and get to know the people they are with. Plus, just going to a movie doesn't win any creativity or originality points with your date. Sorry big screen.

Keep in mind another way to double the fun is to plan dates that will not only help us have fun, but also help serve others.

Five Great Service Dates

- Make care packages and take them to the hospital.
- Visit the elderly at a retirement center.
- Volunteer to serve food at a homeless shelter or work for a day for Habitat for Humanity.
- Participate together in a formal walk/run/bike ride for a charitable cause.
- Hold a service scavenger hunt. Make a list of services that need to be done (for example, sweep the floor, do dishes, vacuum a room) and spread out across town as you try to serve others. The first group to accomplish all the service items on the list wins.

Invitation to Act

If you are sixteen, plan a "service date" where you and a group of people can perform a service for somebody else.

Plan Dating Activities That Are Inexpensive

Aside from the "there is nothing to do" excuse, the next most common excuse we hear young men give for not dating is that it is too expensive. In an address to young single adults, Elder Dallin H. Oaks encouraged them to go on simple, inexpensive dates.[5] And as most young women will tell you, "It doesn't matter how much the date costs, just please ask us out!" A little creativity and planning can make up for a lack of money. Unique dates are usually more memorable than expensive ones anyway.

FIVE Inexpensive Dates

- Go on a "free samples" dinner date. Before the date, research which stores in your area offer free samples or demos of food. Large warehouse stores often have multiple people offering samples of their food products. Drive around to as many stores as you can and feed yourself for free.
- Go to a local bookstore and browse through some of the cool books they have. It's relaxing, and you'll feel smart.
- Make up a survey, then go out and get people to answer your questions. The more creative your survey, the better.
- Create your own mini-golf course in someone's backyard. Instead of a hole, place a plastic cup on its side and putt into that.
- Make a movie. Give each group a plotline to film in about an hour. Go out and shoot your film, then come back and show each other your final product.

It goes without saying that our dates should be uplifting experiences for everyone involved. Treating our date as a child of God and maintaining righteous standards will help us maintain respect for ourselves and our date.

And, guys—don't be shy. Get out there and start asking ladies on dates! There are lots of things you can do to have a fun and uplifting date.

HOW *should I react if nobody asks me out?*

We've met awesome young ladies who waited to date until they were sixteen, but then were sad when the phone didn't start ringing. If boys aren't asking you on dates, don't let that stop you from planning fun group outings with your friends. Also, take advantage of opportunities for girls to ask boys out on dates, like girls' choice dances. We know many wonderful women who did not get asked on dates in high school, but did date in college. Please remember that your self-worth does not hinge on whether or not boys ask you out.

MORE FUN DATE IDEAS!

- Photography contest: Use a digital camera to take pictures. Upload them all and vote on the best photos. You can have a variety of categories: "Best Nature Picture," "Cutest Baby," "Most Random," and so forth.

- Go "people watching" at the mall.

- Go to a museum.

- Create some fine art together (make a one-hour painting or sculpt something).

- Walk down a busy road or sit in a busy public place eating M&M's. Wave at the cars that pass by or at people who are wearing the same color as the M&M you just ate.

- Fly a kite.

- Have "lawn Olympics" and play a handful of fun lawn games (croquet, lawn bowling, badminton, etc.).

HOW *can I find other dating ideas?*

There are tons of fun dating ideas online. Just type in "group dating ideas" in your favorite search engine and choose the ones that meet the requirement of a good, clean, fun date.

TELL ME ONE MORE TiME!

How Can I Have a Fun and Clean Date?

- When you begin dating, go in groups or on double dates.
- Avoid going on frequent dates with the same person.
- Make sure your parents meet those you date.
- Plan dating activities that are inexpensive.

How Can I Have More Meaningful Prayers?

ROAST, ROAST, ROAST!

To see a short video that teaches what roast has to do with having effective prayers, visit http://ldswhy.com.

President Henry B. Eyring, then a member of the Quorum of the Twelve, said, "Most of us have had some experience with self-improvement efforts. My experience has taught me this about how people and organizations improve: the best place to look is for small changes we could make in things we do often. There is power in steadiness and repetition. And if we can be led by inspiration to choose the right small things to change, consistent obedience will bring great improvement."[1]

Improving our prayers is one of the "small changes" we can make in something that we do often. Many people pray at least a couple of times each day, offering hundreds and hundreds of prayers a year. However, as we've all experienced, some of those prayers are more powerful than others. Why is that the case? How can we have more effective prayer on a daily basis?

Follow the Prophets: Go Somewhere Private, Kneel, and Pray Out Loud

We can gain powerful insight into how to make our prayers more meaningful by studying the prayers of prophets. Notice some patterns of prayer in these three scriptures. (We've highlighted some of them for you.)

Enos: "Behold, **I went** to hunt beasts in the forests; and the words which I had often heard my father speak concerning eternal life, and the joy of the saints, sunk deep into my heart. And my soul hungered; and **I kneeled down** before my Maker, and **I cried unto him** in mighty prayer and supplication for mine own soul" (Enos 1:3–4).

Joseph Smith: "In accordance with this, my determination to ask of God, **I retired to the woods** to make the attempt. It was on the morning of a beautiful, clear day, early in the spring of eighteen hundred and twenty. It was the first time in my life that I had made such an attempt, for amidst all my anxieties I had never as yet made the attempt to **pray vocally**. **After I had retired to the place where I had previously designed to go**, having looked around me, and finding myself alone, **I kneeled down** and began to offer up the desires of my heart to God" (Joseph Smith–History 1:14–15).

Nephi: "[Nephi] went out and bowed himself down upon the earth, and cried mightily to his God in behalf of his people, yea, those who were about to be destroyed because of their faith in the tradition of their fathers. And it came to pass that he cried mightily unto the Lord all that day" (3 Nephi 1:11–12).

Did you catch the patterns? First, these prophets went somewhere private when they prayed. Second, they knelt down to pray. Kneeling is a sign of submissiveness to God, a willingness to do what God tells us, and a show of respect and reverence. Finally, the prophets cried out, or prayed vocally. There is great power in vocal prayer: it helps us to concentrate and verbally express our true feelings and desires. Perhaps it isn't coincidental that Joseph Smith's First Vision burst upon him after his first vocal prayer on the subject (see Joseph Smith–History 1:14). The Lord has also instructed us to pray vocally: "And again, I command thee that thou shalt pray vocally as well as in thy heart; yea, before the world as well as in secret, in public as well as in private" (D&C 19:28).

CAN YOU STAY FOCUSED?

Try to think of nothing but vanilla ice cream for one minute straight. Ready? Go!

How did you do? Odds are, your thoughts started to wander, didn't they? Maybe your thoughts ran something akin to this:

Vanilla ice cream, vanilla ice cream, vanilla ice . . . hey, wasn't there a rapper named Vanilla Ice? Whatever happened to him? He's probably hanging out with MC Hammer. Hammer time! Hammers. Where is our hammer in our house? I need to hang up a picture. Oh, yeah, vanilla ice cream!

Sometimes it can be hard to keep our concentration, especially when we are praying silently. Praying vocally can help us focus on our prayer.

ON YOUR KNEES!

Our friend Laurel Christensen shared the following insight with us. A couple thousand years ago a Chinese emperor had his people create an army of more than 8,000 terra-cotta soldiers. These warriors were hand-made statues; each one was unique. There were five different types of statues. Over time many of the warriors were damaged and in need of repair. Only one type of warrior has been discovered that did not need any repair work. Any guesses to which one it was? The archer. *And he was on his knees.*

Choose one of the principles discussed in this chapter and implement it in your personal prayers over the next week. For example, you could try saying your personal morning and evening prayers on your knees.

Invitation to Act

SAY WHAT?

Look at these letters. In your mind, try to figure out what they mean:

1. SA
2. XS
3. NV
4. NTT
5. DK
6. XTC

If you're struggling to figure it out, simply say each letter *out loud* and listen to the words they make. Notice how you got more meaning when you spoke out loud? Vocal prayers are much the same.

Answers: 1. Essay 2. Excess 3. Envy 4. Entity 5. Decay 6. Ecstasy

Speak to God Openly as Your Loving Father

Elder Richard G. Scott said, "Don't worry about your clumsily expressed feelings. *Just talk to your Father.*"[3] In the same talk he also said, "What seems most helpful [in prayer] is seeing in my mind a child approaching trustingly a loving, kind, wise, understanding Father, who wants us to succeed."[4] When "the Lord spake unto Moses face to face," he spoke "as a man speaketh unto his friend" (Exodus 33:11). God is both our friend (see D&C 84:63), and our Father; our prayers are more effective when we speak to him openly and freely as we would our closest friends. Speaking to God in this way will also help us avoid using "vain repetitions" (Matthew 6:7), or prayers without meaning.

Although we should speak to God freely and openly, we should still do it with respect and reverence in our language. Elder Dallin H. Oaks said, "When we go to worship in a temple or a church, we put aside our working clothes and dress ourselves in something better. This change of clothing is a mark of respect. Similarly, when we address our Heavenly Father, we should put aside our working words and clothe our prayers in special language of reverence and respect."[5]

Pray for Others

DO TRY THIS AT HOME!

One of the glasses in the picture above has sugar mixed in it. One has salt mixed in it. Since you can't taste them, how can you tell the difference?

Answer: If you are coming up with complicated science experiments, you are missing the easiest way. Just ask us! We created the picture. The glass on the right has the sugar in it. Remember, Heavenly Father is in charge of everything. Turning to him in prayer and asking him for answers makes solving life's problems a little easier.

Another pattern we can find in the prayers of prophets is that they prayed for others. Notice this pattern in the following verses:

- "Lehi . . . prayed unto the Lord, yea, even with all his heart, *in behalf of his people*" (1 Nephi 1:5; emphasis added).
- "[Enos] prayed unto him with many long strugglings *for [his] brethren, the Lamanites*" (Enos 1:11; emphasis added).
- "[Captain Moroni] prayed mightily unto his God for the blessings of liberty to rest upon *his brethren*" (Alma 46:13; emphasis added).

Sometimes, in the midst of our problems and needs, the greatest solution is to focus on the needs of others. In doing so, we not only serve others, but we find solutions to our own needs. Remember, the Lord promised that "he that loseth his life for my sake shall find it" (Matthew 10:39).

Thank More

For many years Elder F. Michael Watson served as the secretary to the First Presidency. Elder Watson said, "Each morning in the meeting of the First Presidency, the Brethren take turns praying. I always liked to listen to President Ezra Taft Benson pray. His prayers were almost entirely in thankfulness instead of asking for blessings."[6]

Once Elder David A. Bednar and his wife were instructed by a member of the Quorum of the Twelve to offer a prayer in which they only gave thanks. Although they had some pressing matters they wished to pray for, they followed his counsel. Elder Bednar said that as they prayed, only expressing thanks, not asking for any blessings, that they received both insight and inspiration.[7]

> "The most meaningful and spiritual prayers I have experienced contained many expressions of thanks and few, if any, requests. . . . Let me recommend that periodically you and I offer a prayer in which we only give thanks and express gratitude. Ask for nothing; simply let our souls rejoice and strive to communicate appreciation with all the energy of our hearts."—Elder David A. Bednar[8]

Texting or Morse Code—Which Is Faster?

A television show had a competition between two people doing Morse code and two people texting each other to see which pair could communicate more quickly. Which method do you think was the fastest? (Hint: it wasn't texting.) The host of the show joked to the texters that they had been beaten by a 170-year-old technology.[9] But there's something even better than texting or Morse code for communicating important messages—prayer!

Listen More

Imagine if your friend called you and said, "Hi, (insert your name)! Thanks for being my friend. Could you please help my acne go away and also get me some money? And while you're at it, could you help me do better in school? Bye." And then your friend hangs up before you can respond. How would you feel?

In a similar way, we sometimes do this with our prayers. President Gordon B. Hinckley said, "The trouble with most of our prayers is that we give them as if we were picking up the telephone and ordering groceries—we place our order and hang up."[10]

Don't hang up too soon! Elder M. Russell Ballard wrote, "The most important part of prayer is not what we say but how well we listen."[11] We need to take time after we pray to really listen for communication from the Lord. Prayer, after all, should be a *two-way* conversation. If we ask the Lord a question in our prayers, we also need to be still and listen for an answer throughout our prayer and throughout the day.

> "My father [President Henry B. Eyring] has told us that there are two things that he prays for every night. The first is, 'What blessings do I have that I am not aware of?' and the second is, 'Whom can I help?' . . . Dad says there has never been a day that his prayers haven't been answered."—Matthew Eyring[12]

Listen to What the Spirit Tells Us to Pray For

Not only do we need to listen for God's *answers* to our prayers, but the best prayers are the ones in which *we listen to what God is telling us to pray for through the Holy Ghost.* Elder Bruce R. McConkie wrote: "Perfect prayers are those which are inspired, in which the Spirit reveals the words which should be used."[13] The Lord's prophets have repeatedly taught this principle of the Holy Ghost telling us what we should pray for. President J. Reuben Clark said, "I should like to testify to the power of prayer, and to say that it is a wise man who knows what to pray for. One of the things that we should seek in going before the Lord and in going upon our knees, *is his inspiration and his wisdom to tell us what to ask for.*"[14]

This may be what Paul meant when he said, "I will pray with the spirit" (1 Corinthians 14:15), and "Likewise the Spirit also helpeth our infirmities: *for we know not what we should pray for as we ought: but the Spirit itself maketh intercession for us*" (Romans 8:26; emphasis added). If we are humble, have faith, and desire to know and follow God's will, as we listen to the promptings of the Holy Ghost we can know what we should and should not pray for, and therefore pray according to what God desires for us.

HOW can I start praying in the morning, and not just at night?

Although all prayers are important, it is possible that our morning prayers are more important than the prayers we say before we go to bed. Why? Because in the morning we are getting ready to start our day, to face the tests and trials of life, and to perform our work. At night, we are usually concluding the day and then getting into bed. We probably don't need a lot of spiritual direction while we snore! However, most youth (and probably adults) admit that they skip their morning prayer more often than their nighttime prayer. This is because they either forget in the morning or are in too big of a hurry.

Something you might consider trying is getting up a few minutes earlier each day and to pray first thing when you get out of bed. Sometimes the hardest part of developing a habit of morning prayer is simply remembering to pray. You could put a sign on your bathroom mirror or in another place where you will see it to remind yourself to pray each morning. We have one good friend whose reminder is the doorknob. If he touches the doorknob to leave in the morning and hasn't prayed, he gets down on his knees there in front of the door and does so before he leaves. Don't skip out on the vital morning prayer!

"Can I have an iPod? Please give me an iPod. I want an iPod, please give me an iPod . . ."

Does this resemble our prayers? Remember, one of the purposes of prayer is to get ourselves in tune with what God wants for us, and not just to ask what we want for ourselves.

Follow the Pattern Set in the Savior's Prayers

Ultimately, we gain powerful insights into how to make our prayers more meaningful by studying the recorded prayers of our Exemplar, Jesus Christ. His longest prayer in the Book of Mormon is in 3 Nephi 19:

19. And it came to pass that Jesus departed out of the midst of them, and went a little way off from them and bowed himself to the earth, and he said:

Notice that the Savior went to a private place to pray.

Notice that even the Savior showed reverence in his posture.

20. Father, I thank thee that thou hast given the Holy Ghost unto these whom I have chosen; and it is because of their belief in me that I have chosen them out of the world.

The first thing the Savior did after addressing the Father was to express gratitude.

21. Father, I pray thee that thou wilt give the Holy Ghost unto all them that shall believe in their words.

Notice that the Savior is praying for *others*, not himself. The Savior's prayer consisted of expressing gratitude and asking for others to be blessed.

It is also important to note that after this prayer was finished, the Savior offered two more prayers (see verses 27–31). In fact, it appears from the scriptural account that his third prayer was the most powerful prayer of the three. Isn't that interesting? Some of us have had the experience of praying, climbing into bed, and having something else pop into our mind to pray for. We shouldn't say, "Well, I've already prayed tonight." Instead, pray again! The Savior teaches us that we should continually offer prayers and that sometimes it is the second or third prayer that is the most powerful.

Another important lesson from the prayers of the Savior is that he taught we should pray saying, "Thy will be done" (Matthew 6:10). President Boyd K. Packer said, "I have learned to conclude all my prayers with 'Thy will be done.'"[15]

Elder H. Burke Peterson summarizes much of what we have discussed about how to have more effective prayer: "As you feel the need to confide in the Lord or to improve the quality of your visits with him—to pray, if you please—may I suggest a process to follow: go where you can be alone, go where you can think, go where you can kneel, go where you can speak out loud to him. The bedroom, the bathroom, or the closet will do. Now, picture him in your mind's eye. Think to whom you are speaking, control your thoughts—don't let them wander, address him as your Father and your friend. Now tell him things you really feel to tell him—not trite phrases that have little meaning, but have a sincere, heartfelt conversation with him. Confide in him, ask him for forgiveness, plead with him, enjoy him, thank him, express your love to him, and then listen for his answers."[16] We testify that if we will pray in such a manner, we can go from "just saying a prayer" to really praying.

"If you have had trouble getting answers to your prayers, try asking today, 'What is there that you would have me do?' That prayer will be answered if you are sincere and if you listen like a little child, with *real intent to act.*"

—President Henry B. Eyring[17]

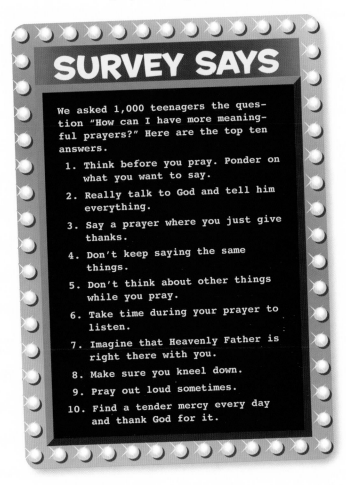

SURVEY SAYS

We asked 1,000 teenagers the question "How can I have more meaningful prayers?" Here are the top ten answers.

1. Think before you pray. Ponder on what you want to say.
2. Really talk to God and tell him everything.
3. Say a prayer where you just give thanks.
4. Don't keep saying the same things.
5. Don't think about other things while you pray.
6. Take time during your prayer to listen.
7. Imagine that Heavenly Father is right there with you.
8. Make sure you kneel down.
9. Pray out loud sometimes.
10. Find a tender mercy every day and thank God for it.

TELL ME ONE MORE TIME!

How Can I Have More Meaningful Prayers?

- **Follow the prophets: Go somewhere private, kneel, and pray out loud.**
- **Speak to God openly as your loving Father.**
- **Pray for others.**
- **Thank more.**
- **Listen more.**
- **Listen to what the Spirit tells us to pray for.**
- **Follow the pattern set in the Savior's prayers.**

18 ch
How Can I Get More from My Scripture Study?

John Says:

In junior high school, I was a huge football fan. I grew up in Seattle, and posters of the Seahawks' star wide receiver Steve Largent hung in my room. I played little league football and was a wide receiver. I had big dreams of going pro, but unfortunately I wasn't on Mr. Largent's level. In fact, one day my dad told me that I wasn't going to be a professional football player.

I was really bummed! Why did my dad say that? Aren't your parents supposed to encourage you in your dreams? But my dad taught me an important lesson—he said, "John you won't be a professional football player because you're not willing to put in the required effort."

At first I was offended, but then I realized that he was right. I enjoyed playing football, but I didn't like to do drills or run laps. (I was also afraid of getting tackled!) I wasn't willing to do what it took to go pro.

In a similar way, I have sometimes found myself acting like an "amateur" in my scripture study. I know I'm supposed to read each day, and I do, but do I put in the required effort to *really* be spiritually nourished?

Go Pro

We can use the acronym PRO (as in "professional") to help us know how to get more out of our scripture study.

Pray

Regular Schedule

Obey

The P is for **"Pray."** Praying before we start reading will help us be able to be in tune and learn what the Lord would have us learn. President Howard W. Hunter said, "There is nothing more helpful than prayer to open our understanding of the scriptures."[1]

In addition to praying before studying, we should pray after we read to thank the Lord for the scriptures and to ask for help in remembering what we've learned. The Lord has commanded us to "pray always" to gain an understanding of the scriptures (D&C 32:4).

The R is for **"Regular Schedule."** Instead of saying, "I'll read whenever I have time and can fit it in," we should have a set time of day to study the scriptures. It could be the first thing when we wake up in the morning, or perhaps just before we go to bed, or any time in

"Getting good results from your study depends on having a strong desire to learn."

PREACH MY GOSPEL[2]

HOW can I get anything from my scripture study if I don't understand all the big words?

Sometimes the unique vocabulary of the scriptures can make the scriptures hard to understand. One thing you can do is to use the seminary student study guide for the book of scripture you are studying. Ask your local seminary teacher for a copy, or you can download a free copy at http://seminary.lds.org/.

Each chapter has descriptions and definitions of difficult words to help make the language more understandable. It also has good quotes and activities throughout it to help you truly study instead of just read.

Others have found that it helps to listen to somebody read the Book of Mormon out loud while they follow along in their own scriptures. Perhaps the most important thing we can do to understand the words is to pray for the Spirit to enlighten us as we study. Elder Bruce R. McConkie said, "There is only one way to *understand* the scriptures. That way is by the power of the *Holy Ghost.*"[3]

between, but having a set time is very helpful because it establishes a routine or habit.

In addition, we should plan to read for a certain amount of *time* each day. President Howard W. Hunter said, "We should not be haphazard in our reading

"If possible, set a consistent time and place to study when you can be alone and undisturbed."

ELDER M. RUSSELL BALLARD[4]

but rather develop a systematic plan for study. There are some who read to a schedule of a number of pages or a set number of chapters each day or week. This may be perfectly justifiable and may be enjoyable if one is reading for pleasure, but it does not constitute meaningful study. It is better to have a set amount of time to give scriptural study each day than to have a set amount of chapters to read. Sometimes we find that the study of a single verse will occupy the whole time."[5]

Sometimes people ask the question, "What if I'm really busy, so I just read one or two verses a day. Is that okay?" Elder M. Russell Ballard said, "I have heard many well-intentioned Church leaders and teachers instruct congregations to find time for daily scripture study, 'even if it's only one or two verses per day.' Though I understand the point they are trying to teach and applaud the sincerity of that conviction, may I

BUT I'M TOO BUSY!

In a study of 103 high school seminary students in Utah who answered the question "When you don't read the scriptures, what is your primary reason for not reading?" the number one response (at 34.95 percent) was "too tired," and the number two reason (at 23.30 percent) was "not enough time" or "too busy."[6]

We need to admit that those aren't the *real* reasons why we don't study the scriptures. After all, we almost always find time each day to eat, to dress ourselves, and to shower or bathe (we hope!) no matter how tired or busy we are. When we see that feeding our soul through scripture study is just as necessary as feeding our body through food, we will make it a priority and make the time for scripture study.

gently suggest that if we are too busy to spend at least a few minutes every day in the scriptures, then we are probably Too Busy and should find a way to eliminate or modify whatever activities are making that simple task impossible."[7]

HOW *can I help my family study the scriptures?*

Modern Church leaders have asked that families give "highest priority" to family scripture study.[8] If your family does not study the scriptures every day, talk to your mom and dad and ask if you can help organize a daily family scripture study. If, for whatever reason, you cannot have scripture study with your parents, consider organizing family scripture study with some of your brothers and sisters.

The O is for **"Obey."** President Henry B. Eyring taught, "The effect of . . . careful scripture study is to *always* feel an urging to *do* things."[9] A major purpose of our study should be to look for insights from the scriptures that help us more fully obey God's commandments. Sometimes the most meaningful parts of scripture study come after we've read the scriptures and ask ourselves, "What can I *do* to apply what I've learned?"

Invitation to Act

Go PRO with your scripture study this week. For the next seven days pray before you study, choose a regular time to study the scriptures each day, and at the end of each study session, decide what you will *do* as a result of your study.

ARE YOU USING YOUR SAFETY EQUIPMENT?

Sister Ann M. Dibb told of a terrible accident where four people were killed while working on a bridge. These individuals had safety equipment, *but chose not to use it.* Sister Dibb taught that Heavenly Father has given us safety equipment—including the scriptures. Are we using it?[10]

"My experience suggests that a specific and scheduled time set aside each day and, as much as possible, a particular place for study greatly increase the effectiveness of our searching through the scriptures."

ELDER DAVID A. BEDNAR[11]

HOW can I get an audio copy of the scriptures to listen to on my iPod? ?

There are a lot of free audio scripture downloads available on the Internet. The Church has provided a free download for each book at http://scriptures.lds.org/.

Click on the book you want to download and then click on "listen." Instructions are given on how to get a free audio copy to listen to on your iPod.

Write Down What We Learn

Another key to getting more from our scripture study is to write down what we learn. There are more than fifty places in the scriptures where the Lord has commanded his children to write his words. For example, the Lord said, "I command all men . . . that they shall write the words which I speak unto them" (2 Nephi 29:11). The Lord is speaking to us through the scriptures—are we recording the impressions we receive?

We've found that when we study the scriptures with paper and pen in hand we receive direction and revelation more easily. Perhaps having a piece of paper and a pen ready sends a signal to the Lord that we expect to learn things worth being written down. Another form of writing as we learn is simply by marking our scriptures and writing impressions or appropriate thoughts in the margins of the scriptures. We know some people who have even purchased the larger set of the scriptures so they can have more room in the margins to write. Whatever our method of writing, the process of recording impressions and thoughts as we study can lead to greater spiritual guidance in our scripture study.

"Please . . . read more slowly and more carefully and with more questions in mind. . . . Ponder, [and] examine every word, every scriptural gem."

ELDER JEFFREY R. HOLLAND[12]

IS ELDER CHRISTOFFERSON ENVISIONING YOUR SCRIPTURE STUDY?

Sometimes we get confused about the purpose of scripture study and think we're just supposed to "read the scriptures." The purpose of scripture study is not just to read the words on the page, but to get the word of God deep in our hearts. Elder D. Todd Christofferson explained what it could mean to seriously study the scriptures. As you read this description, ask yourself: Does this describe my scripture study? He said, "I see you sometimes reading a few verses, stopping to ponder them, carefully reading the verses again, and as you think about what they mean, praying for understanding, asking questions in your mind, waiting for spiritual impressions, and writing down the impressions and insights that come so you can remember and learn more. Studying in this way, you may not read a lot of chapters or verses in a half hour, but you will be giving place in your heart for the word of God, and He will be speaking to you."[13]

GETTING MORE FROM THE SCRIPTURES

Want to continue learning about how to get more from the scriptures? Check out *Please Pass the Scriptures* by John Hilton III. You can download a chapter of the book for free at http://ldswhy.com.

"Study at a desk or table where you can write (not lying down or sitting on your bed), organize your study materials, and remain alert."

PREACH MY GOSPEL[14]

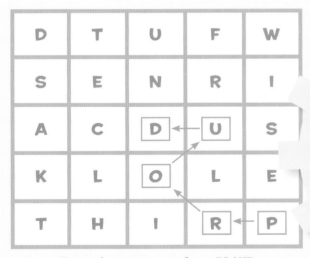

Here is an example: PROUD

Look at the chart to the left. How many words can you find? Here are the rules: 1. You can go in any direction. 2. The letters need to be next to each other (you can't skip over rows or columns to get to the next letter. 3. The words must have at least three letters.

Did you find all the words we found? (See page 136 for answers.)

DO TRY THIS AT HOME!

The Big Picture

Take a look at this picture— what do you see?

Not sure? Let's zoom out a little bit.

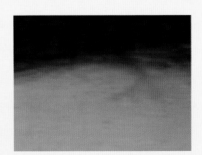

Still don't know? Let's zoom out a little bit more.

At first it was hard to tell what the picture was, but when we zoomed back to see "the big picture" it was much easier. In a similar way, we can sometimes gain more from our scripture study if we stop to see the big picture. One way we can do this after we read from the scriptures is to ask, "What does this mean to me? Why did the Lord put this in the scriptures? What can I learn right now from these scriptures? What do these verses teach me about the Savior? What do these verses teach me about the plan of salvation?"

Answers to "Do Try This at Home" on page 135.

The point of this object lesson is that there are way more words than we think there are. We might have gotten ten words and thought we did pretty well—but there are so many more! (We didn't even list them all here.) In the same way, we may find some insights from the scriptures and think we have found everything—but there is so much more. We need to keep on searching. (Special thanks to Robert Eaton for the idea for this activity.)

hole	house	plod	wiser	dunes	stun	cast
holes	dock	douse	rod	rise	set	core
lode	lock	role	lore	riser	seal	cores
ore	clod	proud	roles	louse	salt	rule
ores	cloud	cent	dole	nurse	ace	rules
teal	clouded	cents	doles	deal	aces	surf
ruler	lace	steal	cod	dolt	dent	cole
hire	laces	tune	send	aloud	colt	dents
our	laced	tunes	hires	end	loud	hilt
ours	scent	ire	tuned	ten	round	dealt
ascent	hour	run	case	rune	tend	rounded
rock	nest	hours	fun	runes	ceased	net
last	sack	old	dour	fund	wise	dune
nets	lasted	lack	hold			

TELL ME ONE MORE TiME!

How Can I Get More from My Scripture Study?

- **Pray before and after you read.**
- **Have a regular schedule.**
- **Find ways to act on or obey the verses you read.**
- **Write down what you learn.**

How Can I Find Answers in the Scriptures?

"We will find answers in the scriptures. The Lord seemed to antici-
pate all of our problems and all of our needs, and He put help in the
scriptures for us—if only we seek it."—President Henry B. Eyring[1]

Look at the picture below until you have found him.

...THE
PREMORTAL LIFE!
  Wow! He can't tell if
he's looking at the book
or if he's *in* the book.
And he can't turn the
page until he finds
himself. You can help
Norman find himself
among the zillions of
spirits waiting to be

squeezed into babies'
bodies for the trip to
earth. You may be
surprised by what you
run across in your
search. Who knows, you
may even find yourself
sliding into your very
own family prennion.
  When Norman finds
himself, he turns the
page to...

   Got him? No? What's wrong? Don't you know what you
are searching for? Let us help you out: You are searching for a
guy named Norman the Nephite. He looks like this:

Now that you know who and what you are searching for, find Norman the Nephite again.

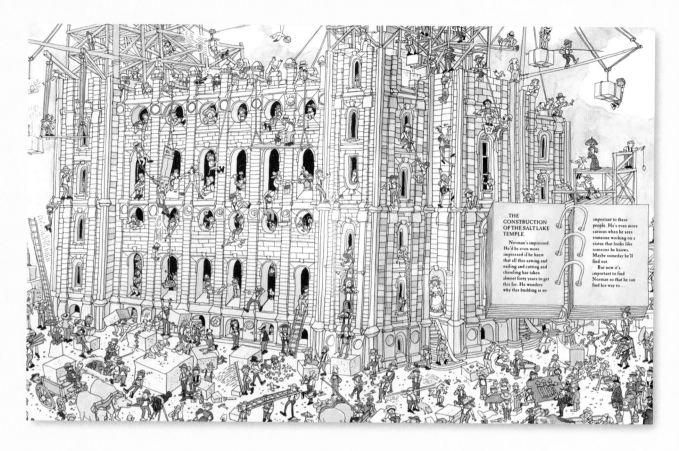

A little easier this time, isn't it? If you need a hint turn the book upside down and read this secret message:

Hint: Take a look in the middle window on the third level of windows.

If you called up your friend on the phone and said, "Hey, what are you doing?" and they answered with, "I'm searching my room," what would your logical follow-up question be? Probably, "What are you looking for?" What if your friend said, "I have no idea. I was just told to search my room, so I'm doing it. I don't know really what I'm looking for, but when I find it—whatever it is—I'll let you know"? You might start to seriously wonder about your friend's health if you had a conversation like that.

But sometimes we do the same thing with the scriptures! The Lord has commanded us to "search the scriptures" (John 5:39), but what are we searching for when we open up those holy pages? Are we looking for cool names? Battle scenes? Are we looking for how many verses are in the chapter so we can know how quickly we can be done reading it? Notice that the Lord used the word *search* and not *read* the scriptures. The scriptures are meant to be studied, feasted upon, and searched—not read like a novel or story or a regular book. Nephi specifically told us to "liken all scriptures unto us" (1 Nephi 19:23). But how can we do that as we search and study the scriptures? It all depends on knowing what we are searching for.

HOW do I know where to look in the scriptures to find the answers I need?

A great place to start is the Topical Guide (it's in the back of the LDS edition of the Bible). That's the *Topical* Guide, not the *tropical* guide (we're not telling you how to get to Hawaii!). The Topical Guide is full of thousands of scriptures organized by topics (such as "trials" or "friendship"). A useful way to start your study of the scriptures is to "start by choosing a subject in the Topical Guide that [you] need to know more about."[2] However, many times what we want to study and the problems we are facing are not necessarily found in the Topical Guide. There is nothing specific in there that will tell us which university to attend, which person to ask to homecoming, or where to get a job. This is when we need to search the scriptures for eternal truths and principles and apply them to ourselves, no matter where we are studying. Answers can be found anywhere in the scriptures, and often—if we are prayerful and hearken to the Spirit's guidance—we are led right to the chapters we need to study. That has happened for us numerous times. We testify it is real and it can and will happen for you too.

DO TRY THIS AT HOME!

Think about how many pennies you have handled in your life. Probably hundreds. But do you know what is on a penny? Find a clean penny and study it for two minutes, trying to find or notice things you've never seen before. We bet you will be able to find some things that you skipped over. The scriptures are the same! If we just read them, like handling a penny without thinking, we'll miss things, but when we take the time to really look into the scriptures and study them, we will find hidden treasures and things we have never noticed before.

1. There is a small "D" or "S" on the face of the penny under the year. 2. Lincoln is wearing a bow tie. 3. There are small dots separating the words E Pluribus Unum. 4. The "o" in "United States of America" is lowercased. 5. There is a statue of Lincoln inside the Lincoln Memorial. 6. The initials "FG" are located at the bottom right-hand corner of the Lincoln Memorial steps. 7. If you flip the penny directly over, the opposite side is upside down.

Search for Eternal Truth in the Scriptures

President Thomas S. Monson instructed us to "find truth in the scriptures."[3] Although there are many possible definitions of truth, we think of "truth" as the eternal and unchanging fundamentals of the gospel of Jesus Christ.

QUICK QUIZ

Which of these would be considered ETERNAL TRUTHS?

a. Today is a nice day.
b. God can control the weather.
c. BYU has a great football team.
d. God the Father has a resurrected body.
e. Jesus has a beard and long hair.
f. There is a temple in Salt Lake City.
g. My body is a temple.
h. In order to be exalted you need to be sealed by priesthood authority.

(Answers: b, d, g, h. Answers a, c, e, and f are not eternal truths because they are relative and can change.)

Let's take a look at this verse of scripture and identify some eternal truths that we might find.

"Wherefore, I the Lord, knowing the calamity which should come upon the inhabitants of the earth, called upon my servant Joseph Smith, Jun., and spake unto him from heaven, and gave him commandments" (D&C 1:17).

What are some eternal truths you found in that verse? Here are a few we found:

- God knows the future ("knowing the calamity which should come").

- God speaks to his prophet ("spake unto him from heaven").

- The teachings of the prophets are from God ("gave him commandments").

Notice how each of those statements are eternal, unchanging, simple truths of the gospel. If those are the truths we found in one verse, think how many statements of truth we can learn from some entire chapters of scripture! Okay, so we've got some eternal truth . . . now what do we do to find answers in the scriptures?

Make Statements of PRINCIPLE from the Eternal Truths Found in the Scriptures

Elder David A. Bednar defined gospel "principles" this way: "Principles are *doctrinally based guidelines for what we ought to do.*"[4] In other words, take a truth and write it in such a way that it can govern our general behavior. That is what we mean by a *principle.* Elder Richard G. Scott taught, "As you seek spiritual knowledge, *search for principles.* Carefully separate them from the detail used to explain them. *Principles are concentrated truth, packaged for application to a wide variety of circumstances.* A true principle makes decisions clear even under the most confusing and compelling circumstances. *It is worth great effort to organize the truth we gather to simple statements of principle.*"[5]

For example, let's take one of the truths we found in Doctrine and Covenants 1:17: *God speaks to his prophet.* What are some simple statements of principle we can make from that doctrine? What should we *do* because of the truth that God speaks to his prophet? Here are a few we came up with:

- Listen and take notes when hearing the prophet speak.

- Live the teachings of the prophet and do what he asks us to do.

- Always sustain the prophet.

WANNA HAVE A LOVE AFFAIR?

Yes, that title is correct. We want you to have a love affair. As a matter of fact, President Gordon B. Hinckley wants you to as well. He said, "I am grateful for emphasis on reading the scriptures. I hope that for you this will become something far more enjoyable than a duty; that, rather, it will become *a love affair with the word of God.* I promise you that as you read, your minds will be enlightened and your spirits will be lifted. At first it may seem tedious, but that will change into a wondrous experience with thoughts and words of things divine."[6]

Let's fall in love with the scriptures!

❓ HOW *can I make more time to study the scriptures?*

One way to find time might be in our television watching. A 2008 study by Neilsen Media Research shows that the average American watches more television than ever—about 142 hours a month—that's an average of more than four hours a day![7]

Elder William R. Bradford tells us what we could do with that time: "If you have a twenty-hour-a-week television habit and would repent and convert it into a gospel-study habit, in one year you could read the Book of Mormon, the Doctrine and Covenants, the Pearl of Great Price, and the entire Bible. In addition, you could read *Jesus the Christ, The Articles of Faith, Gospel Principles,* the . . . priesthood manual, the [Relief Society] manual, the basic children's manual, all three volumes of *Doctrines of Salvation, The Miracle of Forgiveness, The Promised Messiah,* and *Essentials in Church History,* and could then reread the Bible, Book of Mormon, Doctrine and Covenants, and Pearl of Great Price. This would still leave time to read the *Ensign,* the *New Era,* and the *Friend* each month and the *Church News* each week. This is based on your ability to read only ten pages an hour. The average person can read twenty pages or more an hour."[8]

We are not saying that we should cut television completely out of our life, but surely when we stand before the Lord at the judgment bar the excuse that we didn't study the scriptures because we were "too busy" won't hold much weight if we are watching too much television.

Let's practice making principles. Read this verse and see if you can find an *eternal truth* and *a principle that states what we should do* as a result of that truth:

"What? know ye not that your body is the temple of the Holy Ghost which is in you, which ye have of God, and ye are not your own? For ye are bought with a price: therefore glorify God in your body, and in your spirit, which are God's" (1 Corinthians 6:19–20).

Although there are multiple statements of doctrinal truth in there, perhaps a primary one is this: "your body is the temple of the Holy Ghost."

In our modern-day language we might say it like this: **Truth:** Our bodies are sacred. **Principle:** I should not do anything that degrades or harms my body.

Now that we have a principle, we can liken it to our individual lives. Suddenly choices regarding the Word of Wisdom, immorality, modesty, piercings, and tattoos become clearer. We can plainly see the potential violation of this principle in even less clearly defined behaviors like overeating, rash dieting, not getting enough sleep, cutting (self-hurting), or extreme sports that often result in reckless injury. When we have statements of principle, we begin to know how we can specifically apply the scriptures to our lives.

Anthony Says:

Believe it or not, teachers get nervous for the first day of school just as much as students do. One year, on the morning of the first day of the school year, I was particularly nervous because I would be teaching the Old Testament in seminary. I wanted to make sure my students had a powerful experience with the Old Testament, but didn't quite know how to do it. I opened up my scriptures and randomly began reading the following verses:

"And now, ought ye not to tremble and repent of your sins, and remember that only in and through Christ ye can be saved? Therefore, if ye teach the law of Moses, also teach that it is a shadow of those things which are to come—Teach them that redemption cometh through Christ the Lord, who is the very Eternal Father" (Mosiah 16:13–15).

There was my answer right there! The eternal truth I needed to teach was that only through Christ can we be saved. The principle to teach my students was that the law of Moses points to Christ. The application? I was to teach in each lesson how the chapters we were studying in the Old Testament would help us come unto Christ. The answer I received from the Lord through the scriptures made it the best year I've ever had teaching the Old Testament.

THE POWER OF SCRIPTURE MASTERY

There are specific key verses that LDS seminary and institute students are asked to master. These are known as Scripture Mastery verses. These verses are full of powerful truths and principles. Here are a few excellent, short, "power phrases" to master:

"If ye love me, keep my commandments" (John 14:15).

"How then can I do this great wickedness, and sin against God?" (Genesis 39:9).

"Ye are the light of the world" (Matthew 5:14).

"I will go and do the things which the Lord hath commanded" (1 Nephi 3:7).

"I, the Lord, am bound when ye do what I say" (D&C 82:10).

These verses can help you find answers to the questions you have! Check out all the great scripture mastery tools available online at http://semi nary.lds.org/ scripture- mastery/.

Apply (or Liken) the Principle to Your Personal Situation

Remember, Nephi told us to liken the scriptures to ourselves (see 1 Nephi 19:23). A similar word to "liken" is "apply." Once we have a general principle we can then ask ourselves, "How does that relate to me? What should *I* do specifically because of that principle?" The difference between statements of principle and statements of application is that principles are general, and application is specific to your life as the Holy Ghost tells you how to liken it personally.

For example, when you read the principle "I should do what the prophet asks me to do," what specific things do you feel prompted to do? Maybe you think, "I should stop gambling with my buddies," while your parents might think, "We should really get out of the consumer debt we got ourselves into." When you read the principle "Don't do anything that intentionally degrades or harms the body," you might think, "I should stop drawing on myself with a permanent marker," while your friend might be prompted with the thought, "I really need to talk to my bishop about the immorality problems I've been having with my girlfriend." Both are specific applications of the general principle of not degrading the human body.

?

HOW *can having a specific question in mind help my scripture study?*

One great way to apply the scriptures to our lives is to go to the scriptures searching for answers to personal questions we have. Many of Joseph Smith's revelations were the direct result of going to the scriptures with questions. If we go into the scriptures with questions on our mind, we more easily find direction. President Henry B. Eyring said, "You will be taught more easily as you approach the scriptures *if you search with a question and with a determination to act on the answer*. We can receive what seems to us new truth when we go back to the same scripture with new questions."[9]

Your Muscles Are Like . . .

Having a hard time likening the scriptures? Just remember that to liken something is to compare it to something else. You can use this one on your brother: Your muscles are like diamonds . . . rare and hard to find.

When he gets mad, you can use this one to make up for it: Your muscles are like gold . . . soft and yellow.

Likening the scriptures to us is simply taking the truths and principles and comparing them to our lives.

When we approach scripture study by searching for eternal truths, creating statements of principle from those truths, and then applying those principles to our individual lives, the scriptures begin to speak to us and we find answers! We aren't just reading stories about people who lived thousands of years ago—we are finding truths about what we should do in our individual lives today. We're not just trying to get through a chapter; instead, we are discovering truths! We won't be confused about what to do, because "the words of Christ will tell [us] all things what [we] should do" (2 Nephi 32:3).

Invitation to Act

Practice what we have discussed in this chapter. The next time you study the scriptures—search for eternal truth, write down principles, and find ways to liken the principles you find to your personal situation.

"Do you read the Scriptures, my brethren and sisters, as though you were writing them a thousand, two thousand, or five thousand years ago? Do you read them as though you stood in the place of the men who wrote them? If you do not feel thus, it is your privilege to do so, that you may be as familiar with the spirit and meaning of the written word of God as you are with your daily walk and conversation." —Brigham Young[10]

TELL ME ONE MORE TIME!

How Can I Find Answers in the Scriptures?

- **Search for eternal truths in the scriptures and write them down.**
- **Make statements of principle from the eternal truths found in the scriptures.**
- **Apply (or liken) the principle to your personal situation.**

How Can I Keep the Sabbath Day Holy?

Perhaps no other commandment is as difficult to interpret as the command to "Remember the sabbath day, to keep it holy" (Exodus 20:8). We know that we should "not do any work" (Exodus 20:10) on that day, but even that can be difficult to figure out. What is *work* after all? If you pick up around the house on Sunday, is that work? The Pharisees in Jesus' time struggled with this question, and started to make strict rules about what is and is not "work" on the Sabbath, and therefore what is and is not keeping the Sabbath day holy.

WALKING AS WORK?

Did you know the Pharisees in Jesus' day used how many steps a person took in a day to define if they "worked" on the Sabbath?¹ What would happen if you hit the walking limit and weren't all the way home yet?

"What are you doing in the middle of the road?"

"Keeping the Sabbath day holy."

It seems that the Pharisees started to use their *traditions* rather than the *purposes* of the Sabbath to define what is and is not okay to do on the Sabbath (see Mark 7:9).

We may not be so different in the latter days. Instead of using the principles of the Sabbath day to determine what is and is not okay, sometimes we simply use the traditions of our family.

HOW should I dress on the Sabbath?

For the Strength of Youth says, "Your dress before, during, and after church meetings should show respect for the Sabbath."²

Elder David A. Bednar taught, "I know a young man who was taught in his home to dress appropriately for his Sunday meetings—and then to remain in his Sunday attire throughout the

entire Sabbath day."³ Although Elder Bednar made it clear this was not a rule everyone has to follow, it is an idea worth considering.

Should you need further clarification, *For the Strength of Youth* says, "If you are not sure what is appropriate, ask your parents or leaders for help."⁴

THERE'S NO SUCH THING AS THE FAMILY CLAUSE

Sometimes we hear teenagers say that something is okay to do on Sunday because they do it with their family. While we should spend quiet time with family on the Sabbath, "family" isn't necessarily the deciding principle of what is or isn't appropriate for the Sabbath. What if the family wanted to skip church and go to a movie instead—is that okay? What if the family wanted to go wakeboarding on Sunday—is that okay? We hate to break it to ya . . . the "Family Clause" may be more a tradition than a truth.

For example, one family might think it's just fine to go on a long Sunday walk, even in the woods, while another family might think that a long walk is like hiking and should be avoided. How do we know which one is Sabbath worthy? Our internal thoughts might go like this: "Going on a walk? That's fine! But what if we go on a walk in the mountains? No, that is not Sabbath approved. That's hiking, and we hike on Saturdays because we get all sweaty. So, not being sweaty is the key to keeping the Sabbath day holy. Yeah, no hiking. That is, unless you live in the mountains and are hiking to church. Then it's fine!"

To alleviate some internal Sabbath difficulty, and to help us make more *principled* decisions regarding keeping the Sabbath day holy, Doctrine and Covenants 59 gives us a few principles by which to judge our Sunday behavior.

"Hey, there's the church over there . . . keep hiking to keep the Sabbath day holy!"

Does the Activity Keep Me "Unspotted from the World"?

Doctrine and Covenants 59:9 says that one of the purposes of the Sabbath is to "more fully keep thyself unspotted from the world." A good question to ask ourselves is: "Does this activity help keep worldly ideas, thoughts, images, and desires out of my mind and heart?"

HOW does doing homework on Sunday affect my ability to keep the Sabbath day holy?

President James E. Faust addressed this question saying, "I would counsel all students, if they can, to arrange their schedules so that they do not study on the Sabbath. If students and other seekers after truth will do this, their minds will be quickened and the infinite Spirit will lead them to the verities they wish to learn. This is because God has hallowed his day and blessed it as a perpetual covenant of faithfulness."[5]

President Henry B. Eyring spoke about his experience participating in a very competitive graduate program. He was in a program where one-third of the students would fail—and he did not want to be one of the failing students. The competition was fierce though, and most of his classmates studied on Sunday. But President Eyring said, "For me, there was . . . no studying on Sunday."[6]

Instead, President Eyring devoted his Sunday time to the Lord's service, and he saw the blessings of his obedience: "In the few minutes I could give to preparation on Monday morning before classes, ideas and understanding came to more than match what others gained from a Sunday of study. . . . I cannot promise academic success . . . [b]ut I can promise you that if you will go to Him in prayer and ask what He would have you do next, promising that you will put His Kingdom first, He will answer your prayer and He will keep His promise to add upon your head blessings, enough to spare."[7]

Remember, schoolwork is usually the main daily labor for students; the Sabbath is designed to have us rest from our daily labors. When we use Sunday for a homework day, often our thoughts are more on the things of chemistry than the things of eternity.

Does the Activity Allow Me to Attend My Church Meetings and Partake of the Sacrament?

In Doctrine and Covenants 59:9 the Lord says that on the Sabbath we are to "go to the house of prayer and offer up [our] sacraments upon [his] holy day." Of all the meetings and appointments and classes we have during the week, sacrament meeting and partaking of the sacrament is "the greatest and most important meeting in the Church."[8] This is because we are able to renew covenants, recommit ourselves to following the Lord, and "then cometh a remission of your sins by fire and by the Holy Ghost" (2 Nephi 31:17). If an activity prevents us from attending sacrament meeting, it probably isn't an appropriate activity.

The Commandment Is to Keep the Sabbath Day WHOLLY

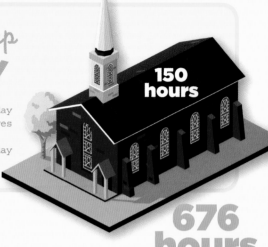

150 hours

676 hours

In one year of going to Church each Sunday, the average Latter-day Saint will spend around 150 hours in Church. But that still leaves us with 676 hours of Sabbath-day activity (if we are awake for sixteen hours a day). There is way more to keeping the Sabbath day *wholly* (for the whole day) than just going to Church.

Does the Activity Help Me Rest from My Regular Work?

Doctrine and Covenants 59:10 teaches that another principle of the Sabbath is "to rest from your labors." We need to ask ourselves: what are my daily labors that this day is designed to allow me to rest from in order to concentrate on more holy things? It seems that resting from our work and drawing closer to the Lord are connected: The more we are able to take a break from our daily work, the more time we have to give ourselves to worship God on the Sabbath. The less we rest from our daily work, the less time we seem to have to worship. That is one of the reasons why the prophets counsel, "Whenever possible, choose a job that does not require you to work on Sundays."[9]

HOW should I respond when my employer wants me to work on Sunday?

For the Strength of Youth simply says, "When seeking a job, share with your potential employer your desire to attend your Sunday meetings and keep the Sabbath day holy. Many employers value employees with these personal convictions. Whenever possible, choose a job that does not require you to work on Sundays."[10] Follow that prophetic counsel and share with your employer your desire to keep the Sabbath day holy by not working on Sunday, and place your faith in the Lord and see what happens.

A young woman named Diane had her dream job—she was a trainer of sea lions and would give performances with them. The only bad thing was that she was required to work on Sundays. After praying about her situation, she felt prompted to tell her boss that she would need to quit if she had to work on Sundays. Her boss told her she had to work Sundays—so Diane quit her job. Later Diane said, "I'm so glad I chose to keep the Sabbath day holy. Although it was hard to leave a job I loved, since then I have been blessed in so many ways." In fact, Diane found a new job, one that allowed her to maintain her standards as well as allowing her to spend time with the man she would eventually marry.

Does the Activity Help Me Draw Closer to God?

One of the primary purposes of the Sabbath day is to "pay thy devotions unto the Most High" (D&C 59:10). A good question to ask ourselves with our Sunday behavior is this: Does the activity help me draw nearer to God? Does it allow me to worship him, make covenants with him (see D&C 59:9), understand him and his purposes more, or help me become more like him?

Does the Activity Allow Me to Serve God's Children?

On the Sabbath we should "offer [our] oblations" of "time, talents, or means, in service of God and fellowman" (see D&C 59:12, footnote *b*). In other words, does a particular Sabbath activity help me give of myself in selfless service to God's kingdom and those around me? Does it help me serve in my calling, visit the needy, and give of myself?

Does the Activity Help Me Repent of My Sins?

Doctrine and Covenants 59:12 says that on Sunday we should be "confessing [our] sins unto [our] brethren, and before the Lord." The Sabbath day is a good day to work on overcoming those sins and temptations that are limiting our progress in becoming more like God. Does the activity we are choosing to do help us repent, or make it more difficult?

ASK YOURSELF: IS IT THE BEST THING?

There are lots of things that probably are not "wrong" to do on the Sabbath. But we've found it helpful to pause and ask ourselves, "Is this *the best* thing I could do with the Sabbath?" Honestly answering this question can give powerful guidance to making the Sabbath more meaningful.

Invitation to Act

Take a few minutes and plan your entire Sabbath day activities, not just the three hours at Church. Latter-day prophets give some suggestions on how we can fill our Sabbath-day time: "Worship the Lord, attend church, spend quiet time with your family, study the gospel, write letters, write in your journal, do family history work, and visit the sick or homebound."[11] Think of the *best* things that you can do to make the whole day holy.

DO TRY THIS AT HOME!

To the right are some activities that, depending on the situation, *might* be questionable to some, and *might* be okay to others, if done on a Sunday. Review each activity in light of the six Sabbath-day principles taught in this chapter and discuss with your family if/when each activity might or might not be in harmony with keeping the Sabbath day holy.

1. Surfing the Web
2. Making a purchase online
3. Buying something from a store
4. Playing a board game with your family
5. Going to a friend's house
6. Talking to a friend on the phone
7. Watching sports on television
8. Watching a movie
9. Fixing something that broke
10. Playing sports outside
11. Doing homework
12. Doing yard work
13. Doing the dishes
14. Going on a walk
15. Going on a hike
16. Taking a drive as a family
17. Going boating as a family
18. Helping someone change a flat tire
19. Reading a book
20. Taking a nap

What NOT to Do

It is significant to note that neither the Lord nor his modern prophets gives us lists of hundreds of things we can't do on Sundays. They have simply stated that "Sunday is not a holiday or a day for recreation or athletic events. Do not seek entertainment or spend money on this day."[12]

If we understand the divine purposes, doctrines, and principles of the Sabbath day, then we will be able to understand how to keep it holy. We testify that as we keep this day pure, blessings flow (see D&C 59:15–19), and it truly becomes a holy day—the highlight and best day of the week.

TELL ME ONE MORE TiME!

How Can I Keep the Sabbath Day Holy?

When considering whether you should do a certain activity on Sunday, ask yourself:

- **Does the activity keep me "unspotted from the world"?**
- **Does the activity allow me to attend my Church meetings and partake of the sacrament?**
- **Does the activity help me rest from my regular work?**
- **Does the activity help me draw closer to God?**
- **Does the activity allow me to serve God's children?**
- **Does the activity help me repent of my sins?**

How Can I Get More from My Church Meetings?

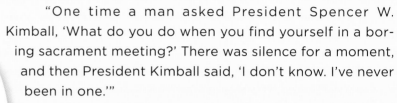

"One time a man asked President Spencer W. Kimball, 'What do you do when you find yourself in a boring sacrament meeting?' There was silence for a moment, and then President Kimball said, 'I don't know. I've never been in one.'"

Some may read that and think, "He's never been to my ward!" ☺

Elder Gene R. Cook, who related this story in an address to BYU's Department of Religious Instruction, said, "That's interesting, isn't it? That tells me that the real meeting was between President Kimball and the Lord. . . . If you enter a meeting with your heart prepared to be written upon by the Lord, then that will happen."[1]

Notice the phrase, "If you enter a meeting with your heart prepared to be written upon by the Lord." When we go to a church meeting, it is our responsibility to make sure that our heart is prepared.

THE PARABLE OF JELL-O

A war story illustrates an important principle connected to getting more from our church meetings: During World War II, U.S. Navy ships would be out at sea for several months at a time, and it was the duty of the head chef to order enough food for those deployments. On one mission, a chef forgot to order enough cherry Jell-O, so he served lemon Jell-O instead. This would seem like a minor issue; however, many crew members were upset. There were fights about the Jell-O, and some even suggested that the chef should lose his job.

Faced with this situation, the chef came up with an idea. He injected red food coloring into the lemon Jell-O and served it as cherry Jell-O. The crew members complimented the chef for "finding" more cherry Jell-O, and the difficulties were avoided.[2]

It's amazing that although the Jell-O didn't change, what the people saw changed and that made all the difference. In a similar way, what we see (our perspective) when we go to church meetings makes all the difference in the world. Do we think that our good or bad experience at church is dependent on someone else? Or do we see that gaining spiritually from our church meetings is *our* responsibility?

DO TRY THIS AT HOME!

Yawn. How do yawns make you feel? Look at that picture of a yawn. Yawn. Yawn. Yawn. Think about yawns. Odds are, you might have yawned just now. That's because seeing yawning is contagious. A researcher at New York University simply showed videos of yawns to sixty-five college students, and the yawning video caused the students to yawn 41.5 percent of the time.[3] Most researchers agree that yawning is mentally contagious. Similarly, if we enter a church meeting and think it will be boring, it probably will be. Try having a positive attitude and being excited to learn in the next church meeting you go to, and it will make a . . . yawn . . . noticeable difference.

President Boyd K. Packer said, "It is important that you know this: The inspiration you may draw from [your church meetings] depends only partly on the effort [the teachers] have expended in the preparation *of* their sermons; it depends much more considerably on what preparation you have made *for* their message."[4]

MAYBE IT'S NOT THE MEETING THAT'S LAME . . .

President Spencer W. Kimball taught: "*If the service is a failure to you, you have failed.* No one can worship for you; you must do your own waiting upon the Lord."[5]

Welcome to Church!

IT'S ABOUT EDIFICATION
. . . Not Entertainment

Sometimes we hear people say they didn't think their class or meeting was very fun. Although everyone likes to laugh and have fun, remember, we can have fun anywhere. We might as well hold church at a giant water park if all we are looking for is friends and fun.

As Elder Dallin H. Oaks said, "If persons are simply seeking a satisfying social experience [at church], they might be disappointed."[6] Sometimes we need to leave the fun behind to understand and feel the sacred, the pure, the holy, and the heavenly. Church isn't about entertainment, it's about edification.

Once we *see* that what we gain from church meetings is our responsibility, how can we do our part? What can we do to make sure we feel the POWER of the Lord during our meetings? Let's use that word "POWER" to help us.

POWER

Pray for yourself and the speaker
Open your scriptures
Write what you learn
Be **E**arly
Raise your hand to participate

First, **P**ray for yourself and for the teacher that you both will have the Spirit. President Henry B. Eyring, then of the Quorum of the Twelve, said, "You may not know who your Sunday School teacher . . . will be next Sunday . . . but you can . . . pray specifically that the Holy Ghost will come to them as they prepare to teach, and then again as you sit at their feet to listen. . . . I know it works. . . . I think you can have faith and confidence that you will never need to hear an unprofitable sermon or live in a ward where you are not fed spiritually."[7]

One young woman shared the following experience: "[I attended a class] and thought it was the most boring class. [I said that] I wasn't going to go to it again . . . [but I did, and I] prayed for that speaker . . . and I also prayed for myself that I [could]

HOW can I help others in my classes be more reverent?

It can be pretty tough when we are trying to enjoy a spiritual class and others are not being reverent. We bet you've got some great answers to this question. E-mail us your best answers at answers@ldswhy.com and we'll post them online.

DON'T PULL A EUTYCHUS!

Think there is no harm in falling asleep in a church meeting? Think again: "And there sat in a window a certain young man named Eutychus, being fallen into a deep sleep: and as Paul was long preaching, he sunk down with sleep, and fell down from the third loft, and was taken up dead" (Acts 20:9).

Better get more involved next time you feel your head bobbing in church. Paul might not be around to raise you from the dead (see Acts 20:10–12)!

. . . get what I needed to learn from his teachings. I had two pages of notes from his class and learned a lot."

Second, we need to **O**pen our scriptures and turn to the verses we are learning about. We will find that we learn much more if we are ready to mark in our own scriptures the verses that are most meaningful to us. Sometimes it can be tempting to not bring our own scriptures to church. However, Elder Joseph B. Wirthlin taught, "The more class members read their scriptural reading assignments . . . [and] bring their scriptures to class . . . the more will be their inspiration, growth, and joy as they try to solve their personal concerns and challenges."[8]

Third, **W**rite down the things we learn. In a school class we would take notes if we expected to really learn, right? A scripture class works the same way. Elder Richard G. Scott taught, "I will seek to learn by what I hear, see, and feel. *I will write down the things I learn and will do them.* . . . Every student who consistently would do that would be blessed with greater inspired direction in . . . life."[9]

Later, Elder Scott taught, "Write down in a secure place the important things you learn from the Spirit. You will find that as you record a precious impression, often others will come that you would not have otherwise received. . . . Have available a piece of paper or a card to record such guidance."[10]

When we make the effort to have paper and pen ready to take notes, we send a signal to the Lord that we want to learn. Remember that the most important thing is to write down the feelings and impressions we receive from the Holy Spirit, and then we need to act on them.

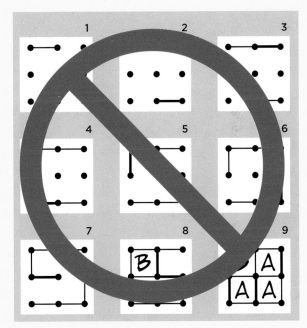

TAKE NOTES, NOT DOTS

You'll get more out of a meeting if you take notes than if you take dots.

Go to Church for Others, Not Just for Yourself

Elder Dallin H. Oaks taught an important truth about attending church: "Some say 'I didn't learn anything today' or 'No one was friendly to me' or 'I was offended' or 'The Church is not filling my needs.' All those answers are self-centered, and all retard spiritual growth.

"In contrast, a wise friend wrote:

"'Years ago, I changed my attitude about going to church. No longer do I go to church for my sake, but to think of others. I make a point of saying hello to people who sit alone, to welcome visitors, . . . to volunteer for an assignment. . . .

"'In short, I go to church each week with the intent of being active, not passive, and making a positive difference in people's lives. Consequently, my attendance at Church meetings is so much more enjoyable and fulfilling.'"[11]

Fourth, be **E**arly. When we arrive early we feel more prepared to learn. The following quote from Elder M. Russell Ballard helps us understand the importance of arriving early:

"We have noticed a growing trend in the Church, but especially among young adults, to arrive late at sacrament meeting, priesthood, and other meetings. . . . Occasionally, there may be a legitimate excuse for not arriving on time (such as an emergency appendectomy), but in most cases it is because you simply plan poorly or do not care enough. The ideal would be to arrive five or ten minutes early so you can sit in the chapel quietly listening to the prelude music and preparing yourselves to worship. . . . When you arrive late, it not only interrupts the reverence of others, but it is a sign of your own disrespect and apathy."[12]

Invitation to **Act**

M ake a special effort to prepare for the next sacrament meeting you attend. Pray for yourself and for the speakers. Bring your scriptures, paper and pen. Arrive early. Afterward evaluate and see if your efforts made a difference in what you got out of the meeting.

HOW *can I make partaking of the sacrament more meaningful?*

Elder M. Russell Ballard remarked, "Our sacrament meetings belong to the Savior. . . . Far too often we see young adults who persist in whispering during the administration of the sacrament. Their minds and hearts are obviously not focused on the emblems of which we partake. It is hard for me to comprehend how anyone who has an understanding and an appreciation for the Atonement of the Lord Jesus Christ could allow this to happen."[13] We can focus on the Savior by offering a silent prayer. We can sing the hymns with our whole hearts. We can avoid texting. These simple steps of preparation invite the Holy Spirit to be with us. Perhaps the most important thing we can do to make the sacrament more meaningful is to focus our attention on the Savior.

MST TIME ZONE

There is a running joke that MST doesn't stand for mountain standard time, but for *Mormon* standard time. The joke is that Mormons show up to everything fifteen to twenty minutes late. (There's even a Facebook page dedicated to it!) It is a time zone that usually belongs to those in the twilight zone. Don't live on MST; come to church meetings and activities on time and get more out of your church meetings.

I'M LATE, I'M LATE!

Top five excuses for being late to church:

1. I got lost with the other ten tribes.

2. I was studying Lehi's dream.

3. I wasn't ten minutes late. In terms of Kolob time, I was only .0001 seconds late.

4. I thought the Millennium started and "time is no longer" (D&C 84:100).

5. If you would have stopped to help the old lady, you would have been late too.

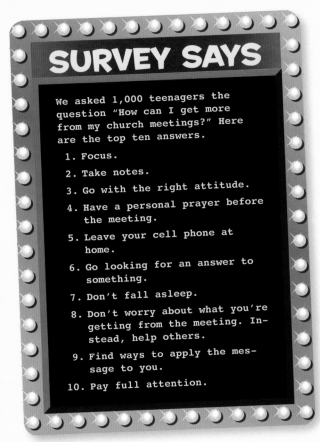

SURVEY SAYS

We asked 1,000 teenagers the question "How can I get more from my church meetings?" Here are the top ten answers.

1. Focus.
2. Take notes.
3. Go with the right attitude.
4. Have a personal prayer before the meeting.
5. Leave your cell phone at home.
6. Go looking for an answer to something.
7. Don't fall asleep.
8. Don't worry about what you're getting from the meeting. Instead, help others.
9. Find ways to apply the message to you.
10. Pay full attention.

Fifth, **R**aise our hand—or in other words participate and share our thoughts and feelings on what we are learning. Elder Richard G. Scott explained, "When you . . . raise [your] hand to respond to a question, [you] signify to the Holy Ghost [your] willingness to learn. That use of [your] moral agency will allow the Spirit to motivate . . . and give [you] more powerful guidance. . . . Participation allows [you] to *experience* being led by the Spirit."[14]

What we get out of church meetings and classes is our responsibility. Let's do everything we can to feel the POWER that can come from these meetings.

TELL ME ONE MORE TIME!

How Can I Get More from My Church Meetings?

- **Realize that you are in control of what you gain from church meetings.**
- **Pray for yourself and the speaker.**
- **Open your scriptures.**
- **Write what you learn.**
- **Be Early.**
- **Raise your hand to participate.**

22 ch How Can I Keep a Meaningful Journal?

Journal writing has been around for a long time—actually, from the time of Adam and Eve. Of our first parents we read, "And a book of remembrance was kept . . . in the language of Adam" (Moses 6:5).

We've all had more than one lesson on the importance of writing in our journal, but the question is how to do it meaningfully, consistently, and well.

John Says:

When I was in Primary, my teacher Sister Drake gave me my very own journal. It was a nicely bound journal that probably cost ten dollars. That made it one of my most expensive possessions. Because I had a journal, I thought I should start writing in it—and I did. For me, it was the simple act of getting a journal that motivated me to write in it regularly. Thanks to Sister Drake, I've been able to keep up that habit ever since.

Decide on a Specific, Convenient Time and Place to Write

One of the first steps to keeping a journal is to figure out some basics. For example, where and how are we going to record our journal? Some people like to type their journal on a password-protected word processing document on a computer. Others would rather blog. Scrapbooking is another form of journaling. Some simply prefer writing on paper. Some like to write topically, others like to write about their day-to-day experiences. Remember, keeping a journal is actually just keeping some form of a record, just like what Adam and Eve did. However the decision of how to keep a record of our lives is up to us individually. We simply need to find the avenue that is most natural and appealing to us because then it will most likely happen.

Elder M. Russell Ballard taught that in order to have good scripture study it's important to have a regular routine, such as a specific time and place to study.[1] The same principle is true when it comes to journal writing. Set a regular schedule for yourself (every night or every Sunday, for example). It's good to have a daily or at least weekly opportunity to write, so we can write while our experiences and thoughts are still fresh and we are "in the Spirit" of the moment (see D&C 76:28, 80, 113, 115). Don't forget important details. We know that this sounds simple and basic; however, if we don't make a specific plan for writing in our journal, it's likely that we won't actually make room for journaling. As the old saying goes, failing to plan is planning to fail.

HOW can I make use of technology in journal keeping?

First of all, keep in mind that you do not need to use technology—use it only if you feel it will help you in your journal-writing efforts. There have been times that we have used a simple word processor to keep our journal. Some of the advantages of doing this are that it is faster, it can be protected by a password, and it's easier to read than our handwriting! Some people find success using online journals that give them e-mail reminders to write in their journal. Still others find that keeping a simple notebook by their bed is the best way to consistently write in their journal.

SHOULD I KEEP A JOURNAL? ANSWER: IT'S OBVIOUS!

Directions:
Use like regular soap

Serving suggestion:
Defrost

Fits one head.

Think these directions are obvious? These are actual labels and directions. So think how about this statement: If you write in your journal you'll be more likely to remember the events and blessings of your life. It's obvious.

COUNT THE Fs

How many Fs are in the following sentence?

"Finished files are the result of years of scientific study and plenty of frugal planning."

How many did you get? There are seven. Often people miss the Fs in the word "of," which appears three times in the sentence. Somehow there is something about those little words that gets overlooked. Similarly, some people may overlook the importance of writing in their journal, thinking it's just a "little thing." Don't make that mistake!

Write Stories and Record Experiences

One thing that is helpful is to write down stories and experiences of things that have happened to us. For example, most people could write a personal experience based on each of the following questions:

- When was a time that the Lord answered your prayers?
- When was a time that the scriptures or words of the prophets helped you find an answer to a problem?
- When was a time that you felt your testimony was strengthened?
- When was a time you did special service for somebody?
- When was a time you followed a prompting from the Holy Ghost, and how did it bless you?

As we begin writing down our experiences and stories, we'll often think of additional events from our life that we could write about.

Tell a parent, sibling, or friend that you want them to remember a secret combination of letters and numbers—1N37M1045. Don't suggest that they write it down (but if they ask if they can write it down, tell them that they can). An hour later, ask them if they remember the secret combination. We're pretty sure that if they wrote it down, they will remember. If they didn't write it down, they won't remember! Another reason why we should write in our journals! (By the way, the secret code stands for 1 Nephi 3:7 and Moroni 10:4–5, the first and last Scripture Mastery verses in the Book of Mormon!)

DO TRY THIS AT HOME!

ATTENTION GUYS!

Guys, feel like keeping a "journal" isn't manly enough for you? We recommend you pick up a copy of the *Manly Book of Experiences* and start to record your life in its pages so you can show your posterity you were a true man.

Write Feelings

One way to make our journals more meaningful is to write down how we *feel*, not just what we *did*. A journal that reads like a robot—"Got up, got dressed, went to school, took test, went to work, ate, did homework, going to bed"—lacks meaning. Compare it to this journal entry: "I took my dreaded algebra test today. Man, math is tough for me. But guess what? All my studying paid off and I pulled off an A! I'm glad I didn't give up on this class . . . it's paying off."

Writing how we feel helps us and any future readers better understand our lives. Think how different the scriptures would be if the prophets had only recorded events! We would have missed Nephi's beautiful psalm in 2 Nephi 4, Paul's statement that he is "not ashamed of the gospel" (Romans 1:16), and Joseph Smith pleading, "O God, where art thou?" (D&C 121:1). Writing down feelings can happen in lots of ways. For example, try writing journal entries based on the following questions:

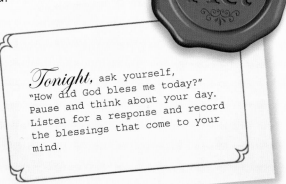

- When was a time that you were afraid?
- How do you feel about your family?
- When was a time you were really embarrassed?
- What does it feel like for you to be led by the Holy Ghost?
- When was a time you felt like you were in the presence of a prophet?
- When was a time you felt loved?
- How are you feeling today, right now?

Taking the time to write down our feelings will often prompt additional insights into life experiences we may have forgotten. When Nephi passed on the records to Jacob, he gave Jacob a "commandment that [he] should write upon these plates a few of the things which [he] considered to be most precious; that [he] should not touch, save it were lightly, concerning the history of this people which are called the people of Nephi" (Jacob 1:2). Let's make sure we don't get so caught up in writing about the facts of our day-to-day life that we forget to record how we feel about life.

Record How the Lord Has Blessed Us

One thing we can always write about is how the Lord has blessed us. President Wilford Woodruff (himself a great journal-keeper) said, "Should we not have respect enough to God to make a record of those blessings which [God] pours out upon us . . . ? I think we should."[2]

President Henry B. Eyring suggested, "As you start to write, you could ask yourself, 'How did God bless me today?' If you do that long enough and with faith, you will find yourself remembering blessings. And sometimes, you will have gifts brought to your mind which you failed to notice during the day, but which you will then know were a touch of God's hand in your life."[3]

Invitation to Act

Tonight, ask yourself, "How did God bless me today?" Pause and think about your day. Listen for a response and record the blessings that come to your mind.

Record *Reality*—The Good and the Bad

Sometimes we are tempted to record only positive events and thoughts, leaving out anything that might make us appear less than perfect. Maybe we are trying to make ourselves appear *more than* we really are. We need to keep in mind that "truth is knowledge of things as they are, and as they were" (D&C 93:24). How many millions of people have taken inspiration from knowing that even the great Nephi struggled with sin and temptation yet overcame it (see 2 Nephi 4:17, 28)?

In recording the reality of our lives we should be careful. President Spencer W. Kimball said, "Your journal should contain your true self rather than a picture of you when you are 'made up' for a public performance. There is a temptation to paint one's virtues in rich color and whitewash the vices, but there is also the opposite pitfall of accentuating the negative. Personally I have little respect for anyone who delves into the ugly phases of the life he is portraying, whether it be his own or another's. The truth should be told, but we should not emphasize the negative."[4]

Most of our lives are not all sunny days and blue skies, or dark thunderclouds and storms. If we record our journals to make them appear as such, then those who might read them down the road won't get a true feel for the events that shaped and molded us, nor will they be able to learn how to overcome their own adversity by learning from us.

JOURNAL OF THE JOURNEY

Consider if Lewis and Clark had only recorded the good of their epic journey. We would have missed all of the struggles and adversity they endured as they traveled across the entire western wilderness of the uncharted United States, and the simple journal entry of 6 November 1805 would have lacked its emotional meaning: "Great joy in camp. We are in view of the ocean, this great Pacific Ocean which we have been so long anxious to see."[5]

President Spencer W. Kimball, one of the great journal-keepers of our time, said, "Begin today and write . . . your goings and your comings, your deeper thoughts, your achievements, and your failures, your associations and your triumphs, your impressions and your testimonies. We hope you will do this . . . for this is what the Lord has commanded, and those who keep a personal journal are more likely to keep the Lord in remembrance in their daily lives."[6]

TELL ME ONE MORE TIME!

How Can I Keep a Meaningful Journal?

- **Decide on a specific, convenient time and place to write.**
- **Write stories and record experiences.**
- **Write feelings.**
- **Record how the Lord has blessed you.**
- **Record *reality*—the good and the bad.**

How Can I Create a Living Area That Invites the Holy Ghost?

Do you know people who find their clothes for the day by reaching down onto the floor, picking up a pair of pants and a shirt, and then taking a whiff to see if they don't smell too bad? Do you not know what color of carpet your best friends have in their rooms, because you can't see the carpet underneath the mess?

Why is having a clean room such a big deal anyway?

There are many reasons. For example, did you know that scientific studies show you can get more accomplished if your room is clean? (We aren't making this up.)[1]

The *New Era* pointed out that even more important than productivity, "a clean room is more likely to invite the influence of the Spirit."[3] That's a very powerful reason. And although having a clean room is important, there is a lot more that we can do to create a living environment that will invite the companionship of the Holy Ghost. In this chapter, we're referring to your bedroom, but please know that these principles apply to every room of the house, or whatever living space you might call home. Here are some "how's" that will help us create an atmosphere where the Spirit can be present in our living spaces.

STUDIES SHOW A CLEAN ROOM IS GOOD FOR YOU

Studies have shown that if you are working in a clean room you will get more done![2]

30%

| how much you got done in a clean room | how much you got done in a messy room |

Keep Things Clean and Organized

President Spencer W. Kimball put it plainly when he said, "We ask you to clean up your homes."[4] President Gordon B. Hinckley taught that a clean home brightens our spirits. He reported that after his family worked to have the house clean that "the result was wonderful. The house was clean, our spirits renewed. The whole world looked better."[5] When your bedroom is clean, you really will feel better.

We often hear comparisons between our homes and the temple. There can be no doubt that part of the reason the temple is a place of revelation is because it is a place of cleanliness. And because "only the home can compare with the temple in sacredness,"[6] we should work to make our living environment similar to that of the temple.

IN WHICH ROOM WILL YOU BE MORE LIKELY TO RECEIVE REVELATION?

Remember, "Only the home can compare with the temple in sacredness."[7]

How Good Does Your Room Smell?

A study done by a BYU scholar showed that people made more ethical decisions when they were in rooms that smelled clean.[8]

Being organized is tied to cleanliness. Have you ever had the frustrating experience of being late for school, but you can't find matching socks? An organized living space can be a benefit in many ways. The prophet Brigham Young was so organized that he said, "I labored many years as a mechanic, and in the darkest night I could put my hand upon any tool I used. You may call this boasting, but it is not. It is merely mentioning the order in which I kept my shop."[9]

One can see the importance of organization in the creation of the earth. Notice this scriptural pattern in Abraham 4:

"The Gods, *organized* and formed the heavens and the earth" (v. 1; emphasis added).

"And the Gods *organized* the earth to bring forth grass from its own seed" (v. 12; emphasis added).

"And the Gods *organized* the lights in the expanse of the heaven" (v. 14; emphasis added).

"And the Gods *organized* the two great lights" (v. 16; emphasis added).

Taking the time to get things organized can be a godly activity. God himself has declared, "Mine house is a house of order . . . and not a house of confusion" (D&C 132:8). Taking the time to clean and organize our rooms will make it so our house is more like his.

DO TRY THIS AT HOME!

Take a look at the following fifteen letters:

J F KFB IC IAL DSC TR.

Spend twenty seconds trying to memorize them. Then, set this book down, wait for one minute and see how many letters you can remember. Then turn to page 170. to see how many you got right.

? HOW can I have a gospel-centered room if I share it with someone else?

Here are a couple of ideas: First, set an example by creating a gospel-centered living space with things you are in control of. You can hang up inspirational pictures and quotes, play good music, and keep your belongings organized and clean. Next, try talking with your roommate or sibling and explain the principles that we have discussed in this chapter. Maybe he/she will feel a desire to change. Another suggestion is to divide the room in half and ask that your roommate keep all of his/her belongings on his/her half of the room. Perhaps then you will at least have half of a clean room!

IF WORSE COMES TO WORST, THROW IT IN THE FRIDGE!

President Thomas S. Monson recounts a time when Spencer W. Kimball was hurrying to clean up his office in preparation for a meeting. He moved some papers to his closet. Others he moved to his secretary's desk. "And then he picked up that big stack of papers he usually carried and threw it in his refrigerator."[10] Not a bad idea if you're in a rush!

Place Things on Your Walls That Uplift You and Reflect Gospel Priorities

President Ezra Taft Benson said that when you enter the homes of those who live the gospel "*the pictures on their walls,* the books on their shelves, the music in the air, their words and acts reveal them as Christians."[11]

Some good questions to ask ourselves are: *What's on my walls? Does it represent the things that are most important to me in my life? Do the images or messages on my walls inspire me to be better and to be more Christlike?* We are not saying that our bedrooms need to be decked out wall-to-wall with images from the Gospel Art Kit, but neither should our rooms look like they belong in the great and spacious building. Imagine if a stranger had to determine our priorities in life simply by observing what we choose to put up on our bedroom walls. What would our room say we think about, dream about, care about, or focus on most?

WHAT'S ON YOUR WALL CAN AFFECT YOU FOR GOOD OR FOR BAD

Marjorie Hinckley said that when she was growing up there was a picture in her room. She wrote that it was "a large picture of the boy Jesus teaching the wise men in the temple. [Mother] had positioned the picture so that the first thing [my] eyes saw when [I] awakened each morning was the beautiful face of Jesus. I was grown and long gone from the home before I realized what a profound effect this had had on my life."[12]

The story is told "of a mother who was saddened because her three sons had left home and gone to sea instead of preparing for further schooling and missions for the Church. Her bishop went to visit her, and upon entering her home immediately saw a large painting of a ship in full sail—the only piece of art in the living room.

"'There is your reason,' he told the mother. 'As your sons have grown up, you have told them every day through this painting of the romance and adventure of the sea. You have taught them well.'"[14]

It isn't only pictures that can uplift us. We can put inspiring scriptures and quotes on our walls as well. Remember, what we see often determines what we think about, and what we think about determines what we desire, and what we desire, often determines our actions.

Anthony Says:

On my wall in my office I have the saying by the philosopher Johann Wolfgang von Goethe: "Treat a man as he is and he will remain as he is. Treat a man as he can and should be, and he will become as he can and should be."[13] I read this statement often, and it reminds me to treat people as sons and daughters of God—future exalted beings. What a great influence a few words on the wall have been for me!

HOW can I have a gospel-centered car, backpack, locker, computer, or cell phone?

Never really thought you could have a gospel-centered car, did you? And no, a gospel-centered car doesn't necessarily have the CTR shield painted on it.

Sometimes we are out and about so much that we actually spend more and more of our time living out of our cars, lockers, backpacks, or desks. But your car can

adhere to the principles we've talked about in this chapter, and so can your backpack, locker, cell phone, iPod, or desk. They can all become gospel-centered living spaces if you keep them clean, organized, filled with good books, quotes, and media, and decorated with gospel-centered pictures and wallpapers.

WHEN WAS THE LAST TIME YOU SWALLOWED?

Swallowing. You know, when your throat kind of lumps up and you contract those muscles to swallow. When was the last time you swallowed? Are you thinking about swallowing right now? Go ahead and try it! We're guessing that reading about swallowing has made you want to swallow. If a few printed words on this page affected your actions, imagine how the printed words or images in our bedrooms will affect what we do!

IT'S NOT JUST WHAT YOU SEE

What we listen to is part of our environment as well. Does the music in our room invite the Spirit? Have you downloaded hymns or talks from general conference, or prophetic addresses from http://speeches.byu.edu? Try adding them to your room environment and see what happens! On Sundays, play music that isn't worldly or loud, or not in harmony with the purposes of the Sabbath day (see chapter 20).

Our friend Darrell Robinson suggested that we "tithe our iPod" by filling at least 10 percent of it with spiritually uplifting messages or music. Not a bad idea!

Limit Media Usage to a Few Open Rooms

Some may be surprised to learn that modern prophets have given guidance on what types of media we should have in our rooms. Specifically, Elder M. Russell Ballard taught, "We need to have TVs and computers in a much-used common room in the home, not in a bedroom or a private place."[15]

Not surprisingly, academic studies back up prophetic warnings. The media we allow into our rooms can have a significant relationship with the actions we take. Dr. Randal Wright conducted a study that showed that there was a relationship between the amount of media in a teenager's room and the willingness of that teenager to have sexual relations outside of marriage. Check it out:

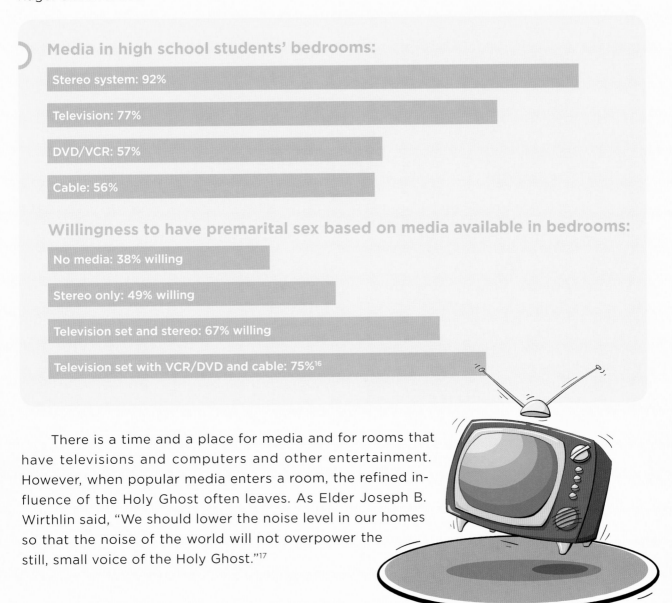

Media in high school students' bedrooms:

Stereo system: 92%

Television: 77%

DVD/VCR: 57%

Cable: 56%

Willingness to have premarital sex based on media available in bedrooms:

No media: 38% willing

Stereo only: 49% willing

Television set and stereo: 67% willing

Television set with VCR/DVD and cable: 75%[16]

There is a time and a place for media and for rooms that have televisions and computers and other entertainment. However, when popular media enters a room, the refined influence of the Holy Ghost often leaves. As Elder Joseph B. Wirthlin said, "We should lower the noise level in our homes so that the noise of the world will not overpower the still, small voice of the Holy Ghost."[17]

FOLLOW THE PROPHETIC "ROOM DECORATION" CHECKLIST

Here are a few specifics the Lord's servants have told us to have in our rooms:

- "Keep a picture of a temple in your home." —President Howard W. Hunter[18]

- "I challenge the homes of Israel to display on their walls . . . scenes from the Book of Mormon." —President Era Taft Benson[19]

- "I wish that every member of this church would put [the] words: . . . 'God hath not given us the spirit of fear; but of power, and of love, and of a sound mind. Be not thou therefore ashamed of the testimony of our Lord' . . . where he might see them every morning as he begins his day." —President Gordon B. Hinckley[20]

- "I challenge the homes of Israel to display on their walls great quotations . . . from the Book of Mormon."—President Ezra Taft Benson[21]

- "College students can create a gospel-sharing home when they adorn the walls of their apartments with pictures that reflect spiritual pursuits instead of the things of the world." —Elder M. Russell Ballard[22]

- "We need to have TVs and computers in a much-used common room in the home, not in a bedroom or a private place."—Elder M. Russell Ballard[23]

√ Picture of a temple

√ Pictures of Book of Mormon scenes

√ Quotation from 2 Timothy 1:7-8

√ Quotes from the Book of Mormon

√ Things on your wall that represent gospel-centered priorities and principles

√ No TV or computer in your bedroom

Invitation to Act

Is there something on the Prophetic "Room Decoration" Checklist you should implement? Select a specific goal of changing something in your room. Maybe you need to move a television or computer out of your bedroom, or perhaps replace some of your pictures of athletes with pictures of Nephi (hey, they both have big muscles!). Maybe you simply need to organize your living space a little more and keep it a little cleaner.

(Continued from page 166.) You might have had a hard time remembering all those letters. But what if we had organized them like this: **JFK FBI CIA LDS CTR?**

They would have been a lot easier to remember! Now, stop reading this book and go organize your room!

Invite the Spirit into Our Rooms through Our Actions

Finally, our actions will have an important influence on what we feel in our rooms. If we have a picture of Jesus up in our rooms, but aren't trying to keep his commandments, we still won't have a very gospel-centered living space. Here are a few things we can practice in our rooms and homes to invite the Spirit:

- Don't "tease, fight and quarrel"[24] as these things are offensive to the Spirit. The Savior taught us that "contention is not of me, but is of the devil" (3 Nephi 11:29).

- Don't raise your voice, yell, or and talk in loud or harsh tones. President David O. McKay said that we should "never speak in loud tones to each other, 'Unless the house is on fire.'"[25]

House on fire? The only time we should ever "speak in loud tones."

- Do productive things around the room and the house, as hard productive work is a value of the gospel (see D&C 58:27), while idleness and laziness are not (see Alma 38:12).

- Do tell your family and friends that you love them. Elder David A. Bednar taught: "Children, when was the last time you told your parents [or siblings] that you love them? . . . We should tell the people we love that we love them. . . . We need to say it, we need to mean it, and most importantly we need consistently to show it. We need to both express and demonstrate love."[26]

- Do small acts of service and kindness for those you live with. It is amazing what doing a small chore without being asked will do to soften hearts and invite the Spirit.

- Above all, keep the commandments. There is no place for the Spirit to dwell in the great and spacious building, no matter how much room there is (see 1 Nephi 11:36)! The Spirit dwells in holy temples, holy rooms, and holy people (see Mosiah 2:37).

It is important to remember that we can turn any space into a gospel-centered living space, no matter how rich or poor, old or young we are. Having the beauty of the Spirit where we live depends on us. Let's make sure that all we do and are—from cleanliness and order down to the decorations, music and even the smells—invites the Spirit and creates gospel-centered living spaces!

TELL ME ONE MORE TiME!

How Can I Create a Living Area That Invites the Holy Ghost?

- **Keep things clean and organized.**
- **Place things on your walls that uplift you and reflect gospel priorities.**
- **Limit the amount of media to a select few "open" rooms, and try to minimize the amount of media in your room.**
- **Follow the Prophetic "Room Decoration" Checklist.**
- **Invite the Spirit into your room through your actions.**

How Can I Stay Faithful When Life Is Hard?

On a summer day in 2002, our good friends Peter and Michelle lost their only daughter, Alex, in a tragic accident. This kind of trial is among the most difficult tests of faith that anyone can face in mortality. It can bring grief, sorrow, despair, pain, regret, frustration, anger, bitterness, and darkness. Peter and Michelle were faced with those feelings and more in the moments and subsequent days after the accident. Peter says, "That evening when my wife and I were left to mourn and to cry, we began to pray for strength and peace. Then a very real choice came to us: we could right then choose darkness and hate and hurt, or choose light, peace, and love. That night we chose to trust in God and to lean on His power and grace. We felt such comfort and peace—no answers to our 'why's' came, but we felt peace."

When hard times come our way, we, like Peter and Michelle, have a choice. We can become bitter and angry and lose faith and the peace of the Spirit in our lives, or we can choose light and truth and remain faithful. We've asked hundreds of teenagers what hard things they face in their lives. Here are some things we've heard.

- I come from an extended family that is all involved in street gangs. They want me to become a part of it. It's really hard to avoid gang life and still be part of my family.

- I want to earn enough money for college and a mission, but it's hard because my parents need help paying the bills.

- My brother didn't go on a mission and is not active in the Church. It really hurts to see how his bad choices affect our family.

- Last year an older boy took advantage of me. I have talked to my bishop about it, but I still feel so bad.

- I have cancer and it is not curable. I have to live with it every single day.

- My dad just cheated on my mom and was excommunicated from the Church. My parents argue all the time and my younger sisters all depend on me for support. It is hard to even want to be at home.

"Though faced with struggles, you can overcome."
—Nick Vujicic, born with no arms or legs.[1]

HOW can God love us if he lets bad things happen to us?

This is perhaps one of the most often asked questions regarding trials. If God loves us so much, then why does he let bad things happen? President Spencer W. Kimball answered this question by saying: "Could the Lord have prevented [all] tragedies? The answer is yes. The Lord is omnipotent, with all power to control our lives, save us pain, prevent all accidents, drive all planes and cars, feed us, protect us, save us from labor, effort, sickness, even from death. . . . But . . . the basic gospel law is free agency. To force us to be careful or righteous would be to nullify that fundamental law, and growth would be impossible. . . . Is there not wisdom in his giving us trials that we might rise above them, responsibilities that we might achieve, work to harden our muscles, sorrows to try our souls? Are we not permitted temptations to test our strength, sickness that we might learn patience, death that we might be immortalized and glorified? . . . We know so little. *Our* judgment is so limited."[2]

YOU CAN HANDLE IT!

One of the great promises in the scriptures is that God "will not suffer you to be tempted [or tried] above that ye are able" (1 Corinthians 10:13).

WHO IS GOING THROUGH THE HARDER TRIAL?

It is easy to think that the good-looking, active person probably isn't going through as hard of a trial as the sick person, but consider this quote from President Boyd K. Packer: "Some are tested by poor health, some by a body that is deformed or homely. Others are tested by handsome and healthy bodies. . . . *All are part of the test, and there is more equality in this testing than sometimes we suspect.*"[3]

How might someone with a handsome, healthy body be tried? Perhaps with increased tests of immorality and pride. Keep in mind that a trial is anything that tests us spiritually, and those spiritual tests come in many forms and ways. Don't mistakenly think that trials always come in the form of misfortune or tragedy.

Staying faithful when life is difficult is no easy task. But it *is* possible. When we asked Peter and Michelle what they did to remain faithful during their trials, they said for them there was one main key: *They did things that invited the Spirit of God.* This is because the Spirit brings peace (see D&C 19:23), eternal perspective (see Jacob 4:13), and comfort (see John 14:16). The following are some keys to inviting the Spirit during hard times so we can come through our trials faithfully.

Ask "What" and Not "Why"

In hard times it's tempting to question God and ask "Why?" "Why me?" "Why now?" "Why didn't you stop this?" Elder Richard G. Scott said, "When you face adversity, you can be led to ask many questions. Some serve a useful purpose; others do not. To ask, Why does this have to happen to me? Why do I have to suffer this, now? What have I done to cause this? will lead you into blind alleys. It really does no good to ask questions that reflect opposition to the will of God."[4] This is what our friends Peter and Michelle said about asking "why," and about what questions we *should* ask:

Peter: "'Why's do not carry comfort with them—they only carry bitterness and anger. You are not trying to understand God when asking 'why'? It's when you can accept and say, 'Thy will be done' that the comfort comes. 'Thy will be done' is the opposite of 'why'? One brings darkness, the other brings light."

Michelle: "'Why' made me feel horrible. We need to ask, 'What do I have to learn from this?' When you take that question to the Lord, he is willing to give you an answer. At the beginning I was having a really hard time with 'why'—'Why is this little girl alive and ours isn't?' But when we focus on 'thy will be done' and not the 'why,' we learn more about God's timing and how to deal with it."

DO TRY THIS AT HOME!

Get a bucket of ice water, a bucket of hot water, and a bucket of lukewarm water. Place your left hand in the bucket of cold water, and your right hand in the bucket of hot water, and leave them there for a minute. After your hands have gotten used to the feel of the water, pull out each hand and instantly place them both into the bucket of lukewarm water. You will have an interesting experience. The hand that was in the cold water will feel like the lukewarm water is hot, and the hand that was in the hot water will feel cold. How is that possible? How can the same water be felt as two different temperatures? It is because of the environment the hand was originally placed in.

Similarly, what we surround ourselves with during times of trial will greatly affect how we feel during our trial. Depending on whether we surround ourselves with angry "why" questions or faithful "thy will be done" statements will greatly change how we feel about the hard time we are going through.

HOT   LUKE WARM   COLD

Elder Richard G. Scott gives us some questions we *should* ask during hard times: "What am I to do? What am I to learn from this experience? What am I to change? Whom am I to help? How can I remember my many blessings in times of trial? . . . [W]hen you pray with real conviction, 'Please let me know Thy will' and 'May Thy will be done,' you are in the strongest position to receive the maximum help from your loving Father."[5]

REMEMBER, TRIALS CAN BLESS YOU

"No pain that we suffer, no trial that we experience is wasted. It ministers to our education, to the development of such qualities as patience, faith, fortitude and humility. All that we suffer and all that we endure, especially when we endure it patiently, builds up our characters, purifies our hearts, expands our souls and makes us more tender and charitable, more worthy to be called the children of God."—Elder Orson F. Whitney[6]

Search, Ponder, and Pray

One of the blessings of scripture study, pondering, and prayer is that it opens us up to receive direction, comfort, and peace from the Holy Ghost. It also helps us understand God's purposes, and gives us hope.

Our friend Peter said, "When I would doubt I would go back to the scriptures. It literally was a continual return to God's word that gave us hope. The only thing that relieved the suffering was the promises and the assurances in the scriptures and words of the prophets."

Peter and Michelle also said that they began to listen to less worldly music during car rides so that they could ponder and think and have some quiet time to reflect. This is also why temple attendance is recommended during hard times—so we can ponder and help ourselves be in tune with the Spirit.

Elder Joseph B. Wirthlin taught, "Some are distracted by the things of the world that block out the influence of the Holy Ghost, preventing them from recognizing spiritual promptings. This is a noisy and busy world that we live in. . . . If we are not careful, the things of this world can crowd out the things of the Spirit."[8]

Elder Richard G. Scott taught, "Challenges often come in multiple doses applied simultaneously. When those trials are not consequences of your disobedience, they are evidence that the Lord feels you are prepared to grow more."[7]

Take Two . . . They'll Help You Grow

Serve Others

Some might read that heading and think, "Serve others? When I'm having a hard time I want people to serve *me.* I'm the one who needs help and support." Those are natural thoughts, but remember, the way of the Savior is often different than our natural desires. For example, when the Savior's relative and friend John the Baptist was murdered, Jesus wanted to be alone, and he went "into a desert place apart" (Matthew 14:13). The Savior probably wanted some private time to grieve. But when the people found out that Christ had left them, they followed after him. When the Savior saw them, he "was moved with compassion toward them, and he healed their sick" (Matthew 14:14).

In the next twenty-four hours you will come across somebody who needs service. Maybe it's a formal service project, or perhaps it will simply be smiling at somebody or having a conversation with somebody who is lonely. Whether or not you are going through a hard time, try to make somebody else's life better by serving them.

One great blessing of doing service during hard times is that we are able to feel charity—the pure love of God—for others. As we do so, we also feel the love God has for us.

Michelle was a great example of thinking of others during her time of trial. In the weeks and months after their daughter passed away, she volunteered to help with a special-needs class. Michelle said, "Through serving others I could feel the Spirit. The small acts of service are how I felt peace. When you are helping others you are always feeling more comfort and you can forget about yourself. Because of serving others I was able to feel the love of God."

On February 3, 1993, President Howard W. Hunter was giving a talk to students at Brigham Young University. As he stood to speak, a man rushed to the podium, saying he had a bomb. The man threatened to detonate the bomb unless President Hunter read a message to the crowd.

President Hunter refused. The BYU students began singing, "We Thank Thee, O God, for a Prophet," and the man became distracted. Members of the congregation then tackled the man. President Hunter "resumed his speech by saying, 'Life has a fair number of challenges in it.' He stopped, looked over the audience, and added, 'As demonstrated.'"[9] What a great example of staying faithful in a trying time!

A BOMB AT BYU?

Remember the Blessings We *Do* Have

An important key for staying faithful even when life is hard is to remember the blessings that we *do* have. We're reminded of a favorite saying by an unidentified author:

"I thought I was abused because I had no shoes until I met a man who had no feet."[10]

Show Gratitude

Scientific research has shown that people who express gratitude

- Are more optimistic
- Are healthier
- Sleep better
- Progress better on personal goals
- Serve others more
- Are less likely to say they are "bitter"[12]

"There's nothing to feel sorry for. I'm this way for a reason. . . . I'm happy the way I am, and I'm prepared to live that way."—Burgon Jensen, blind and partially deaf[11]

There are several ways that we can be more grateful during times of trial. Consider doing these as you go through hard times:

1. Keep a "gratitude journal" and make a list of everything you are grateful for.
2. Specifically look for positive things in the world and attempt to really enjoy these things.
3. Write a letter of gratitude to an important person in your life.

One woman reported that a psychological expert told her that if she did these things she would feel happier, which is what happened.[13]

HOW *can I overcome feelings of ingratitude?*

When we feel ungrateful we should pause and counter those feelings by thinking of things we are grateful for. It's easy to overlook simple things that we should be thankful for. For example, do we send text messages? If so, think of how much we use our thumbs to send text messages, among other things (try buttoning your shirt without using your thumbs)! But when was the last time we thanked Heavenly Father for our thumbs? When we pause to think of the many things we *have* been given, it helps us overcome ungrateful feelings for the few things we may not have.

NO NEED TO WHINE

Sometimes there is a temptation to complain when life is hard. But remember, although some things are difficult we still have much to be grateful for. Elder Jeffrey R. Holland said, "No misfortune is so bad that whining about it won't make it worse."[14] When we are tempted to complain about the hard things we face, counting the blessings that we do have will help us through hard times.

We know that there are and will be hard things that happen to each of us in life. Some of us may have experienced some severe trials already. Some things we cannot change. We cannot change what has happened in the past. We cannot control the actions of others. But we can choose to focus on those things that are in our control. We can choose to seek help from trusted parents or friends. We can choose to serve others. We can choose to go to the scriptures and find direction and assurance. We can choose to remember the blessings we do have. We can say "thy will be done" and choose light rather than darkness. Like Peter, Michelle, and thousands of other faithful Saints, we can choose to remain faithful during hard times.

TELL ME ONE MORE TiME!

How Can I Stay Faithful When Life Is Hard?

- **Ask "What" and not "Why."**
- **Search, ponder, and pray.**
- **Serve others.**
- **Remember the blessings you *do* have.**

How Can I Overcome Feelings of Fear and Doubt?

It is dark, and the ship is being violently tossed in the raging storm. A handful of men scatter about the ship, pulling ropes to steady sails and grabbing buckets to bail water. The ship is sinking in the water, and fear is rising in their hearts. It is a tense moment, and it looks like the ship, and its crew, will go down. Over the noise of the wind and waves one of the men shouts to another, "Go wake him up! We are going to drown!"

With that, a soaking man scrambles hurriedly to the back part of the ship, where, under some covering, a lone man is asleep on a pillow. With fear and doubt in his voice, he wakes him and says, "Master, carest thou not that we perish?"

The man is roused from his sleep by the question, and wakes up to see a boat of chaos, confusion, and concern. He calmly rises, and turning his gaze from his terrified friend, speaks three simple words to the sea, "Peace, be still." And suddenly, there is a great calm.

Most of us are familiar with this story from Christ's life, found in Mark 4:36–41. Part of the lesson learned from this story is that Jesus has control over the elements of the earth and can command the winds and the waves to be still. That very truth leads to an important question: Did his disciples know Jesus could do that? If not, then why did they wake him? If so, then why were they afraid? Perhaps the most important line from the story comes in Jesus' rebuke to his disciples, "Why are ye so fearful? how is it that ye have no faith?" (Mark 4:40).

Having moments of fear and doubt as we go through life is normal. Whether we doubt our testimony, doubt our abilities, or are afraid of failing, we have all experienced doubt and fear. Elder Neil L. Andersen said, "There are also days when we feel inadequate and unprepared, when doubt and confusion enter our spirits, when we have difficulty finding our spiritual footing. Part of our victory as disciples of Christ is what we do when these feelings come."[1]

We need to recognize that doubt and fear are not feelings from God, and we should strive to overcome those feelings. Paul plainly taught, "For God hath not given us the spirit of fear; but of power, and of love, and of a sound mind" (2 Timothy 1:7). In addition, "Doubt is a negative emotion related to fear. . . . It is inconsistent with our divine identity as children of God."[2]

So as we go through our day-to-day lives, striving to be faithful but sometimes faltering, how can we overcome our feelings of doubt and fear?

TOP 10 FEARS IN AMERICA[3]

1. Snakes—**51%**
2. Speaking in public—**40%**
3. Heights—**36%**
4. Being closed in a small space—**34%**
5. Spiders and insects—**27%**
6. Needles and getting shots—**21%**
7. Mice—**20%**
8. Flying on a plane—**18%**
9. Dogs; thunder and lightning; crowds—**11%**
10. Going to the doctor—**9%**

DO YOU FEEL FEAR? THE BRETHREN DON'T

"Fear is the antithesis of faith. In this Church, we do not fear. I have been sitting in the councils of the Brethren now for many years. I have seen disappointment, shock, and concern. Never once, for one second, have I ever seen any fear. And you should not."—President Boyd K. Packer[4]

The phrases "fear not" and "fear ye not" together appear more than one hundred times in the scriptures. Using electronic scriptures at http://scriptures.lds.org find some of these references and make a collection of your favorites.

DO TRY THIS AT HOME!

Do You Have Theophobia? You Shouldn't.

Theophobia is the scientific name for the fear of God. When the scriptures speak about "fearing God," it means to repect and revere him. But we don't need to be afraid *of* him. Remember, God loves you and wants to bless you![5]

Know That God Is Aware of Us, Loves Us, and Desires to Bless Us

The same great God who holds the universe in his hands is aware of the smallest flower and tiniest sparrow (Matthew 10:29). Jesus lovingly taught, "Fear ye not therefore, ye are of more value than many sparrows" (Matthew 10:31). If God cares about sparrows and flowers and provides for them, he definitely cares about us and desires to bless us (see D&C 76:5).

Knowing that "the very hairs of [our] head are all numbered" (Matthew 10:30) to God will help move

OVERCOME YOUR FEARS STEP BY STEP

Erik Weihenmayer startled the world by climbing Mt. Everest . . . blind. When asked how he did it, Erik said, "I just kept thinking . . . keep your mind focused. Don't let all that doubt and fear and frustration sort of get in the way." Then, most importantly, he said, "Just take each day step by step."[6]

the fear of the unknown and the fear of the uncontrollable out of our minds. As we increase our testimony about the reality of God and his love for us, our fears will naturally begin to subside as faith increases, just as it did for Jesus' disciples in the boat.

HOW *can I worry less and stress less?*

Sometimes we think that we are the only ones with problems and worries, but that is not true. Everyone has worries—even General Authorities. Elder Richard G. Scott shared an experience from his life that caused him stress and worry. He was married and had a good job, but had so much stress in his life that he had serious health problems. The solution he found was this: "I was prompted to divide mentally and physically, where possible, all of the challenges and tasks and assignments given to me into two categories: First, those for which I had some ability to control and to resolve, I put into a mental basket called 'concern.' Second, all the rest of the things that were either brought to me or I imagined I had the responsibility to carry out, but over which I had no control, I put in a basket called 'worry.' I realized I could not change them to any significant degree, so I studiously strove to completely forget them. The items in the 'concern' basket were ordered in priority. I conscientiously tried to resolve them to the best of my ability. I realized that I could not always fulfill all of them on schedule or to the degree of competence I desired, but I did my conscientious best."[7]

We would invite you to do the same with the things you are stressing out about: create concern and worry baskets of the stresses in your life and focus on the things that you have control over. It will decrease your stress and worry!

Concern   Worry

Keep Our Focus Fixed on the Savior

When our minds turn too much from the things of God to the things of the world, we begin to lose faith and gain doubts and fears. Consider another scriptural account of boats, storms, waves, and the Savior. This time it involves the Apostle Peter. In the middle of a raging storm, the disciples saw a man walking out to them, on the water! The man called out to them and said, "Be of good cheer; it is I; be not afraid.

"And Peter answered him and said, Lord, if it be thou, bid me come unto thee on the water.

"And he said, Come. And when Peter was come down out of the ship, he walked on the water, to go to Jesus.

"But when he saw the wind boisterous, he was afraid; and beginning to sink, he cried, saying, Lord, save me.

"And immediately Jesus stretched forth his hand, and caught him, and said unto him, O thou of little faith, wherefore didst thou doubt?" (Matthew 14:27–31).

As long as Peter was focused on the Savior he was able to walk on water—but when he feared, he began to sink. Similarly, we will sink into feelings of doubt and despair if we take our eyes off the gospel of Jesus Christ and focus too much on the trials and pressures of life and the things of the world—losing our faith as we do so. However, "If we, like Peter, keep our eyes fixed on Jesus and our eternal destination, we, too, may 'walk triumphantly over the swelling waves of disbelief, and unterrified amid the rising winds of doubt.'"[8]

HOW should I respond if I have doubts about the Church?

President Dieter F. Uchtdorf said, "Is it all right to have questions about the Church or its doctrine? . . . Some might feel embarrassed or unworthy because they have searching questions regarding the gospel, but they needn't feel that way. Asking questions isn't a sign of weakness. It's a precursor of growth. . . . Fear not; ask questions. Be curious, but doubt not! Always hold fast to faith and to the light you have already received."[9] When you have doubts, talk with your parents or trusted youth leaders. They will help you!

DO YOU HAVE HEXAKOSIOIHEX-EKONTAHEXA-PHOBIA OR HAM-ARTOPHOBIA? YOU SHOULD.

Hexakosioihexekontahexaphobia is the fear of the devil's number—666—and hamartophobia is the fear of sin.[10] The fear of the devil and sin is about the only good fear we can have. Elder Neal A. Maxwell tells us: "The only things we should really fear are those things which can keep us from going where there is no fear."[11]

Know That in the Strength of the Lord, We Can Do All Things

Sometimes feelings of doubt and fear creep into our lives when we are faced with tasks that seem too big for us or are out of our control. Perhaps we are faced with a problem that seems to have no immediate solution, or maybe we are starting a new job or church calling that is demanding, or a situation has arisen in our life that places us in circumstances that seem impossible to handle. In these moments, it is easy for doubt and fear to creep in, trying to paralyze us from doing what we know we should do. The Book of Mormon prophet Ammon—who knew a thing or two about facing tough challenges—teaches us a great truth about overcoming our fears when faced with intimidating situations. Upon returning from his successful mission to the Lamanites, he said, "I will boast of my God, for in his strength I can do all things" (Alma 26:12).

Remember, the Lord will never ask us to accomplish or do something that we cannot do (see 1 Nephi 3:7). Rather, through the atoning grace of Christ, he will "expand your vision, and strengthen you. He will give you the help you need to meet your trials and challenges."[12] Having faith that "with God all things are possible" (Matthew 19:26) dispels our doubts and fears when we are faced with challenging situations.

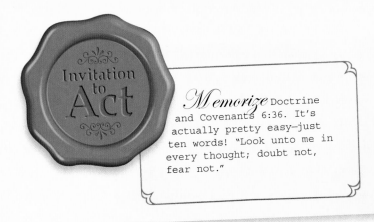

Memorize Doctrine and Covenants 6:36. It's actually pretty easy—just ten words! "Look unto me in every thought; doubt not, fear not."

Pray and Be Filled with the Holy Ghost

Some of the gifts of the Spirit are feelings of peace, joy, and love (see Galatians 5:22). These feelings are also not compatible with fear. As we fill our lives with the things of the Spirit, the gift of the Holy Ghost will help dispel our fears and fill us with hope and confidence (see D&C 121:45–46). Brigham Young said, "The testimony or witness of the Holy Ghost . . . destroys fear and doubt."[13] Just as we should not surround ourselves with bad friends or influences, we should not be surrounded with doubts and fears either, for "fear and faith are not good companions."[14]

In the early days of the Restoration, the Lord repeatedly told—even commanded—the Saints to "fear not." In one section alone the Lord tells them not to fear three different times: "Fear not to do good, my sons" (D&C 6:33), "Therefore, fear not, little flock" (D&C 6:34), and the classic line that we hope this chapter has helped solidify in our hearts: "Look unto me in every thought; doubt not, fear not" (D&C 6:36).

Anthony Says:

While working on my PhD, I had to take a high-level and very difficult (for me) statistics course. It was demanding, we moved at a fast pace, and my mind struggled to keep up and grasp the concepts. During one of our major take-home tests, I came across a problem I couldn't solve. I worked on this one problem for four hours and just couldn't figure it out. As I went to bed that night, I prayed, "Heavenly Father, please help me to understand this. I need to do well on this test for my studies. I've given it my all and don't get it. You know statistics . . . you are the author of all knowledge! Will you please help me, strengthen me, and enlighten my mind so I can understand this problem and do well on this exam."

During the night I didn't sleep well. I was doing statistical calculations all night long in my dreams. I remember seeing formulas and working through pages of hand calculations. When I woke up, I got an impression to go try to rework the problem I had struggled with for hours the day before. I went immediately to my study room and upon looking at the problem, it was crystal clear to me what I had been doing wrong and how I should rework the problem. I solved the calculation in fifteen minutes. It suddenly became clear to me: the Lord had answered my prayer and enlightened my mind during my statistics dreams in the night to solve that problem. I thanked God in prayer for enabling my mind to understand, and for being so kind. With God, all things are possible, even statistics!

HAVING A BAD DAY? THAT'S OKAY!

President Boyd K. Packer taught, "It helps a great deal if we realize that there is a certain healthy element in getting the blues occasionally. It is quite in order to schedule a good, discouraging, depressing day every now and again just for contrast."[15]

HOW *can I be happy?*

Nephi tells us that he and his people "lived after the manner of happiness" (2 Nephi 5:27). Even though they lived in a hard time, they found happiness. Read 2 Nephi 5 carefully and you will find several keys for happy living. Some that we found include the following: (1) surround yourself with righteous family and friends, (2) keep the commandments, (3) make the scriptures part of your life, (4) create things, (5) make the temple the center of your life, and (6) work hard.

"The future is as bright as your faith."—President Thomas S. Monson[16]

TELL ME ONE MORE TiME!

How Can I Overcome Feelings of Fear and Doubt?

- **Know that God is aware of us, loves us, and desires to bless us.**
- **Keep our focus fixed on the Savior.**
- **Know that in the strength of the Lord, we can do all things.**
- **Pray and be filled with the Holy Ghost.**

How Can I Handle Anti-Mormon Teachings in a Christlike Way?

FREE SPEECH GOES BOTH WAYS

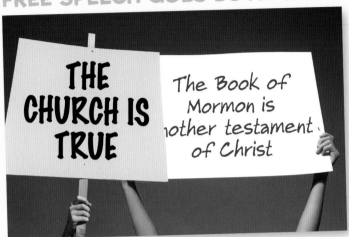

When Joseph Smith related his First Vision to a local Methodist preacher, the preacher treated the vision with "great contempt, saying it was all of the devil" (Joseph Smith–History 1:21). This encounter was perhaps the beginning of hostility and opposition to the Church. Since then, the church Joseph restored has faced similar opposition and persecution. Much of the opposition that is directed toward the Church and its members comes through "anti-Mormon" people and organizations. The *Encyclopedia of Mormonism* defines anti-Mormonism as "any hostile . . . opposition to Mormonism or to the Latter-day Saints."[1] Anti-Mormons often create literature or foster ideas that mock and distort the beliefs of Latter-day Saints with the intent to stop the Church's growth or influence.

Most Latter-day Saints have had to deal with anti-Mormon literature, propaganda, or people at some point in their life, and likely will in the future. Sometimes it is difficult to know what to do, or what to say—or if we should say anything at all. In this chapter, we will give you some principles that may be useful in knowing how to handle anti-Mormonism in a Christlike way when you come across it.

Be Respectful of Other People's Opinions, Ideas, Experiences, and Beliefs

Remember that just because someone might think differently than Latter-day Saints do on points of belief or religious doctrine does not make him or her an anti-Mormon or a bad person. Currently 99 percent of the world are *not* Latter-day Saints and therefore have different perspectives and ways of thinking.

As Joseph Smith said, "We claim the privilege of worshiping Almighty God according to the dictates of our own conscience, and *allow all men the same privilege,* let them worship how, where, or what they may" (Articles of Faith 1:11; emphasis added). We don't like it when people persecute, revile, or belittle us for our beliefs and doctrines—we shouldn't do the same to them.

Avoid Contention at All Costs

Arguing, yelling, and being demeaning is not in harmony with the gospel of Jesus Christ. We simply can't call an anti-Mormon protestor an idiot and feel in tune with the Holy Ghost. The Savior taught, "He that hath the spirit of contention is not of me, but is of the devil, who is the father of contention" (3 Nephi 11:29). It doesn't matter how right we might be, or how wrong someone else may be, our conversations with others about the gospel of Jesus Christ must be done in a spirit of humility and kindness. The Savior said, "A commandment I give unto you, that ye shall declare whatsoever thing ye declare in my name, in solemnity of heart, in the spirit of meekness, in all things" (D&C 100:7). In some cases this may mean that we must avoid talking to those who are purposely making inflammatory comments. In these situations it's best to just stop, drop, and roll: *Stop* what you were going to say, *drop* the prideful desire to prove right/wrong, and *roll* on outta there!

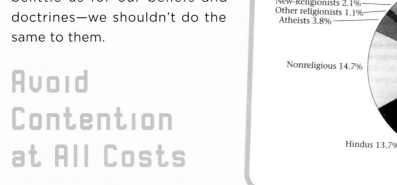

MEMBERSHIP OF WORLD RELIGIONS*

(Compiled from information from *1996 Britannica Book of the Year*, s.v. "Religion: World Religious Statistics"; information current mid-1995.)

Buddhists 5.7%
Orthodox 3.8%
Chinese folk religionists 3.9%
Protestants 6.9%
Ethnic religionists 2 %
New-Religionists 2.1%
Other religionists 1.1%
Atheists 3.8%
Roman Catholics 16.9%
Nonreligious 14.7%
Anglicans 1.2%
Latter-day Saints** .17%
Other Christians 4.6%
Jews .2%
Hindus 13.7%
Muslims 19.2%

*Based on a world population of 5,716,425,000
**Computed using 10,000,000 as membership

STOP, DROP, & ROLL

HOW should I respond if I see people protesting against the Church?

We've both had experiences at general conference in Salt Lake City or visiting Nauvoo where we had to walk past people who were holding signs protesting against the Church. Often the best thing to do is to walk past the people and ignore them. In Alma 30 a high priest and chief judge were faced with an anti-Christ. We read, "Now when the high priest and the chief judge saw the hardness of his heart, yea, when they saw that he would revile even against God, they would not make any reply to his words" (Alma 30:29).

Many times talking to those who are trying to put down our religion leads to contention—and that won't help anyone.

To Learn the Truth, Search the Scriptures and Words of the Prophets— Not Anti-Mormon Literature

President Ezra Taft Benson said, "The Book of Mormon exposes the enemies of Christ."[2] Anti-Christs are featured in both Jacob 7 and Alma 30. Read these two chapters side by side and compare the similarities and differences in (1) The arguments the anti-Christs used, and (2) How the prophets Jacob and Alma handled the situation. What do you learn from these two prophets about how to handle those who oppose the Church?

To find truth the Lord commanded us to "search the scriptures . . . they are they which testify of me" (John 5:39). The scriptures are the greatest source of truth we have to teach us the gospel of Jesus Christ. If we want to know if Joseph Smith was a prophet of God, then read, study, pray about, and live what is taught in the Book of Mormon. This will do infinitely more for our testimony than reading any anti-Mormon publication about Joseph Smith or Church history that claims to uncover a hidden "truth" about the Prophet or the Church.

As President Marion G. Romney said, "'When I drink from a spring I like to get the water where it comes out of the ground, not down the stream after the cattle have waded in it. . . . I appreciate other people's interpretation, but when it comes to the gospel we ought to be acquainted with what the Lord says.'"[3]

WHERE YOU WOULD GO . . .

If you wanted to learn how to make Chinese food would you go to McDonald's or a Chinese restaurant? If you wanted to learn to speak French would you ask a German to teach you? If you want to learn about The Church of Jesus Christ of Latter-day Saints don't go to anti-Mormon sources.

If It Doesn't Edify or Uplift You . . . Don't Touch It

Sometimes members of the Church are tempted to read anti-Mormon literature so they can "know what it says" or simply because they are curious to see how things are being distorted. Some even think they need to read anti-Mormon material so they can know what is being said so they know how to answer the charges and defend the Church. This is like someone saying that they need to watch filthy movies to really understand what kind of media is out there, or jump off a cliff to see if gravity really works. The Doctrine and Covenants teaches clearly "that which doth not edify is not of God, and is darkness" (D&C 50:23). In other words, if it doesn't uplift you, don't touch it! Many people literally feel "darkness" inside of them after reading or listening to anti-Mormon propaganda. Pay attention to how you feel. If it doesn't feel right, it probably isn't right.

Be Aware of Subtle Tactics That Anti-Mormons Use to Make Inflammatory Statements about the Church

If you are faced with someone expressing anti-Mormon ideas, remember a common tactic of anti-Mormon literature is to take things out of context. For example, what if we said, "Did you know that Mormons aren't Christians? Their very own Book of Mormon teaches that 'there should be no Christ' (Alma 30:12)."

Now, before you go and suddenly lose your testimony about the Book of Mormon, realize the context of the actual verse that was just cited. The person who said "there should be no Christ" was Korihor . . . an anti-Christ! In the verses that follow, Alma rebukes him and testifies that he knows there will be a Christ (see Alma 5:48). You may laugh and say this is a silly and unrealistic example, but it was on an actual piece of anti-Mormon literature.

Another tactic is to exaggerate the truth and make inflammatory statements: "Joseph Smith wasn't martyred . . . he was killed in a blazing gun battle in Illinois!" This is an actual exaggerated statement that has been made by some anti-Mormons trying to discredit the martyred Prophet of the Restoration because a mob of 150 to 200 armed men—with their faces painted black—attacked four cornered men who had nothing but two small pistols and a walking stick to defend their lives. The statement is both exaggerated and inflammatory and shouldn't be believed, but is an example of a common anti-Mormon tactic.

Don't Be Afraid to Correct Statements That Are Incorrect, Exaggerated, or Taken Out of Context

When false statements are made, simply provide the actual truth, if you can do it in a non-confrontational way. Alma's encounter with Korihor, the anti-Christ, is an excellent example of this. Korihor accuses Church leaders of binding the believers down "even as it were in bondage, that ye may glut yourselves with the labors of their hands" (Alma 30:27). Alma quickly corrects him and says, "We do not glut ourselves upon the labors of this people; . . . notwithstanding the many labors which I have performed in the church, I have never received [any money] for my labor; neither has any of my brethren" (Alma 30:32–33). There are so many falsehoods and lies and misinformation spread about the Church that some people repeat it simply because it is all they have heard ("Mormons don't believe in Christ, they have one hundred wives, and they can't use electricity!"). In a humble yet sure way, we should do as Alma and others have done and correct the "lying reports abroad, over the world" (D&C 109:29). Let them know we do believe in Christ, we don't practice polygamy anymore, and we do use electricity!

DO TRY THIS AT HOME!

People have been trying to discredit the Book of Mormon ever since it was published. Take a look at this newspaper clipping from a paper in New York on May 15, 1830. How many errors can you find?

Answers: They only got one of the books of the Book of Mormon right, the page count is wrong, and there were eight witnesses, not six.

IMPOSITION AND BLASPHEMY !!—MONEY-DIGGERS, &c.

The book comes before the public under the general title of the "Book of Mormon," arranged under different heads, something as follows. The book of Mormon—containing the books of Nephi, Nimshi, Pukei, and Buckeye—and contains some four or five hundred pages. It comes out under the 'testimony of three witnesses,' and of 'six witnesses,' who say they 'have seen and hefted the plates,' that

Anthony Says:

When I was on my mission, we had a person tell us that the Book of Mormon obviously wasn't true because it contained a French word, "Adieu," in Jacob 7:27. This anti-Mormon said, "French wasn't even invented as a language until hundreds of years *after* Christ, and yet here it is in a portion of the Book of Mormon that supposedly took place around 500 B.C.? Ha!" Being young and naïve, I wasn't sure how to answer that, and it troubled me. Until a companion who was a little wiser than I was, said, "The Book of Mormon is a *translation*, and Joseph Smith simply used whatever words were available to him to express the ideas that were written on the plates, whether it was an English word or a French word." This answer made complete sense, and helped me say *adieu* to my previous worries. Sometimes, it pays to simply talk to faithful people who know a little more than we do. (By the way, we've since learned that *adieu* was in the English dictionary at the time Joseph Smith was translating the plates and was a common way of saying good-bye.)

Let us not be surprised when the Church is attacked, nor troubled by it. President Brigham Young said, "Every time you kick 'Mormonism' you kick it upstairs; you never kick it downstairs. The Lord Almighty so orders it."[4]

THE BEST WEAPON OF ALL: PERSONAL TESTIMONY

"You can argue or debate about the scriptures; you can explain away the works that are performed by prophets and say they were done by this power or that. But you cannot argue with a testimony; there is no issue to debate; there is no defense against the testimony that rests in the hearts of living witnesses who go out and certify of the divinity of this work."—Elder Bruce R. McConkie[5]

?

HOW should I respond if I hear an anti-Mormon statement that brings up something I've never heard of before?

When you are talking to somebody who brings up something you aren't sure about, follow this counsel from Elder Jeffrey R. Holland: "When there is something you do not know, testify of what you do know."[6] For example, if somebody says to you, "Did you know that Joseph Smith was a Freemason?" you could say, "I don't know much about that, but I do know that he in reality saw God the Father and Jesus Christ and that he is a prophet." The most powerful thing you can share is your testimony. After you've responded, talk to a parent or leader who knows more and can help you out (like in Anthony's "Adieu" experience). (By the way, in case you didn't know, being a "Freemason" is like being part of a social club, and was common in Joseph Smith's day.)

TELL ME ONE MORE TIME!

How Can I Handle Anti-Mormon Teachings in a Christlike Way?

- Be respectful of other people's opinions, ideas, experiences, and beliefs.
- Avoid contention at all costs.
- To learn the truth, search the scriptures and words of the prophets—not anti-Mormon literature.
- If it doesn't edify or uplift you . . . don't touch it.
- Be aware of subtle tactics that anti-Mormons use to make inflammatory statements about the Church.
- Don't be afraid to correct statements that are incorrect, exaggerated, or taken out of context.

27^{ch} How Can I Set Meaningful Personal Goals?

"In order to accomplish the things we desire . . . we must have positive and definite goals in mind. Success in life, school, marriage, business, or any other pursuit doesn't come by accident, but as the result of a well-defined plan and a concentrated effort to bring about a realization of the plan."
—President Howard W. Hunter[1]

When we were children, we would sometimes make up our own recipes. Sometimes they went well, other times they didn't. Anthony once made a potato chip sandwich, and John created "cornflake cookies"—they were pretty disgusting. Some things were just not meant to be combined.

When you create and cook from a recipe, you actually create the food twice. There is the recipe, where it's created on paper, and then the actual food that is cooked. In a similar way when God created the earth he created everything twice—spiritually and then physically. In Moses 3:5 we read, "For I, the Lord God, created all things, of which I have spoken, spiritually, before they were naturally upon the face of the earth."

In other words, before the animals or plants were put on earth they were spiritually created. Before humans were made physically, we were created spiritually. All things were spiritually created first. A recipe is sort of a "spiritual creation"; the dish, when prepared, becomes the second, physical creation. Similarly, before a house is physically built, there are blueprints drawn up. Before a dress is made there is a sewing pattern.

How does this relate to our lives? Setting goals is a form of pre-planning and life direction. As we make plans for what we want to become in our lives we are creating a blueprint of what we desire to happen. We shouldn't passively let life happen to us; rather, we should be proactive in setting and achieving goals.

Are We DRIVING or Being DRIVEN by Conditions?

Oliver Wendell Holmes said, "To reach the port of heaven, we must sail sometimes with the wind and sometimes against it, but we must sail, and not drift, nor lie at anchor."[2]

President Ezra Taft Benson said, "Every accountable child of God needs to set goals, short- and long-range goals."[3] Even our Heavenly Father has the overall goal, "to bring to pass the immortality and eternal life of man" (Moses 1:39). So how do we set meaningful personal goals to plan and give direction to our lives?

Involve God in Your Goals

As we set goals we should remember to include our Father in Heaven. He has a plan for each of us individually that he will reveal line upon line if we ask him. Elder Richard G. Scott said, "The Lord has a purpose for you. . . . Discover it and fulfill it."[4]

We should talk directly to God and ask him what goals he wants us to set. As we tap into the vision of what he wants us to become we will be better able to set goals that will help us fulfill our potential. Elder Jeffrey R. Holland explained, "I believe that in our own individual ways, God takes us to the grove . . . and there shows us the wonder of what his plan is for us."[5] Elder M. Russell Ballard simply said, "Pray for divine guidance in your goal setting."[6] When you know you are working on a goal that God wants you to accomplish, it is easier to achieve it.

? HOW can I know where to begin setting goals?

Elder M. Russell Ballard quoted Benjamin N. Woodson as saying: "'All you need to do is this: Beginning this very day, stop doing one thing you know you should not do.' After you have written this one thing down, stop doing it! . . . Write down one thing that you are going to start doing that you have been meaning to do for a long time but that you just haven't gotten around to. I don't know what it might be, but place into your life, beginning tonight, one thing that you are going to do that is going to make you a better person. I believe if you make this a regular practice, you will start to fulfill the Savior's teaching when He asked us, 'Be ye therefore perfect, even as your Father which is in heaven is perfect.'"[7]

ANYBODY WANT A MARSHMALLOW?

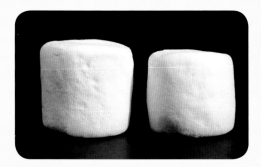

An academic study at Stanford University in the late 1960s tested young children on their ability to delay gratification. These children were told that they could have either a marshmallow at that moment or, if they would wait a few minutes while the professor left the room, two marshmallows when the professor returned. When the professor left the room, some kids ate the marshmallow. Other kids made themselves wait (sometimes for as long as fifteen minutes) and eventually got two marshmallows. About ten years passed and the researchers again contacted the parents of the same children (now teenagers) and discovered that the children who didn't wait to eat the marshmallows "seemed more likely to have behavioral problems, both in school and at home. They got lower S.A.T. scores. They struggled in stressful situations, often had trouble paying attention, and found it difficult to maintain friendships. The child who could wait fifteen minutes had an S.A.T. score that was, on average, two hundred and ten points higher than that of the kid who could wait only thirty seconds."[6]

One lesson we learn from this study is that the ability to put off what you want right now for a more worthy future goal says a lot about your ability to succeed. When you have a goal, do not be distracted from achieving it. If your goal is to write in your journal every day, and one day you want to stay on Facebook for a few more minutes instead of writing in your journal, say no to that Facebook marshmallow. Don't trade the goals you have set for something that only gratifies you in the moment.

Set Well-Rounded Goals

We would be wise to set goals and strive to be well-rounded in our lives. A good pattern to begin with is the only verse about the Savior's teenage years: "And Jesus increased in wisdom and stature, and in favour with God and man" (Luke 2:52). Notice that this verse describes four primary areas of focus to live a balanced life: wisdom (intellectual), stature (physical), favour with God (spiritual), and favour with man (social).

Set goals related to intellectual development. These goals can be anything that stimulates, expands, or enlarges your mind. In other words, do things that make you smarter. Goals in this area might include getting better grades, doing homework, reading books, going to college, learning a new skill, playing an instrument, writing, painting, building, or creating things.

Set goals related to physical development. Losing weight is the most common New Year's resolution, but physical development involves much more than dropping pounds. Physical development concerns caring for the overall gift of your physical body, not necessarily how toned or ripped your right bicep is. Goals in this area might include obeying the Word of Wisdom; exercising daily; participating in sports; learning to play a new sport; completing a 10K, marathon, or triathlon; hiking; biking; eating more nutritious meals; packing a healthier lunch (a candy bar and a soft drink doesn't cut it!); or eliminating caffeine, excess sugar, or energy drinks from your diet.

Set goals related to spiritual development. Goals in this area can include doing better at daily scripture study, having more meaningful personal prayer, attending family home evenings, partaking of the sacrament each week, serving in our callings, participating in Sunday School and seminary, fasting, attending the temple, repenting of our sins, developing faith in Jesus Christ, sharing the gospel with others, or preparing for missions.

Set goals related to social development. To move the kingdom of God forward, we need to develop our social skills and abilities as best as possible. Goals in this area could be connected to doing service projects; being involved in school government or community leadership; being part of formal school groups, teams, or clubs; having a job and contributing to society through meaningful employment; going on dates (if you are older than sixteen); keeping yourself well groomed and modestly dressed; attending performances and uplifting concerts; and limiting the time you spend texting and social networking so that you can actually talk and socialize with living human beings face to face!

Setting goals in all these areas will help us create and maintain a well-balanced life.

ARE YOUR GOALS ON TARGET?

Ready for a challenge? Stand up over this book, hold a pen or pencil, point down, over the target and try to drop it in the bull's-eye. Do it five times. How accurate were you? How consistent were you? It is important to realize that to truly be "on target" we need to be both accurate and consistent. If we are consistent in achieving our goals, but our goals are on the periphery (like constantly hitting the edge of the target, not the middle) then consistency may not be a good thing. For example, if your goal is to watch twenty hours of television each week, and you consistently meet your goal, that may not be good! Make sure your goals are on target with righteous living and what the Lord desires for you—and then consistently hit them!

Invitation to Act

Set one personal goal in each of the four areas (intellectual, physical, spiritual, and social). Keep in mind that setting and meeting goals in all of these areas can count toward Personal Progress and Duty to God awards.

Set SMART'R Goals

To reach our goals in these four areas of our lives, it is important that we set *S.M.A.R.T.* goals.[9]

Specific: Goals that are specific give us focus and direction. It is the difference between saying "I think I'll go visit Europe" and "I'm going to go to Europe in January to snowboard the Swiss Alps." In spiritual terms, "I'll study my scriptures" could more specifically be stated as "I'll study from the Book of Mormon each day for fifteen minutes and finish the book by the end of the year." Answer these questions about your goals: who will be involved, what will be accomplished, where it will take place, when will it be finished, and how will I make it happen.

*M*easurable: President Thomas S. Monson has said, "When performance is measured, performance improves."[10] How can we know if we reached a goal, or know our progress, if it isn't measurable—if we can't see the results? Measuring a goal helps us stay focused and evaluate our success in the specified goal. For example, if our goal is to study the scriptures daily, we can measure it by checking off a box on a calendar.

*A*chievable: A goal that is achievable or attainable is one that is realistically in the realm of reaching. It would be silly to set a goal to walk from your house to your mailbox this year, but it would also be unrealistic to think "I'm going to walk to the moon." Elder M. Russell Ballard said, "Set short-term goals that you can reach. Set goals that are well balanced—not too many nor too few, and not too high nor too low. Write down your attainable goals and work on them according to their importance."[11]

*R*elevant: Set goals based on their order of importance to you in your life. Pick the top few in each of the four categories that are most relevant to the overall direction you want your life to go and that have the most important areas to progress in. *Most importantly, make sure the goal is relevant to what you can control!* Setting goals based on other people's performance is not in harmony with the principle of agency. For example, don't set a goal that Jennifer will go to prom with you—you cannot control what Jennifer does. Instead, set a goal that you can control, such as, "I will ask Jennifer to prom."

Elder Dallin H. Oaks taught that this same principle applies to missionaries who are setting goals. He said, "Some of our most important plans cannot be brought to pass without the agency and actions of others. A missionary cannot baptize five persons this month without the agency and action of five other persons. A missionary can plan and work and do all within his or her power, but the desired result will depend upon the additional agency and action of others. Consequently a missionary's goals ought to be based upon the missionary's personal agency and action, not upon the agency or action of others."[12]

*T*ime-bound: A goal must have a definitive time frame to be accomplished by to provide motivation and goal completion. A great example of this was when President Gordon B. Hinckley challenged the members of the Church in August of 2005 to read the entire Book of Mormon by the end of the year.[13] That time frame

DO TRY THIS AT HOME!

Get up and count how many steps it takes you to walk across the room. Got it? Now, try to beat your normal stride by taking two fewer steps. Now, try to beat that by two fewer steps. See how far you can lengthen your stride and stretch yourself. . . . It's probably a lot farther than you think.

We can all try a little harder, and do a little better, than we are now doing. We can all improve in some area. Let's set some goals and push ourselves in some areas in life that we could stretch a little more in.

gave people motivation and context to evaluate how well they did, and many people upped their scripture study performance because of it. If President Hinckley had simply said, "Read the Book of Mormon," it might not have had the same effect or outcome.

HOW often should I set goals?

As often as you feel you want to improve in an area of your life. You don't need to wait until New Year's Day, that is for sure. Speaking of New Year's resolutions, Elder Jeffrey R. Holland said we should "take stock of our lives and see where we are going" but that we should have our "eye toward *any* time of transition and change in our lives—and those moments come virtually every day."[14]

We could even add an "R" and make "SMART'R" goals by adding in "Reportable."

Reportable: President Thomas S. Monson said, "Where performance is measured, performance improves. Where performance is measured and reported the rate of improvement accelerates."[15] You can probably see how this would be the case. If you have to report to somebody else on how you are doing with your goal, you're more likely to want to achieve it so that you can give a good report. Suppose you have a goal to read your scriptures every day. You could tell your parents about your goal and give them a report every week on how many days you read.

THE COOKIE MONSTER!

Elder Bruce C. Hafen and Sister Marie K. Hafen wrote, "Our family once watched a segment of the children's television program *Sesame Street* in which the Cookie Monster won a quiz show. . . . After Mrs. Monster joined her spouse on the stage, the emcee congratulated the couple and offered them their choice among three big prizes—a $200,000 dream home next month, a $20,000 new car next week, or a cookie right now. . . . As the timer buzzed, a big smile broke across Mr. Monster's face, and he greedily announced his choice: 'Cookie!'"[16] The cookie monster wasn't able to delay gratification to pursue more important goals. Are we?

We should take the time to study out what our goals should be and then talk with the Lord about them. Additionally, we should write our goals down and post them where we can see them to constantly be reminded of our intentions. We hope the principles in this chapter will help us act on and accomplish our goals so that we can progress in our ultimate goal of becoming like God and obtaining eternal life through the Atonement of Jesus Christ.

PUT YOUR GOALS WHERE YOU CAN SEE THEM

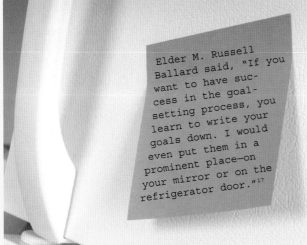

Elder M. Russell Ballard said, "If you want to have success in the goal-setting process, you learn to write your goals down. I would even put them in a prominent place—on your mirror or on the refrigerator door."[17]

"This time is a precious window of opportunity to prepare for your future. Do not waste this time away. Get out a paper and pencil and write down the things that matter most to you. List the goals that you hope to accomplish in life and what things are required if they are to become a reality for you. Plan and prepare and then do."—Elder M. Russell Ballard[18]

WHICH PATH?

Don't think you need to set goals? Listen to President Thomas S. Monson's analogy: "Let us not find ourselves as indecisive as is Alice in Lewis Carroll's classic *Alice's Adventures in Wonderland*. You will remember that she comes to a crossroads with two paths before her, each stretching onward but in opposite directions. She is confronted by the Cheshire cat, of whom Alice asks, 'Which path shall I follow?'

"The cat answers: 'That depends where you want to go. If you do not know where you want to go, it doesn't matter which path you take.'"[20]

GOOD, BETTER, BEST GOALS

Good: "I'm going to get better grades."

Better: "I'm going to pull my math grade up from a B to an A."

Best: "By the end of the first semester I will earn an A in math. I will accomplish this by doing my math homework each afternoon from 3:00 p.m.–4:00 p.m., turning all homework assignments in on time, not intentionally missing any class, taking notes each day, and forming a study group to prepare for tests."

Memorize This Poem!

The heights by great men reached and kept were not obtained by sudden flight, but they, while their companions slept, were toiling upward in the night. –Henry Wadsworth Longfellow[19]

TELL ME ONE MORE TiME!

How Can I Set Meaningful Personal Goals?

- **Involve God in your goals.**
- **Set well-rounded goals—intellectual, physical, social, and spiritual.**
- **Set SMART'R goals—specific, measurable, achievable, relevant, time-bound, and reportable.**

How Can I Resist Negative Peer Pressure?

Elisa had been invited to a swim party. She knew that all of her other friends would be wearing two-piece swimsuits. She felt that if she were the only person wearing a one-piece suit the other girls would laugh at her. She decided to do what she knew was right and wear her one-piece to the party. It turned out that it was no big deal. Nobody came up to her and said, "You're such a great example," but at the same time, people didn't ridicule her either. Later she

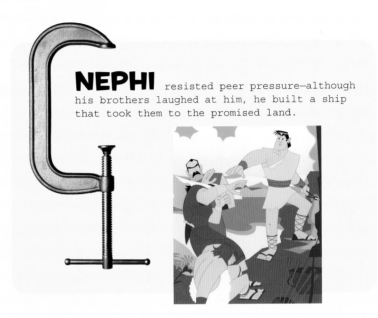

NEPHI resisted peer pressure—although his brothers laughed at him, he built a ship that took them to the promised land.

said, "I felt so good that I did what was right, even though I was worried about what others would think."

David was out with a group of friends—one of whom was a returned missionary; the rest of them were preparing to serve missions. It was late at night, and one of the boys said that he had a huge stash of illegal fireworks. "Let's go blow up some mailboxes," the boy said. Everybody else thought that was a great idea—including the returned missionary. But David didn't feel right about it.

"I don't think so," he told his friends. "It's illegal."

"C'mon," they said. "Nobody will know. We're just having fun!"

"I don't want to do it," David said.

"Don't be such a baby. It's no big deal."

Finally David told his friends, "I'm not going to blow up mailboxes. If you guys want to drop me off, I'll walk home." (They were about two miles from his house at the time.) When his friends saw how determined he was, they decided it probably was not a good idea to blow up mailboxes, and they decided to do something else instead.

Elisa and David both faced a very common issue—negative peer pressure. In fact, to one degree or another, we all struggle with this concern. So, how can we more effectively resist negative peer pressure?

Focus on What God Thinks, Not What Your Friends Think

One important key for resisting negative peer pressure is to focus on what God thinks, not what your friends think. Sure your friends may be cool, but ultimately what matters more—what God thinks about you or what your friends think?

What God thinks

What my friends think

Which is more important?

Through the prophet Isaiah the Lord issued this rebuke: "Behold, who art thou, that thou shouldst be afraid of man, who shall die. . . . And forgettest the Lord thy maker . . . ?" (2 Nephi 8:12–13).

In other words, Isaiah says, "Why are you so afraid of man who is mortal? Why do you forget about God who is all-powerful?"

Isaiah also taught that when God is on our side we do not need to fear. Notice the phrase he repeats. He said, *"For the Lord God will help me,* therefore shall I not be confounded. . . . The Lord is near, and he justifieth me. . . . *For the Lord God will help me.* And all they who shall condemn me, behold, all they shall wax old as a garment, and the moth shall eat them up" (2 Nephi 7:7–9; emphasis added).

Even the Prophet Joseph Smith faced peer pressure!

Even the Prophet Joseph Smith faced peer pressure. Martin Harris, a friend who was older and wealthier than Joseph, pleaded with Joseph to give him the first 116 pages of the Book of Mormon so he could show his family. After those pages were lost, the Lord rebuked Joseph saying, "For, behold, *you should not have feared man more than God.* Although men set at naught the counsels of God, and despise his words—*Yet you should have been faithful;* and he would have extended his arm and supported you against all the fiery darts of the adversary; and he would have been with you in every time of trouble" (D&C 3:7–8; emphasis added).

HOW *should I respond when others ask if they can copy my homework or cheat off my test?*

This can be a very tough peer pressure situation. Remember that the eighth commandment is "Thou shalt not steal" and President Gordon B. Hinckley said simply, "To cheat is wrong."[1]

Don't worry about what your friends will think; focus on what God will think. Tell your friend that you are happy to help him or her study, but that you will not cheat.

God told Joseph Smith directly—do not fear man more than God. When we are faithful to God, he will support us and help us through our difficulties—including negative peer pressure. When we are faced with negative peer pressure, remember that what God thinks is more important than what other people think. A good question to always ask ourselves is: "Will this make my Heavenly Father pleased with me?" God *will* help us and strengthen us to resist negative peer pressure if we are more concerned about pleasing him than pleasing others.

ABINADI resisted peer pressure—although he was put to death, he still testified of what he knew was right. His testimony affected generations.

A VOICE MESSAGE FOR WHEN YOU NEED TO CHANGE YOUR FRIENDS

"I am not available right now, but thank you for caring enough to call. I am making some changes in my life. Please leave a message after the beep. If I do not return your call, *you* are one of the changes."

HOW can I know if I should stop hanging out with a certain friend or group of friends?

Proverbs 22:24-25 states, "Make no friendship with an angry man; and with a furious man thou shalt not go: Lest thou learn his ways, and get a snare to thy soul." A principle from these verses seems to be, *if your friends are having a negative influence on you, then do not be around them.*

Elder Robert D. Hales, then a member of the presiding bishopric, said, "A true friend makes it easier for us to live the gospel by being around

him. Similarly, a true friend does not make us choose between his way and the Lord's way."[2]

Another important indicator to know whether you should stop hanging out with a certain group of friends is to talk with your parents. If they recommend you stop hanging out with certain friends, listen to them. As President Boyd K. Packer taught, "Do not run with friends that worry your parents."[3]

DON'T LEAP WITH THE SHEEP!

In his book *Don't Leap With the Sheep*, S. Michael Wilcox recounts the following story. He and his cousins were teenagers, working on his uncle's ranch. He wrote, "One summer . . . we came across six lambs out on the desert. . . . They were wild, and roughly a year old. We decided to try to catch them and take them back to the ranch. . . .

"For over an hour we ran around, making grabs for them as they broke through our tightening circle. After many unsuccessful attempts, we got an idea. There were many cliffs in the area, so we thought we would back them against the edge of a cliff, thus blocking off their escape. We were closing in on them when the biggest one turned and ran for the edge of the cliff. To our amazement, instead of stopping he leaped over the edge

and plunged to his death. We backed off when we saw this, to give the remaining lambs some room, but to our shock the other five raced toward the cliff. One by one all five of them jumped to their deaths."[4]

Don't leap with the sheep. Stand up for what you know is right.

Remember, We're Not Supposed to Be Like Everyone Else

Just like a basketball player practices free-throws, take some time to practice what you will do when you face peer pressure. Role-play with a family member or friend who will pretend to pressure you to do something bad. What will you say to resist peer pressure?

Invitation to Act

It seems that at the heart of peer pressure is the phrase, "Everybody else is doing it." "Dude, relax. Everybody copies their music and software, it's just how it's done." "C'mon, Justin. Everybody else said their parents would let them come to the party." "Please, Jessica? Everybody else lets me copy their homework."

It seems like Corianton used the idea that "everyone else was doing it" to justify why he left his missionary work to be immoral with a young woman. His father, Alma the Younger, let Corianton know this excuse was not acceptable. In Alma 39:4, Alma said, "Yea, she did steal away the hearts *of many; but this was no excuse for thee,* my son" (emphasis added). "Everybody else is doing it" was no excuse for him, and it's no excuse for us.

The scriptures teach us that as faithful Saints, we are "a chosen generation, a royal priesthood, an holy nation, a peculiar people" (1 Peter 2:9). The word "peculiar" has many meanings, some of which are to be different, unusual, distinct, or set apart. If someone tries to persuade us by saying we should be more like everyone else, that should be a sign that the adversary is trying to tempt us to give up our privilege of being a people that are different than the rest because of our divine beliefs and standards.

MORMON

resisted peer pressure—although he lived in a time when wickedness was all around him, he stood firm in what he knew was right.

DO TRY THIS AT HOME!

Take a look at the three geometric shapes below:

Are you smart enough to be able to recognize them? Are you sure? It's harder than you may think. Say out loud all three shapes right now.

Now, take a look at the answers below and see if you were correct:

Circle, Square, Rhombus

If you said it was a circle, square, and a rhombus you were correct! Congratulations. If you didn't, we seriously wonder about your geometry abilities and where you went to school!

Most people think the last shape is a triangle, but anyone who knows anything about geometry knows that it is a rhombus. Did you think it was a triangle? Really?

Actually, we hope you did, because it *is* a triangle. The real question is: Were you second-guessing yourself just now? Did you know it was a triangle all along, but because some guys printed in a book that it was a rhombus, did you start to doubt yourself? Don't let what others say change what you know is right in your mind and heart! We need to stick to what we know to be true, despite outside influences and opinions. Stick to your triangle!

P.S. If you want to have some more fun, show these shapes to a friend or family member and see if you can get them to call the third shape a rhombus. It helps if you have two or three people with you, all of whom insist it's a rhombus.

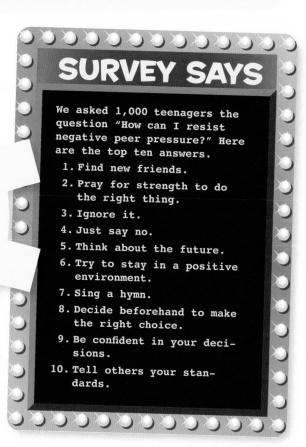

SURVEY SAYS

We asked 1,000 teenagers the question "How can I resist negative peer pressure?" Here are the top ten answers.

1. Find new friends.
2. Pray for strength to do the right thing.
3. Ignore it.
4. Just say no.
5. Think about the future.
6. Try to stay in a positive environment.
7. Sing a hymn.
8. Decide beforehand to make the right choice.
9. Be confident in your decisions.
10. Tell others your standards.

Remember the Power of One

Often it only takes one person to stand up for the right thing. Our friend Courtney described a time she was at a party. The movie they were watching wasn't appropriate, so she left and went into another room. Soon somebody else joined her, and they started playing a game. Before long there were more people in the room with them than were watching the movie. All because one person stood up for what was right.

Consider a scriptural example. The prophet Nephi was teaching a group of people, most of whom were wicked. After he spoke, the people cried out against him. Imagine you were in that setting—would you have the courage to speak up on behalf of the prophet? The scriptures say that "there were some who did cry out: Let this man alone, for he is a good man, and those things which he saith will surely come to pass except we repent" (Helaman 8:7).

How would it have felt to be the first one to stand up for Nephi? It certainly would have taken courage, but when one spoke up, others did too. In fact, because of their words the wicked people were frightened and Nephi was able to finish his message. There is power in being the one who stands up against peer pressure. There is a righteous synergy that comes from being with just one other righteous person, even in the face of a group of negative peer pressure.

SYNERGISTIC STRENGTH

Synergy is when two things coming together combine to create something more than the two things could individually. For example, a single two-by-four board can withhold 605 pounds of pressure before it will break. So how much pressure do you think two two-by-fours put together can withstand? Logic would say 1,210 pounds (twice as much as one on its own). But in reality, they can withstand 5,965 pounds of pressure, almost three times more than a single board can hold! Similarly, having the blessing of being put with one strong friend can produce an enormous amount of spiritual strength to resist negative temptation.

Peer Pressure on American Idol

Carmen Rasmussen was seventeen years old when she entered the *American Idol* competition. One of the challenges she faced was intense peer pressure to go against her standards. For example, at a photo shoot for an upcoming issue of *People Magazine*, the fashion designer had picked out several outfits for her, all of which were immodest. Even though the fashion designer was rude about it, Carmen stuck to her standards and insisted on a modest outfit. When the issue came out, Carmen was the only contestant who got a two-page spread.[5] Who knows, maybe she stood out from the group because of her modesty!

MENTAL VISUALIZATION

Athletes face many high-pressure situations. To help diffuse these situations they use visualization. They picture in their minds what they will do when they have to perform under pressure. We can do the same thing—we can visualize how we will respond when we are offered alcohol, or how we will turn away from pornography when it appears in front of us. Practicing and mentally reviewing what we will do will help us to not crack under pressure. One study reported that "a review of thirty-five studies featuring 3,214 participants showed that mental practice alone—sitting quietly, without moving, and picturing yourself performing a task successfully from start to finish—improves performance significantly. . . . Overall mental practice alone produced about *two thirds of the benefits of actual physical practice.*"[6]

We all face peer pressure. But it really doesn't matter what our peers think or if "everybody else is doing it." What matters is what God thinks. President Thomas S. Monson said, "Make every decision pass the test: 'What does it do to me?' What does it do for me? And let your code emphasize not 'What will others think?' but rather, 'What will I think of myself?'"[7] President Monson also said, "If your so-called friends urge you to do anything you know to be wrong, *you* be the one to make a stand for right, even if you stand alone.[8]

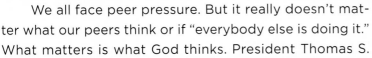

I'VE been making changes in my life and becoming a better person, but my friends make fun of me for being too good. How should I respond?

In the New Testament the Apostle Paul warned that in the last days there would be "despisers of those that are good" (2 Timothy 3:3). Nephi, Abinadi, and even the Savior were all ridiculed for making right choices. It is a frustrating reality that sometimes our friends may put us down for choosing the right. One young woman said while she was at EFY she made several goals for herself as to how she could improve

and be a better person. But when she got home her friends mocked her. She responded by sticking to her standards. Some of her friends eventually began to respect her and followed her example. Other of her friends stopped hanging out with her. But she was very glad that she stuck to her standards.

Remember, when Joseph in Egypt refused to sin with Potiphar's wife, things got worse at first (he was put in prison for it), but in time things got better (he became one of the top rulers in Egypt and saved his family because of it). As you keep the commandments things will get better for you too, even if it's difficult at first.

PEER PRESSURE IN THE RECORDING STUDIO

When LDS musician Alex Boyé joined the Church in his teens, he was kicked out of his house and began living on the streets. After experiencing poverty for many years he got a break when a band he was in was given the opportunity to record a single that was guaranteed to be a hit. The only problem was that some of the lyrics went against Alex's standards. As he sat in the recording studio, getting ready to record the song, Alex had a horrible feeling that he could not continue. He told his manager that he didn't want to sing the song. "What are you talking about?" his manager said. "This song is guaranteed to be a hit. It will bring you fame, money, whatever you want!"

But Alex told his manager he would not sing the lyrics.

"Fine," the manager said. "You're replaceable. We'll hire a new singer."

Alex left the studio. A few weeks later, Alex got a call from his manager. "We really want you to sing," the manager said. "Take out whatever words you want so that you'll sing [the song]."

Alex went back, they recorded the song, and it went on to be a top-twenty hit in several European countries. Best of all, Alex felt good about his decision to resist peer pressure.⁹

YOU resist peer pressure. Your influence can affect literally thousands.

Draw a picture of yourself here.

TELL ME ONE MORE TiME!

How Can I Resist Negative Peer Pressure?

- **Focus on what God thinks, not what your friends think.**
- **Remember, we're not supposed to be like everyone else—we are supposed to be different!**
- **Remember the power of one (righteous synergy). Be that one.**

How Can I Help Friends and Family Who Are Struggling with Serious Problems?

What should we do when someone we care for is in trouble?

Michelle opened her mouth to speak to her best friend Jessica, but no words came. Silent tears began flowing down her cheeks.

"What on earth could have happened?" Jessica thought to herself as she waited for Michelle to speak.

It took a couple of minutes, but Michelle was finally able to speak. "I have an eating disorder," she said over her tears.

"What?" Jessica cried.

"You're the only one I've told, and I don't want you to tell anyone. I feel like I'm dying, and I can't keep this secret inside me anymore. Everyone thinks I'm perfect, but I'm not. Nobody knows except you. I don't know what to do, Jessica, you've got to help me."

Although the previous dialogue is fictional, the challenge presented is all too real. We frequently hear youth ask how they can help friends or family members who are in trouble. Here are some of those questions:

- How can I help an inactive family member come back to church?
- How can I help my friend whose parents are getting divorced?
- How can I help my sister who is starting to do bad things with her boyfriend?
- How can I help my friend who is harming her body by self-cutting?
- How do I help a friend with a pornography problem?
- How can I help my friend who talks about taking his life?

While these are only a few of the many different scenarios our friends might be in, we've found that one question youth desperately want an answer to is: *How can I help friends and family who are struggling with serious problems?*

Strengthen Their Hand in God

An Old Testament account of friendship provides an insight of how to help friends and family in trouble. David (as in David and Goliath) was in serious trouble. Although he was living righteously, the king was trying to kill him. When David was hiding in the forest his friend Jonathan "went to David into the wood, and strengthened his hand in God" (1 Samuel 23:16). Think about that phrase: he "strengthened his hand in God."

Whatever problem our loved ones may have, it is likely that they will need to be strengthened spiritually. We can encourage our friends and family to study the scriptures, to pray, and to attend church. Also, we can teach, remind, and testify to them of eternal gospel truths they may be forgetting or need to hear—truths from the plan of salvation.

One young man shared the following experience. "My friend was going through a really hard time. When she told me about it, she said, 'I just don't know what to do!'

"I asked, 'Have you prayed about it?'

"She said, 'No, I hadn't thought about that.' The next day she sent me a text and told me that after she prayed she had received the answer she needed."

Strengthening our loved ones in God means that we uplift them spiritually and help them turn to the Lord for guidance. We pray with them. We invite them to study the scriptures. We study with them! We invite them to seminary, institute, Young Men or Young Women, and to church. And we can go to all those places with them. All of this will strengthen their hand in God.

Stay on the High Ground

One thing to keep in mind, particularly if the problem our family or friend is struggling with has to do with sin, is that we need to be careful that we stay on the high spiritual ground. A young man who has a friend who is struggling with alcohol might say, "I need to help my friend out, so I'll go with him to the party to keep him out of trouble." He is asking for trouble himself. Remember this truth: The Lord will never require us to break a commandment to save someone else! It would be like trying to pick someone up off the floor when we are lying down right next to them.

President Harold B. Lee said, "You cannot lift another soul until you are standing on higher ground than he is."[1] Staying on higher ground and providing an example will do more for our struggling friends than lowering our standards and getting stuck in sin with them just to try to help them out.

HOW should I respond if my friends want me to "cover" for them?

Satan wants us to hide our sins and participate in "secret works of darkness" (2 Nephi 9:9). If your friends are asking you to help them hide what they are doing, just say no. You should not help your friends make bad choices.

DO TRY THIS AT HOME!

Sometimes people think maybe they can just have some good friends and some bad friends. To see how this doesn't work, try this: With your leg straight, lift up your right foot in the air and swing it in a clockwise direction. Now, with your foot rotating in a clockwise direction, point your right arm straight in front of you and try to draw the number 6 in the air.

Did you notice what happened? Either your foot or your hand changed directions! Similarly, we can't make the mistake of thinking we can be good and go in one direction, yet still hang out with bad friends who are going the other direction. We eventually will change directions with them.

(To check out a video clip of John and Anthony doing this activity in a fireside, visit http://ldswhy.com.)

LIFE SAVING 101

If someone is drowning in a swimming pool, do you jump in the water with them, or do you throw them a rope or extend a pole to them?

We hope you chose to throw them something or give them something to grab onto to pull them in, and not to jump in the pool after them. This is because it is much safer and more effective to *be on firm ground yourself* to save a drowning victim than to be in the water with them. Unfortunately, sometimes those who jump in the water to save a panicking victim simply get pulled under themselves, sadly resulting in two drowning victims. Saving a swimmer and saving a soul are very similar: Staying on firm ground is the best way.

Lovingly Correct When Needed

Sometimes, we mistakenly think that being a good friend means that we accept our friends as they are—that we let them do whatever they want. We may hear misinformed statements like, "My friends just accept me for me."

This is opposite of what *For the Strength of Youth* teaches us: "A true friend will encourage you to be your best self."[2]

Similarly, Elder Richard G. Scott said, "A true friend is not one that always encourages you to do what you want to do, but one who helps you do what you know you ought to do."[3]

Sometimes we hold back on correcting a family member or friend when they are doing wrong because we don't want to offend them or make them feel badly. However, we would do well to ask ourselves in this situation: Who am I *really* concerned about? Most often we will find that we are just trying to protect ourselves from a potentially uncomfortable conversation and are not really trying to help our loved one. Elder Neal A. Maxwell taught that "our capacity to grow and to assist each other depends very much upon our being 'willing to communicate.' (1 Timothy 6:18.) Communication includes proper measures of *counsel, correction, and commendation.* . . . We worry (and understandably so) that some [corrective] communications will only produce more distance. But silence is very risky, too."[4]

Withholding correction when needed is often a sign of selfishness. While we should be as sensitive as possible—and our comments should be uplifting, edifying, and inspired—we can still tell our family and friends we don't approve of inappropriate behavior. Remember, "whom the Lord loveth he correcteth" (Proverbs 3:12). If we love our family and friends and desire to help them, we will do the same.

HOW can I know if I should tell on my friend?

There are some extreme situations in which you might want to seek outside help even if your friend refuses to do so. A young man named Michael was faced with a difficult situation when one of his friends started doing drugs. Michael talked to his friend and encouraged him to make different choices. He tried to help his friend in every way he could. However, his friend continued to use drugs. After praying about it, Michael decided to talk to his friend's parents.

It was a difficult conversation, but at the end his friend's parents said, "Michael, we are so grateful you had the courage to talk to us. We've known something was wrong with our son, but we haven't known exactly what it was. Just today we had a special fast to know what we could do to help our son—you have been an answer to our prayers."

Michael's friend was able to get professional help and get his life back on track. Michael later said, "I'm so glad I had the courage to really help my friend." If you are wondering if you should tell on your friend, seek guidance from your parents (see also the conclusion of this book).

Encourage Them to Seek Help from Others

A lot of times the problems our friends and family are having are serious—they need outside help and quite possibly the help of an adult. For example, suppose we are talking to a friend of ours and she tells that she is struggling with depression. Of course it's good to talk to our friend and to pray for her; however, in this situation she probably needs more help than we can provide alone. The ideal would be to encourage our friend to seek help from a capable adult or professional.

Depending on the situation our friend or family member is in, there are lots of things we could do to encourage them to seek help, such as offering to go with them to talk with the bishop. Perhaps we could invite them to talk with our parents, or even a school counselor. This is especially true if someone's behavior is spiritually or physically self-destructive.

Pray for Our Struggling Friends and Family Members

Perhaps the simplest, yet most effective thing we can do for a struggling loved one is to pray for them. Remember, the prophet Alma had a son known as Alma the Younger. Alma the Younger was struggling spiritually and was making sinful choices. Then an angel of the Lord appeared to him and called on him to repent. Listen to what the angel said about why he came: "Behold, the Lord hath heard the prayers of his people, and also the prayers of his servant, Alma, who is thy father; for he has prayed with much faith concerning thee that thou mightest be brought to the knowledge of the truth; therefore, for this purpose have I come to convince thee of the power and authority of God, *that the prayers of his servants might be answered according to their faith*" (Mosiah 27:14; emphasis added). Our prayers for loved ones make a difference.

Invitation to Act

Do you have a friend or family member who is going through some serious problems? We invite you to pray and ask the Lord what he would have you do to help your friend. Act on the promptings and direction you receive.

HOW can I help friends or family members who don't attend church?

As members of the Church, many of us have parents, siblings, or other relatives who don't attend church. Did you know that many members of the First Presidency and Quorum of the Twelve have come from homes where family members were not active in the Church? For example, Elder Richard G. Scott's mother was less active, and his father was not a member of the Church.[6] Elder Russell M. Nelson's parents were not very active in the Church,[7] and Elder David A. Bednar's father was not a member of the Church while he was growing up.[8]

Perhaps one of the best things we can do for less-active family members is to pray for them (see the example of Alma in Mosiah 27). In some cases that may mean sincerely praying daily for years. As we work to help loved ones come to church, remember this counsel from Elder Richard G. Scott: "Never give up on a loved one, never!"[9]

SURVEY SAYS

We asked 1,000 teenagers the question: "How can I help friends who are making bad choices?" Here are the top ten answers.

1. Be a good example.
2. Tell your friends that you don't approve of what they're doing.
3. Pray for them.
4. Invite them to do good things.
5. Help them see how their choices affect them and others.
6. Ask them to talk to their parents or a bishop.
7. Talk to an adult about the problem.
8. Fast, either with your friends or by yourself.
9. Compliment them when they make right choices.
10. Listen to your friends and then give them advice.

TELL ME ONE MORE TIME!

How Can I Help Friends and Family Who Are Struggling with Serious Problems?

- **Strengthen their hand in God.**
- **Stay on the high ground.**
- **Lovingly correct when needed.**
- **Encourage them to seek help from others.**
- **Pray for our struggling friends and family members.**

How Can I Bear a Powerful Testimony?

Have you ever stopped to think that roughly one in four sacrament meetings are dedicated to the bearing of testimony by the members of the congregation? No assigned speakers, no prepared sermons, no planned program. Just an open mike and a bunch of Saints with testimonies. Almost sounds crazy, doesn't it? But there is something about hearing the testimonies of our fellow ward members that strengthens us and invites the Holy Ghost. In fact, it was a simple, heartfelt testimony that converted Brigham Young![2]

How can we ensure that the testimonies we offer in family home evening, when talking to a friend, and during sacrament meeting, youth conferences, and seminary classes are powerful?

What group activities help youth feel the Spirit most?

Of all the group activities that can help youth feel the spirit—from singing to praying to reading the scriptures to discussing the gospel—the most common activity mentioned in a study of seminary students was hearing others bear testimony. In fact, 46% of the responses specifically mentioned testimony.

The researcher of the study, David Seastrand, concluded: "Testimony sharing is obviously perceived by [youth] as a powerful tool for the elicitation of the Spirit."[1]

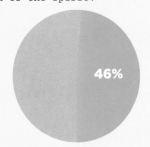

46%

Remember, We *All* Have Testimonies

John the Revelator tells us that—in the premortal council in heaven—the faithful overcame the adversary "by the blood of the Lamb, and by the *word of their testimony*" (Revelation 12:11; emphasis added). We *all* have testimonies. It is not something we are "gaining" here on earth as much as it is something we are "re-discovering." It is inside each of us somewhere—we just need to dig in and re-find it. Additionally, most everyone has a testimony of *some gospel principle.* Perhaps we are still not sure if Joseph Smith was a prophet of God, or even if Jesus is the Christ. But that doesn't mean that we don't have testimonies (plural) of other gospel principles. Perhaps the Spirit has testified to us about the power of service, tithing, forgiveness, or charity. Testify of that then! If we are really stumped . . . then we can at least testify that we know that murder isn't right! ☺

HOW can I bear my testimony when I don't feel very confident in it?

Know that when we bear our testimony, we can expect to not only strengthen other people's testimony, but our own as well. Do not worry if you do not feel confident in your testimony. Share what you do know—and your testimony will increase. President Boyd K. Packer said, "It will be supplied as you share it. . . . As you give that which you have, there is a replacement, with increase!"[3]

WHICH SWITCH?

Sometimes we think of a testimony as either "off" or "on" like a light switch. But if you think about it, it's more like a dimmer switch—it gradually increases or decreases. We're pretty sure your testimony isn't totally "off"—so share what light you do have with others!

Bear a Testimony—Not a Travelimony, Storyimony, Sermonimony, Thankimony, or Lovimony

The definition of bearing testimony is "to bear witness by the power of the Holy Ghost; to make a solemn declaration of truth based on personal knowledge or belief"[4] It is telling how we feel about what we know is true.

Elder M. Russell Ballard said, "We need to replace stories, travelogues, and lectures with pure testimonies."[5]

President Spencer W. Kimball said, "Testimony bearing is not preaching. Do not exhort each other; that is not a testimony. Do not tell others how to live. Just tell how you feel inside. That is the testimony. The moment you begin preaching to others, your testimony ended."[6]

I'd like to bear my travelimony that last month my family went to Hawaii . . .

President Henry B. Eyring noted, "Those who have prepared carefully for the fast and testimony meeting won't . . . give sermons nor exhortations nor travel reports nor try to entertain as they bear witness. . . . Neither will they feel a need to use eloquent language or to go on at length."[7]

We are all excited about your trip to Siberia, but it is more powerful to hear about your inner experiences with the Holy Ghost and gospel of Jesus Christ.

Similarly, a public testimony meeting is not the place to give private thanks or expressions of love. Hopefully, a spouse, a child, or a friend is already hearing such expressions at home or in private conversations. President Henry B. Eyring taught, "Because they will have already expressed appreciation to people privately, they will have less need to do it publicly."[8]

Keep Your Testimony Centered on the Savior and the Truths of the Gospel

Elder M. Russell Ballard gave some great suggestions about the central focus of our testimonies. He said, "Our testimony meetings need to be more centered on the Savior, the doctrines of the gospel, the blessings of the Restoration, and the teachings of the scriptures. . . . Although we can have testimonies of many things as members of the Church, there are basic truths we need to constantly teach one another and share with those not of our faith. Testify God is our Father and Jesus is the Christ. The plan of salvation is centered on the Savior's Atonement. Joseph Smith restored the fulness of the everlasting gospel of Jesus Christ, and the Book of Mormon is evidence that our testimony is true."[9]

BIG FIVE

The following five things are some of the areas our testimonies should consistently be centered on:

DO TRY THIS AT HOME!

Some testimonies have been written to music, like "I Believe in Christ."[10] Get a copy of Hymn no. 134 and, using the same meter, write a verse to the same music that expresses your testimony of Jesus Christ. Send it to us at answers@ldswhy.com

I. God the Father

II. Jesus the Christ

III. The Atonement

IV. Joseph Smith

V. The Book of Mormon

Don't Think That Your Testimony Is "Lame," or That Nobody Cares, or That It Won't Influence Anyone

Sometimes we think that nobody will care what we say, or that what we say doesn't really matter. But it usually does to someone! Upon seeing Jesus one day, John the Baptist bore a simple testimony, "Behold the Lamb of God!" (John 1:36). The result was that "two disciples heard him speak, and they followed Jesus" (John 1:37). That one testimony brought the following disciples unto Christ: Andrew (John 1:40), Peter (the future prophet) (John 1:41), Philip (John 1:43), and Nathanael (John 1:45), and who knows how many more!

Remember that the prophet Alma was converted by the powerful testimony of Abinadi—perhaps Abinadi's only convert. Alma accepted Jesus as the Christ, "repented of his sins and iniquities, and went about privately among the people, and began to teach the words of Abinadi" (Mosiah 18:1). Think of the power of one testimony—and that testimony could be yours!

In the next

Invitation to Act

twenty-four hours, share your testimony with a family member or friend. It can be short and simple—but share what you know with somebody else.

HOW should I respond if I feel I should bear my testimony, but I don't know what to say?

Many of us have had that feeling where the Spirit suddenly prompts us to stand and bear witness. The heart starts racing, the mind starts spinning, and we wonder, "What would I even say?" Unfortunately, because of that, we sometimes try to ignore the prompting, push it aside, and hope it will go away. We need to be obedient to those promptings! Don't worry about what to say. President Boyd K. Packer taught, "A testimony is to be found in the bearing of it!"[11] The testimony will come as you stand and share it.

"ONE DIRTY LITTLE IRISH KID"

One returned missionary felt like his mission was a failure because, as he said, he "'only baptized one dirty little Irish kid. That is all I baptized.'

"Years later . . . Brother Callis, [then] a member of the Council of the Twelve, learned where he was living, this old missionary, and he went up to visit him. And he said to him, 'Do you remember having served as a missionary over in Ireland? And do you remember having said that you thought your mission was a failure because you had only baptized one dirty little Irish kid?'

"He said, 'Yes.'

"Well, Brother Callis put out his hand and he said, 'I would like to shake hands with you. My name is Charles A. Callis, of the Council of the Twelve of The Church of Jesus Christ of Latter-day Saints. I am that dirty little Irish kid that you baptized on your mission.'"[12]

If You Know, Say You Know

There is nothing wrong with saying "I believe" or "I've experienced" or "I feel," if that is the level of your testimony. However, if you *know* through feelings and experiences—if it is sure and undeniable in your heart by the power of the Holy Ghost—then don't hesitate to say, "I know." President Spencer W. Kimball said, "'I know it is true.' Because . . . those few words have been said a billion times by millions of people does not make it trite. It will never be worn out. I feel sorry for people who try to couch it in other words, because there are no words like 'I know.' There are no words which express the deep feelings which can come from the human heart like 'I know.'"[13]

Elder M. Russell Ballard noted, "My experience throughout the Church leads me to worry that too many of our members' testimonies linger on 'I am thankful' and 'I love,' and too few are able to say with humble but sincere clarity, 'I know.' As a result, our meetings sometimes lack the testimony-rich, spiritual underpinnings that stir the soul and have meaningful, positive impact on the lives of all those who hear them."[14]

When the Holy Ghost has witnessed to us that something is true, we have an obligation to share it with others. The prophet Jeremiah couldn't stop bearing his testimony: "[God's] word was in mine heart as a burning fire shut up in my bones, and I was weary with forbearing, and I could not stay" (Jeremiah 20:9). Elder M. Russell Ballard said, "The lesson, I believe, is clear: having a testimony alone is not enough. In fact, when we are truly converted, we cannot be restrained from testifying. And as it was with Apostles and faithful members of old, so is it also our privilege, our duty, and our solemn obligation to 'declare the things which [we] know to be true' (D&C 80:4)."[15]

"I KNOW" vs. "I BELIEVE"

While it is good to say "I believe," consider how different the statements below are when someone doesn't actually "know" but only believes:

- From a master electrician: "I believe that you shouldn't touch the red and black wires together."

- From a math professor: "I believe 2 + 2 = 4."

- From a United States senator: "I believe I live in America."

- From a leading scientist: "I believe the earth revolves around the sun."

- From a famous artist: "I believe that mixing red and yellow make orange."

- From a Latter-day Saint: "I believe Jesus is the Christ."

We would expect industry leaders to *know* these things about their field. Latter-day Saints are the "light of the world" when it comes to spiritual truths. We need to *know!*

TELL ME ONE MORE TiME!

How Can I Bear a Powerful Testimony?

- Remember, we *all* have testimonies.
- Bear a *testimony*—not a travelimony, storyimony, sermonimony, thankimony, or lovimony.
- Keep your testimony centered on the Savior and the truths of the gospel.
- Don't think that your testimony is "lame," or that nobody cares, or that it won't influence anyone.
- If you know, say you know.

31 ^{ch} How Can I Prepare and Give a Powerful Youth Talk?

"Joseph? Hello, this is Brother Johnson from the bishopric . . . "

"Uh, hey, Brother Johnson."

"The bishop asked me to call you and invite you to be our youth speaker in sacrament meeting next month."

"He did?"

"Yes, he did. Is that something that you would be willing to do? If so, we would like you to speak on Christ's visit to the Nephites in the Americas. Could you do that?"

"Um, well, yeah, I could do that, I think."

"Great. I'll tell the bishop you've accepted the assignment, and we'll look forward to a great talk from you, Joseph! Thank you."

"You're welcome, I guess . . . 'bye."

"'Bye."

"Hey, Mom? Um, I just got asked to do a talk in sacrament meeting. But I'm confused . . . Christ came to America?"

Ah, poor Joseph. We've all been there. As active members of the Church, most of us will probably be asked to give a talk in a church meeting at some point. Whether it is in sacrament meeting, or mutual, Young Men or Young Women, Sunday School or seminary, the Josephs and Josephinas of the Church get asked to give talks. So how can we prepare and give a powerful youth talk?

Prepare as Early and as In-depth as Possible

Logic would tell us that if we were in Joseph's situation above, we would start looking into Christ's visit to the Americas in the Book of Mormon as soon as possible, and study it over the next couple of weeks. Unfortunately, we are not logical sometimes. Some of us are procrastinators! In fact, if it were a profession, a few of us could be professional procrastinators. Amulek's words are applicable here with a few word changes: "Therefore, I beseech of you that ye do not procrastinate the day of your [talk preparation] until the end; . . . behold, if we do not [prepare our talk], . . . then cometh the night of darkness wherein there can be no labor performed" (Alma 34:33).

Perhaps the worst thing Joseph can do is wait until his head lifts off the pillow Sunday morning and say, "Oh no. That talk is today. What should I say? Mooooooooom?" The Lord told Hyrum Smith, "Seek not to declare my word, but first seek to obtain my word, and then shall your tongue be loosed" (D&C 11:21). The earlier we begin our study and preparation, the more the words of the Lord can enter our minds and hearts and "distil upon [our] soul as the dews from heaven" (D&C 121:45).

PROCRASTINATION— FIGHTING THE RISING TIDE

According to a ten-year study on procrastination, *USA Today* cites the following:

- "In 1978, only about 5% of the American public thought of themselves as chronic procrastinators. Now it's 26%."

- "Last-minute Christmas shopping with credit cards was five times higher in 1999 than in 1991."

- "In the past quarter century, the average self-score for procrastination (using a 1-to-5 scale with 1 being no delaying) has increased by 39%."[1]

Here are five ways you can fight debilitating procrastination:

- "Precommitment. Force yourself to do what needs to be done, like Ulysses tying himself on the ship's mast to get past the tempting songs of the Sirens.

- "Do unpleasant work when you have the most energy, early and in the morning.

- "Set attainable goals and do the work in steps.

- "Unplug distractions, such as television and computers.

- "The five-minute rule. Commit to doing the job for five minutes. At the end of five minutes, commit to another five minutes."[2]

Seek the Spirit's Influence

The Lord has said that if we are teaching, but not by the Spirit, then it is not of God (see D&C 50:18). Doctrine and Covenants 42:14 tells us how to obtain the Spirit's influence in our teaching: "And the Spirit shall be given unto you by the prayer of faith." The Holy Ghost can "show unto you all things what ye should do" in preparing and giving your talk (2 Nephi 32:5). Ask God to enlighten your mind so you can understand what you are to speak about and how best to present the information.

Prepare an Outline

Elder Richard G. Scott gave a great summary of four simple points, organized in any order, that a youth talk outline should include. Here they are:

1. "A well-expressed statement of the truth to be taught."
2. "An example from everyday life to illustrate more understandably that truth."
3. "A scripture to give power and meaning to the truth."
4. "A personal testimony of the worth of the truth and, where possible, a personal application of it."[3]

It is often better to prepare a simple *outline* of what you are to speak on instead of writing the talk out word for word and reading it. Reading a talk may tie you down to say exactly what is written instead of being able to adapt as the Holy Ghost gives you "in the very moment, what ye shall say" (D&C 100:6). If we follow the four simple points Elder Scott gave we might be surprised to see that it fills a good three- to five-minute youth talk.

Check out Joseph's sample talk outline.

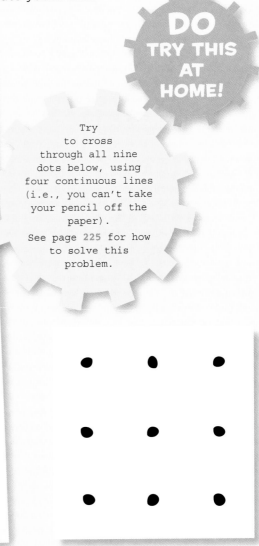

• My statement of truth: After his resurrection, Jesus Christ visited the Americas as recorded in the Book of Mormon. His visit and ministry is in 3 Nephi 11-28.

• Scriptures to give power: Read 3 Nephi 11:13-17 when Christ let all the people feel the marks in his hands, feet, and side.

• Example from everyday life: Maybe talk about how cool it would have been to be there and see Christ. Tell about how I had a similar feeling when I went and stood before the Christus statue at Temple Square in Salt Lake.

• Testimony and application to my life: Bear my testimony about the truthfulness of the Book of Mormon and Christ's visit to the Americas. Testify about how I am excited to meet Jesus one day myself.

P.S. Thanks to my mom for helping me!

DO TRY THIS AT HOME!

Try to cross through all nine dots below, using four continuous lines (i.e., you can't take your pencil off the paper). See page **225** for how to solve this problem.

Teach the Doctrine

Sometimes when we are asked to speak in church we are worried that we won't be funny enough, or interesting enough, so we focus more on humor and jokes and random storytelling than we focus on teaching the truths of the gospel (the doctrine) from the words of the scriptures and modern prophets. Remember, people can go to a movie or sporting event and be entertained. But they can't get the everlasting gospel from those places. Have faith in the fact that teaching gospel doctrines has a "more powerful effect upon the minds of the people than the sword, or anything else" (Alma 31:5). It is the word of God—the doctrine of Christ—that enlightens our understanding and is delicious to our spiritual taste buds (see Alma 32:28). If you want to really have a powerful effect on those who hear you, then help them understand true doctrine. President Boyd K. Packer taught: "True doctrine, understood, changes attitudes and behavior."[4]

Pretend that you have been asked to give a talk on charity based on Moroni 7:45-48. Using the principles from this chapter, prepare a short talk on charity. Give it at your next family home evening.

Invitation to Act

Final Tips

Here are a few last tips:

- Speak clearly, loudly, and slowly. King Benjamin wanted to make sure his people could hear his talk (see Mosiah 2:7). Don't mumble or rush through your material as fast as possible leaving the next speaker amazed that you delivered your talk in 24.5 seconds. Your purpose is to help people understand the gospel, not just to sit down as quickly as possible.

- Don't start by telling everyone how unqualified you are or that you don't want to be up there. Saying things such as "I don't know why they asked me to speak," or "I'm not really that prepared" doesn't give the audience confidence in what you are going to teach them.

- Plan a beginning and an end. Know how you will introduce your topic, and how you will conclude.

- Try not to prepare or review your notes while on the stand. Do that before the meeting. While on the stand, sit back, relax, sing the hymns, take the sacrament with your mind focused on the Savior. Say a prayer in your mind for the Lord to calm your nerves. Doing these things will help you stay in tune with the Holy Ghost, speak comfortably, and not "get shaken from [your] firmness in the Spirit, and stumble because of [your] over anxiety" (Jacob 4:18).

> "I'm glad Joseph left me 49 minutes of the remaining 50 minutes in the block for my talk."

By following these principles we can be better prepared and hopefully have a powerful effect on the hearts of those who hear our talk. As the Spirit loosens our tongues, "he that preacheth and he that receiveth, understand one another, and both are edified and rejoice together" (D&C 50:22). Translation: Both Joseph and those who hear Joseph will get a lot out of his talk, and yours too!

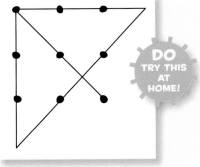

DO TRY THIS AT HOME!

Notice how solving this problem requires you to get outside of the box of nine circles, to go further out than you might have originally thought, in order to cross all nine points with four lines. Similarly, if we are to have powerful youth talks, we must get outside our comfort zone—outside the normal box—of reading our talks word for word with our heads down in a monotone reading voice! We must speak! Try to prepare and give your next talk with only *bullet points!* (Get it?)

TELL ME ONE MORE TIME!

How Can I Prepare and Give a Powerful Youth Talk?

- **Prepare as early and as in-depth as possible.**
- **Seek the Spirit's influence.**
- **Prepare an outline (following the four points suggested by Elder Richard G. Scott).**
- **Teach the doctrine.**

How Can I Share the Gospel with Others?

We constantly have opportunities to share the gospel with family, friends, and others. We know we should share the gospel, and often we want to. The Prophet Joseph Smith said, "After all that has been said, [our] greatest and most important duty is to preach the Gospel."[1] But sometimes we might feel a little guilty because we don't think we are sharing the gospel well enough, or often enough, or even the right way. Elder M. Russell Ballard said, "We often hear members say, 'I know I should share the gospel, but I don't know how to do it.'"[2] So how can we share the gospel with others throughout our life?

Scared of public speaking? Don't worry—there are lots of ways to share the gospel . . . keep reading . . .

Obtain the Word

Before we can effectively share the gospel with others, we must know the gospel. We should study the scriptures diligently and attend our church meetings with the goal of learning things so well that we can clearly explain them to others. Elder M. Russell Ballard said that being an effective missionary *requires that you understand the basic principles of the gospel. It is essential that you are able to offer a clear and correct witness of gospel truths.*"[3]

HOW can I prepare to serve a mission?

Elder David A. Bednar said, "The single most important thing you can do to prepare for a call to serve is to *become* a missionary long before you *go* on a mission."[4] Our recommendation would be to take the missionary preparation course through your stake or through your local institute of religion. We asked this same question "How can I prepare to serve a mission?" to 1,000 youth and here were their top ten responses:

1. Share your testimony with others.
2. Read *Preach My Gospel*.
3. Read the scriptures.
4. Prepare financially (save money).
5. Study and understand the doctrine.
6. Talk to brothers, sisters, or others who have gone on missions.
7. Have clean thoughts.
8. Practice being a missionary now.
9. Go to missionary preparation classes.
10. Home teach and give family home evening lessons.

DO YOU KNOW THE BASIC PRINCIPLES OF THE GOSPEL?

Here is a quiz for you!

1. Which of the following is NOT another name for the Holy Ghost?
   a. The Spirit
   b. The Soul
   c. The Comforter
   d. The Spirit of God
   e. All of the above

2. Through the Atonement of Jesus Christ, everyone will:
   a. Enter the celestial kingdom
   b. Be resurrected
   c. Be forgiven
   d. Become like God

3. Which statement below best describes the creation of the earth?
   a. It was created from nothing.
   b. It was organized from existing matter.
   c. It was established through trial and error.
   d. It randomly evolved over time.

4. The reuniting of the body and spirit after death is known as:
   a. The restitution
   b. The restoration
   c. The resurrection
   d. The reincarnation

Answers: 1-b, 2-b, 3-b, 4-c

One of the measures of how well we know the gospel is how clearly, concisely, and accurately we can explain it to another person. Try doing this exercise with some of the basic doctrines of the Church: Explain the following topics in FIVE WORDS or less in simple and clear terms:

Apostasy
Restoration
Priesthood
Prophets
The Plan of Salvation
The Creation
The Fall
The Atonement
Commandments

DO TRY THIS AT HOME!

Possible answers:

Apostasy—Church taken from the earth

Restoration—Church brought back to earth

Priesthood—God's power given to man

Prophets—Authorized spokesmen for God

The Plan of Salvation—To become like God

The Creation—God made all through Jesus

The Fall—Adam became mortal for us

The Atonement—Jesus overcame sin and death

Commandments—God's laws that bless us

Live the Gospel

Perhaps the easiest way to fulfill the command to share the gospel, and maybe the most powerful, is to simply live what we know. *For the Strength of Youth* says, "Many people have joined the Church through the example and fellowship of their friends."[5]

President Gordon B. Hinckley said, "The example of our living will carry a greater influence than will all the preaching in which we might indulge."[6] The prophet Alma had to rebuke his son Corianton because "when they saw your conduct they would not believe in my words" (Alma 39:11). On the other hand, the great missionary Ammon was able to win the heart of King Lamoni and teach his people because of his great example and Christlike service (see Alma 17–19).

If we have "received [Christ's] image in [our] countenances" (Alma 5:14) we will be effective missionaries simply by the way we are living, and the light of Christ will shine in our eyes. Bishop H. David Burton quoted an unknown author as saying, "'Live in such a way that people who know you but don't know Christ will want to know Christ because they know you.'"[7]

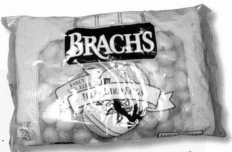

This is an actual bag of candy I've saved since my mission!

John Says: Better Than Jelly Beans

While serving as a missionary we had Mondays as our preparation day to go shopping. On the Monday after Easter my companion and I were at the store buying our usual supply of cold cereal and frozen pizza for the week. While shopping, I noticed that the Easter candy was on sale. Not just on sale, on an AMAZING sale. A bag of jelly beans that usually cost a dollar fifty was on sale for ten cents. I couldn't believe it! Bags of candy—big bags—for ten cents. I was so excited! I wound up buying twenty-seven bags of candy. The whole time I was shopping I was so pumped up. I wanted to run up and down the aisles and tell every shopper that they could buy big bags of candy for only ten cents. As I was riding my bike home from the store, it dawned on me that I was more excited about candy for ten cents than I was about the gospel. I made it a point from then on to be more excited about the gospel message, which is infinitely better than ten-cent bags of candy!

HOW can I know if I should serve a mission?

Recently a seminary student came to one of our classrooms and said, "I'm just not sure if I should serve a mission." This young man needed to hear an important quote from Elder David A. Bednar, who said, "Every man who holds the priesthood was foreordained to that very responsibility in the premortal existence. Does a young man who understands that doctrine have a choice to go on a mission? He made that choice before he was ever born.

. . . We have promised that we will carry this message to the nations of the earth. Brothers and sisters, you and I were born to spend our lives proclaiming the gospel and serving others. . . . Blessing others by proclaiming the gospel is what we were born to do."[8]

If you are male and hold the priesthood you know that unless excused by your bishop you agreed to serve a mission before you were ever born. You already made the choice.

Share Church Literature and Media

The Church has produced some wonderful literature and media that make it easy and convenient to give someone information about the gospel. You could share a copy of the DVD *Joy to the World* with others at Christmastime or give the DVD *Finding Faith in Christ* to a friend as an Easter present.

The Church also produces small pass-along cards. You can give one of these cards to a friend (or a stranger), and they can call and order a free video. We enjoy giving these cards to people we meet on airplanes and sharing them with waitresses who have served us. Elder Dallin H. Oaks suggests that "we can carry a packet of these attractive pass-along cards and give them to persons—even casual acquaintances—with whom we come in contact in the daily activities of our lives. These cards are an ideal way to invite people to investigate the additional truths we have to share."[9]

Use Online Technologies

The Internet provides other ways for us to share the gospel. Elder M. Russell Ballard said, "May I ask that you join the [online] conversation by participating on the Internet to share the gospel and to explain in simple and clear terms the message of the Restoration. Most of you already know that if you have access to the Internet you can start a blog in minutes and begin sharing what you know to be true. You can download videos from Church and other appropriate sites, including newsroom.lds.org, and send them to your friends."[10]

The Church has great Web sites to point interested friends and acquaintances to at www.lds.org, www.mormon.org, www.jesuschrist.lds.org, and www.josephsmith.net. Additionally, there are videos such as "Mormon Messages" that can be sent electronically to friends, family, and acquaintances. You can use online tools such as blogs, e-mail, Facebook, and so forth to point friends and family members to online resources that will help them come unto Christ.

Even if your blog or other online efforts reach only a couple of people, remember that every soul is important to Jesus Christ.

The Greatest Missionary Tool in the World

Pass-along cards, DVDs, and Web sites are great, but they pale in comparison to sharing with someone the greatest missionary tool on earth: The Book of Mormon.

"Now, since we are engaged in the greatest missionary undertaking that has ever been planned as part of Deity's program, he has also placed in our hands the most effective, compelling, and persuasive missionary tool ever given to any people in any age. The name of this tool is the Book of Mormon."—Elder Bruce R. McConkie[11]

Invite Friends to Church Activities

For the Strength of Youth tells us to "invite your friends of other faiths to your Church meetings and activities, where they can learn about the gospel. Help them feel welcome and wanted. . . . Don't be offended if your friends decline your invitation to learn more about the gospel. Just continue to be their friend."[12] There are so many Church functions to invite people to: Sunday meetings, mutual, church dances, seminary, service projects, church pageants, open houses—to name only a few. Elder M. Russell Ballard said, "There is nothing more effective that any of us can do for our friends than to say 'come and see' by joining with us in sacrament meeting. Far too many do not know they are welcome to worship with us."[13]

Look for Natural Opportunities to Share the Gospel

When your friends ask, "How was your weekend?" don't just tell them about Friday and Saturday. Instead say something such as: "My weekend was pretty good. On Friday night I went to the football game, and on Saturday I worked. But on Sunday I went to my church and I heard a great talk about . . ." If it naturally comes up, then naturally talk about the gospel and don't avoid it.

Set a Date

A powerful way to share the gospel with others is to prayerfully set a date by which we will invite somebody to meet with the missionaries. Elder M. Russell Ballard taught, "One way to show your faith in the Lord and His promises is to prayerfully set a date to have someone prepared to meet with the missionaries."[14]

Elder Clayton M. Christensen said, "[In] 1984, I was listening to General Conference, and Elder M. Russell Ballard gave a talk where he invited us as members of the church to set a date, a point in the future, as a commitment to our Heavenly Father. He invited us to not pick a person that we were going to share the gospel with, but to set a date. He promised us that if we would do all that we could to engage in conversations about the gospel, with as many people as we could, that God would bless us by that

ISN'T THIS ORANGE JUICE OFFENSIVE?

Sometimes people are worried about offending someone if they talk to them about the gospel. Elder Robert C. Oaks gave a great analogy to cure this: "Consider that you are invited to a friend's house for breakfast. On the table you see a large pitcher of freshly squeezed orange juice from which your host fills his glass. But he offers you none. Finally, you ask, 'Could I have a glass of orange juice?'

"He replies, 'Oh, I am sorry. I was afraid you might not like orange juice, and I didn't want to offend you by offering you something you didn't desire.'

"Now, that sounds absurd, but it is not too different from the way we hesitate to offer up something far sweeter than orange juice."[15]

Elder M. Russell Ballard said: "Some members say, 'I'm afraid to share the gospel because I might offend someone.' Experience has shown that people are not offended when the sharing is motivated by the spirit of love and concern."[16]

That wasn't too offensive, was it?

date that we would intersect with somebody who would accept our invitation to meet with the missionaries. . . . That night I went home and knelt by my bed and committed to my Heavenly Father that by a certain date I would find somebody for the missionaries to teach. That was in 1984. That year, by the date, Heavenly Father blessed me to find a man who we could bring into our home to teach with the missionaries. I have set a date once, twice, and now three times every year as a commitment to my Heavenly Father that I'm going to be a missionary, and every Sunday I fast that God will help me to intersect with somebody who I can invite to learn of the gospel of Jesus Christ. Every time I pray, I pray that God will put somebody in my path, and I'm grateful to be able to say that God has answered my prayer every time."[17]

Invitation to Act

Choose a principle from this chapter to implement immediately in your life. For example, you could set a date by which you will have somebody prepared to meet with the missionaries or you could use the Internet to share the gospel with others. Pick your principle and then apply it!

We hope these suggestions will help us fulfill the divine command to preach the gospel throughout our lives. Even if we aren't like Dan Jones shouting the Book of Mormon boldly in the middle of the streets, there are still multiple ways we can become capable and active participants in taking this gospel to the four corners of the world.

TELL ME ONE MORE TIME!

How Can I Share the Gospel with Others?

- **Obtain the word.**
- **Live the gospel.**
- **Share church literature and media.**
- **Use online technologies.**
- **Invite friends to church activities.**
- **Look for natural opportunities to share the gospel.**
- **Set a date for missionary opportunities.**

Conclusion: The Holy Ghost Will Tell You *How*

As we have talked to youth in a variety of settings we frequently ask them what questions they have. We have heard literally thousands of questions from LDS youth, and some of the questions we get are hard to give definitive answers to.

For example, one person asked, "I write books. The characters in my books are not LDS, and I'm wondering if it's okay to have them swear and do other things that non-LDS people do."

We realize that some might say, "That's fine, you're depicting real life." Others might say, "No way!" But as far as we know there isn't a firm commandment dealing with this specific question. We believe that if a person has a specific question like this then the best way to gain an answer is through personal revelation.

This principle is taught powerfully in a video called *Ask and Ye Shall Receive: Getting Answers to Gospel Questions.*[2] This video was shown at the 2008 Young Women general broadcast. (If you haven't seen it, you should definitely check it out—we've linked to it at http://ldswhy.com.) The video shows a group of young women who are trying to figure out what kinds of swimsuits are modest. The young women pray, study the scriptures, and by the end of the video feel that they have had their question answered through revelation.

A few weeks after this video aired, Sister Elaine Dalton talked about the video and said that after it was shown in conference many people called and said, "We loved the video, but you didn't answer the question. We want to know, what kinds of swimsuits are modest!"[3]

Sister Dalton helped us see that those people had missed the point of the video. The point of the video wasn't to answer the swimsuit question, but to show that through studying the

WANT AN ANSWER? . . . FIGURE IT OUT YOURSELF!

Elder David A. Bednar said that the greatest teachers in his life "refused to give me easy answers to hard questions. In fact, they did not give me any answers at all. Rather, they pointed the way and helped me take the steps to find my own answers. I certainly did not always appreciate this approach, but experience has enabled me to understand that an answer given by another person usually is not remembered for very long, if remembered at all. But an answer we discover or obtain through the exercise of faith, typically, is retained for a lifetime. The most important learnings of life are caught—not taught."[1]

scriptures and prayer we can find answers through revelation to difficult personal questions. Joseph Smith found an answer to a deep personal question—Which church should I join?—by going to the scriptures and praying. We can find answers to our questions in the same way.

So to the person wondering about if it's okay for non-LDS characters in his or her book to do bad things, or to the person who wonders if it is okay to drink a certain cola or energy drink, or how long a nap is appropriate for Sunday, or whether it's okay to single date when you're 18.23 years old—study it out! Pray, find scriptural doctrines that relate to your questions, ponder on it, and God will help you find the answer through the Holy Ghost.

"THE SINGLE MOST IMPORTANT SKILL"

"The ability to qualify for, receive, and act on personal revelation is the single most important skill that can be acquired in this life."—Sister Julie B. Beck[4]

The Spirit Will Guide You

Nephi taught that "the Holy Ghost . . . will show unto you *all* things what ye should do" (2 Nephi 32:5; emphasis added). With many of the questions you will face you should seek for the personal direction of the Spirit. For example, suppose your question is, "How can I better honor my parents?" Although we talked about that question in this book (and we hope we gave you some good answers), the truth is, we don't know you, your parents, or your specific family situation. But the Lord does. If you will seek personal revelation as to how *you* can honor *your* parents, the Lord will give you specific guidance for your situation. The same principle applies to many of the questions we have discussed in this book. How can you help a friend or family member struggling with serious problems? We gave some suggestions, but ultimately you need the guidance from the Holy Ghost to know what you should do in your specific situation.

WRONG ANSWER!

One of our friends who is a stake president shared the following story with us. He was at a stake conference with a General Authority and they were doing a question-and-answer session. A young man asked a question about whether or not he should start a Christian club at his high school. The General Authority turned to our friend and said, "President, why don't you answer that question." The stake president thought for a few moments and then said, "Yes, I think you should start the club."

Later that night, the General Authority said privately to the stake president, "You gave that young man the wrong answer." Our friend said that he was surprised. The General Authority said, "You should have told him to pray about it and receive his own revelation on that kind of question." Our friend told us he learned a valuable lesson: many of our questions should find their answers not through the advice of others, but directly from the Lord.

Go to the Scriptures

Nephi also taught, "The words of Christ will tell you *all* things what ye should do" (2 Nephi 32:3; emphasis added). We have seen several instances when a person had a *how* question and found an answer in the scriptures. For example, Thomas had a friend who had stopped going to church. He wondered, "How can I help my friend come back to church?" He prayed sincerely and turned to the scriptures, looking for verses that would give him guidance.

As he flipped through the scriptures, he kept coming across verses where one person was writing a letter to another person. The inspiration came into his heart that he should write his friend a letter. When you have a question you're not sure about, turn to the scriptures. They will tell you all things you should do—including how you should act or respond to situations.

"Have Ye Inquired of the Lord?"

As you go through life you will have many questions about how to act. Remembering a question that Nephi asked may help you find direction. Nephi's older brothers didn't understand what their father had taught about the tree of life. When they came to Nephi and asked for an explanation, he asked them a simple question in return that we should ask ourselves: "Have ye inquired of the Lord?" (1 Nephi 15:8).

"Have ye inquired of the Lord?" Often when we have problems we turn to friends or family members and seek their advice. This isn't necessarily bad; in fact, it is frequently part of the process of studying things out. But do we sometimes forget to inquire of the Lord?[5]

The next time you need answers, remember Nephi's simple question: "Have ye inquired of the Lord?" We know God will help you find answers to *your* questions. We testify that God and his Son Jesus Christ live. They know you personally. They love you and want you to become like them. Through the Holy Ghost, prayer, scriptures, modern prophets, and church standards, God will give us the guidance we need to know *how* to live the gospel.

Notes

Russell M. Nelson, "Set in Order Thy House," *Ensign,* November 2001, 69; emphasis added.

INTRODUCTION: "FOR *HOW* TO ACT I DID NOT KNOW"

1. National Weather Service, "Rip Current Safety Tips," http://www.ripcurrents.noaa.gov/tips.shtml.
2. Gordon B. Hinckley, "Reach with a Rescuing Hand," *Ensign,* November 1996, 86; emphasis added.
3. *Encyclopedia of Mormonism,* 4 vols., edited by Daniel H. Ludlow (New York: Macmillan, 1992), 462; emphasis added.
4. Henry B. Eyring, "Prayer," *Ensign,* November 2001, 17; emphasis added.
5. Dieter F. Uchtdorf, "The Love of God," *Ensign,* November 2009, 21; initial capitals in original.
6. Robert D. Hales, "Seeking to Know God, Our Heavenly Father, and His Son, Jesus Christ," *Ensign,* November 2009, 31.
7. David A. Bednar, "That We May Always Have His Spirit to Be with Us," *Ensign,* May 2006, 30.
8. Richard G. Scott, "Now Is the Time to Serve a Mission!" *Ensign,* May 2006, 88.
9. Russell M. Nelson, "Sweet Power of Prayer," *Ensign,* May 2003, 7; initial capitals in original.
10. Henry B. Eyring, "In the Strength of the Lord," *Ensign,* May 2004, 16.
11. Dallin H. Oaks, "The Challenge to Become," *Ensign,* November 2000, 32; emphasis added.
12. David A. Bednar, "More Diligent and Concerned at Home," *Ensign,* November 2009, 17; emphasis added.

CHAPTER 1: HOW CAN I INCREASE MY FAITH IN JESUS CHRIST?

1. Thomas S. Monson, "The Call to Serve," *Ensign,* November 2000, 49.
2. *True to the Faith: A Gospel Reference* (Salt Lake City: The Church of Jesus Christ of Latter-day Saints, 2004), 54.
3. Henry B. Eyring, "Spiritual Preparedness: Start Early and Be Steady," *Ensign,* November 2005, 39.
4. Joseph Smith, *Lectures on Faith* (Salt Lake City: Deseret Book, 1985), 1.
5. David A. Bednar, "Seek Learning by Faith," Address to CES Religious Educators, 3 February 2006, 2.
6. *True to the Faith: A Gospel Reference* (Salt Lake City: The Church of Jesus Christ of Latter-day Saints, 2004), 55.
7. James E. Talmage, *Articles of Faith* (Salt Lake City: Deseret Book, 1981), 87; emphasis added.
8. See Wayne Rice, *Hot Illustrations for Youth Talks* (Grand Rapids, Mich.: Zondervan Publishing House, 1993), 206–7.
9. See Smith, *Lectures on Faith,* 38.
10. Joseph Smith, quoted in Milton V. Backman, Jr., *Joseph Smith's First Vision: Confirming Evidences and Contemporary Accounts,* 2d ed. rev. (Salt Lake City: Bookcraft, 1980), 157.
11. Richard G. Scott, "The Sustaining Power of Faith in Times of Uncertainty and Testing," *Ensign,* May 2003, 76; emphasis in original.
12. Bednar, "Seek Learning by Faith," 2.

CHAPTER 2: HOW CAN I BREAK BAD HABITS?

1. Richard G. Scott, "Finding the Way Back," *Ensign,* 75.
2. Thomas S. Monson, "School Thy Feelings, O My Brother," *Ensign,* November 2009, 68; emphasis in original.
3. Scott, "Finding the Way Back," 75.
4. See "Ivan Pavlov," http://en.wikipedia.org/wiki/Ivan_Pavlov.
5. Scott, "Finding the Way Back," 75.
6. See Brian Wansink, *Mindless Eating* (New York: Bantam Books, 2006), 85.
7. Scott, "Finding the Way Back," 75.
8. See Tara Parker-Pope, "Well; What Are Friends For? A Longer Life," *New York Times,* 20 April 2009, http://www.nytimes.com/.
9. David A. Bednar, "In the Strength of the Lord," *Ensign,* November 2004, 77.
10. Dallin H. Oaks, in "Same-Gender Attraction," http://newsroom.lds.org/ldsnewsroom/eng/public-issues/same-gender-attraction.

11. Boyd K. Packer, *That All Might Be Edified* (Salt Lake City: Deseret Book, 1982), 196; emphasis in original.

12. L. Tom Perry, "'Thy Speech Reveals Thee,'" *New Era,* August 1986, 7.

13. Ibid.

CHAPTER 3: HOW CAN I REALLY REPENT?

1. LDS Bible Dictionary, "Repentance," 760; emphasis added.

2. Neal A. Maxwell, "Repentance," *Ensign,* November 1991, 31.

3. Ibid., 30.

4. Ibid., 31.

5. Richard G. Scott, "The Path to Peace and Joy," *Ensign,* November 2000, 26.

6. *True to the Faith: A Gospel Reference* (Salt Lake City: The Church of Jesus Christ of Latter-day Saints, 2004), 133.

7. Neil L. Andersen, "'Repent . . . That I May Heal You,'" *Ensign,* November 2009, 41.

8. *True to the Faith,* 134.

9. *For the Strength of Youth* (Salt Lake City: The Church of Jesus Christ of Latter-day Saints, 2001), 30.

10. *True to the Faith,* 134.

11. Richard G. Scott, "Finding Forgiveness," *Ensign,* May 1995, 77.

12. Robert L. Backman, "To the Young Men of the Church," *Ensign,* November 1980, 42.

13. Richard G. Scott, "The Power of Righteousness," *Ensign,* November 1998, 70.

14. *True to the Faith,* 135.

15. Maxwell, "Repentance," 31; emphasis added.

16. Jeffrey R. Holland, "For Times of Trouble," in *1980 Devotional Speeches of the Year* (Provo, Utah: Brigham Young University Press, 1981), 42.

17. See LDS Bible Dictionary, "Repentance," 760–61.

18. Marvin J. Ashton, "'Shake Off the Chains with Which Ye Are Bound,'" *Ensign,* November 1986, 15.

19. Maxwell, "Repentance," 30.

20. Spencer W. Kimball, *The Miracle of Forgiveness* (Salt Lake City: Deseret Book, 1969), 203.

21. Scott, "Finding Forgiveness," 76.

CHAPTER 4: HOW CAN I KNOW WHEN I'VE BEEN FORGIVEN?

1. F. Burton Howard, "Repentance," *Ensign,* May 1983, 59; some emphasis added.

2. *For the Strength of Youth* (Salt Lake City: The Church of Jesus Christ of Latter-day Saints, 2001), 29.

3. Jeffrey R. Holland, "'Remember Lot's Wife,'" Brigham Young University Speeches 2008–2009, 13 January 2009, 5; see http://speeches.byu.edu.

4. Dalai Lama, see http://www.achieving-life-abundance.com/inner-peace-quotes.html; accessed 25 January 2010.

5. Henry B. Eyring, *To Draw Closer to God* (Salt Lake City: Deseret Book, 1997), 49–50.

6. See Gordon B. Hinckley, "Forgiveness," *Ensign,* November 2005, 83–84.

7. *For the Strength of Youth*, 28.

8. Richard G. Scott, "Peace of Conscience and Peace of Mind," *Ensign,* November 2004, 18.

9. Henry B. Eyring, "Come unto Christ," in *Brigham Young University 1989–90 Devotional and Fireside Speeches* (Provo, Utah: University Publications, 1990), 45.

CHAPTER 5: HOW CAN I MAKE THE TEMPLE A MORE IMPORTANT PART OF MY LIFE?

1. Anne C. Pingree, "Seeing the Promises Afar Off," *Ensign,* November 2003, 13.

2. Howard W. Hunter, as quoted in Jay M. Todd, "President Howard W. Hunter," *Ensign,* July 1994, 5.

3. *Gospel Principles* (Salt Lake City: The Church of Jesus Christ of Latter-day Saints, 2009), 222–23.

4. Dieter F. Uchtdorf, "See the End from the Beginning," *Ensign,* May 2006, 44.

5. Howard W. Hunter, "Exceeding Great and Precious Promises," *Ensign,* November 1994, 8.

6. David B. Haight, "Temples and Work Therein," *Ensign,* November 1990, 61.

7. Ezra Taft Benson, *The Teachings of Ezra Taft Benson* (Salt Lake City: Bookcraft, 1988), 256.

8. David B. Haight, "Come to the House of the Lord," *Ensign,* May 1992, 15.

9. Glenn L. Pace, "Spiritual Revival," *Ensign,* November 1992, 12.

10. Joseph Fielding Smith, *Doctrines of Salvation,* comp. Bruce R. McConkie, 3 vols. (Salt Lake City: Bookcraft, 1955), 2:242.

11. Joseph Smith, *Teachings of the Prophet Joseph Smith* (Salt Lake City: Deseret Book, 1976), 367; emphasis added; see also Joseph Fielding Smith, *Doctrines of Salvation,* comp. Bruce R. McConkie, 3 vols. (Salt Lake City: Bookcraft, 1955), 2:158, 230.

12. Theodore M. Burton, "Salvation for the Dead—A Missionary Activity," *Ensign,* May 1975, 71.

13. Haight, "Come to the House of the Lord," 16.

14. Howard W. Hunter, *The Teachings of Howard W. Hunter,* ed. Clyde J. Williams (Salt Lake City: Bookcraft, 1997), 236.

15. "From the First Presidency," *Church News,* 22 March 2003; see also http://www.ldschurchnews.com/articles/43389/From-the-First-Presidency.html.

16. Hunter, *Teachings of Howard W. Hunter,* 230–31; emphasis added.

17. Howard W. Hunter, "Follow the Son of God," *Ensign,* November 1994, 88.

18. Boyd K. Packer, *Preparing to Enter the Holy Temple* (Salt Lake City: The Church of Jesus Christ of Latter-day Saints, 2002); see also Russell M. Nelson, "Prepare for Blessings of the Temple," *Ensign,* March 2002, 17.

19. Benson, *Teachings of Ezra Taft Benson*, 251.

20. Richard G. Scott, "Temple Worship: The Source of Strength and Power in Times of Need," *Ensign,* May 2009, 43–44.

21. Ibid., 44.

22. W. Grant Bangerter, "What Temples Are For," *Ensign,* May 1982, 72.

23. Jeffrey R. Holland, "'Abide in Me,'" *Ensign,* May 2004, 31.

24. Hunter, "Follow the Son of God," 88.

CHAPTER 6: HOW CAN I PREPARE FOR AN ETERNAL MARRIAGE?

1. http://192.220.96.182/joke_kquotes.html.

2. Ibid.

3. David A. Bednar, quoted in interview with Sheri Dew; http://radio.lds.org/eng/programs/conversations-episode-1.

4. Spencer W. Kimball, "Oneness in Marriage," *Ensign,* October 2002, 42.

5. Dieter F. Uchtdorf, "The Reflection in the Water," CES fireside talk on 1 November 2009 at Brigham Young University. http://www.ldschurchnews.com/articles/58360/President-Dieter-F-Uchtdorf-The-Reflection-in-the-Water.html.

6. Boyd K. Packer, *Eternal Love* (Salt Lake City: Deseret Book, 1973), 11.

7. Boyd K. Packer, "The Library of the Lord," *Ensign,* May 1990, 38; emphasis in original.

8. Gordon B. Hinckley, "Loyalty," *Ensign,* May 2003, 59.

9. Ezra Taft Benson, "The Law of Chastity," *New Era,* January 1988, 5.

10. James E. Faust, "The Enriching of Marriage," *Ensign,* November 1977, 10.

11. *For the Strength of Youth* (Salt Lake City: The Church of Jesus Christ of Latter-day Saints, 2001), 26.

12. http://www.physorg.com/news166714990.html; see also Galena K. Rhoades, Scott M. Stanley, and Howard J. Markham, "The Pre-engagement Cohabitation Effect: A Replication and Extension of Previous Findings," in *Journal of Family Psychology* 23 (February 2009): 107–11.

13. David O. McKay, "The Choice of an Eternal Companion," *Improvement Era,* April 1965, 284.

14. http://192.220.96.182/joke_kquotes.html.

15. M. Russell Ballard, "Fathers and Sons: A Remarkable Relationship," *Ensign,* November 2009, 50.

16. Howard W. Hunter, *The Teachings of Howard W. Hunter,* ed. Clyde J. Williams (Salt Lake City: Bookcraft, 1997), 199–200.

CHAPTER 7: HOW CAN I STRENGTHEN MY TESTIMONY?

1. Thomas S. Monson, "Be of Good Cheer," *Ensign,* May 2009, 92.
2. Gordon B. Hinckley, "Testimony," *Ensign,* May 1998, 69–70.
3. Robert D. Hales, "Seeking to Know God, Our Heavenly Father, and His Son, Jesus Christ," *Ensign,* November 2009, 32.
4. Ezra Taft Benson, *A Witness and a Warning* (Salt Lake City: Deseret Book, 1988), 18.
5. Ezra Taft Benson, "I Testify," *Ensign,* November 1988, 86; emphasis added.
6. Gordon B. Hinckley, "The Power of the Book of Mormon," *Ensign,* June 1988, 6.
7. List adapted from Kay W. Briggs, *Brother Joseph* (Salt Lake City: Bookcraft, 1994), 13–15.
8. George Cannon, in Jeffrey R. Holland, "Safety for the Soul," *Ensign,* November 2009, 89.
9. Ezra Taft Benson, "The Book of Mormon Is the Word of God," *Ensign,* May 1975, 64.
10. Howard W. Hunter, Conference Report, April 1967, 115–16; emphasis added.
11. Brigham Young, in Junius F. Wells, "Historic Sketch of the Y. M. M. I. A.," *Improvement Era,* June 1925, 715.
12. Richard G. Scott, "The Power of a Strong Testimony," *Ensign,* November 2001, 87.

CHAPTER 8: HOW CAN I KNOW WHEN THE HOLY GHOST IS SPEAKING TO ME?

1. David A. Bednar, "That We May Always Have His Spirit to Be with Us," *Ensign,* May 2006, 30.
2. Spencer W. Kimball, "Revelation: The Word of the Lord to His Prophets," *Ensign,* May 1977, 78.
3. Richard G. Scott, "Using the Supernal Gift of Prayer," *Ensign,* May 2007, 9.
4. Richard G. Scott, "To Acquire Spiritual Guidance," *Ensign,* November 2009, 9.
5. http://www.thefreedictionary.com/enlighten.
6. Bednar, "That We May Always Have His Spirit to Be with Us," 30; emphasis in original.
7. Dallin H. Oaks, "Teaching and Learning by the Spirit," *Ensign,* March 1997, 13; emphasis added.
8. Spencer W. Kimball, *The Teachings of Spencer W. Kimball,* ed. Edward L. Kimball (Salt Lake City: Bookcraft, 1982), 454–55.
9. Howard W. Hunter, *The Teachings of Howard W. Hunter,* ed. Clyde J. Williams (Salt Lake City: Bookcraft, 1997), 184.
10. Franklin D. Richards, "The Importance of Prayer," *Ensign,* July 1972, 66.
11. Boyd K. Packer, "Personal Revelation: The Gift, the Test, and the Promise," *Ensign,* November 1994, 61; emphasis in original.
12. Scott, "To Acquire Spiritual Guidance," 8.

CHAPTER 9: HOW CAN I AVOID BEING DECEIVED WHEN RECEIVING REVELATION?

1. Boyd K. Packer, "Reverence Invites Revelation," *Ensign,* November 1991, 21.
2. Boyd K. Packer, Interview, 20 July 2007; http://newsroom.lds.org/ldsnewsroom/eng/news-releases-stories/president-packer-interview-transcript-from-pbs-documentary; emphasis added and in original.
3. See David A. Bednar, "Receiving, Recognizing, and Responding to the Promptings of the Holy Ghost," Ricks College Devotional, 31 August 1999; and Dallin H. Oaks, "I Have a Question: How can I distinguish the difference between the promptings of the Holy Ghost and merely my own thoughts, preferences, or hunches?" *Ensign,* June 1983, 27.
4. Russell M. Nelson, "Honoring the Priesthood," *Ensign,* May 1993, 39.
5. David E. Sorensen, "The Blessing of Work," CES Fireside, 6 March 2005; http://speeches.byu.edu; see also http://www.ldschurchnews.com/articles/46994/Elder-David-E-Sorenson-The-blessing-of-work.html.
6. *For the Strength of Youth* (Salt Lake City: The Church of Jesus Christ of Latter-day Saints, 2001), 26.
7. Richard G. Scott, "Learning to Recognize Answers to Prayers," *Ensign,* November 1989, 32.
8. The First Presidency, in *Messages of the First Presidency of The Church of Jesus Christ of Latter-day Saints,* James R. Clark, comp., 6 vols. (Salt Lake City: Bookcraft, 1965–75), 4:286.

CHAPTER 10: HOW CAN I RECOGNIZE AND DEVELOP SPIRITUAL GIFTS?

1. Marvin J. Ashton, "There Are Many Gifts," *Ensign,* November 1987, 20.

2. Dallin H. Oaks, "Spiritual Gifts," *Ensign,* September 1986, 68.

3. Ashton, "'There Are Many Gifts,'" 20.

4. See Bryant S. Hinckley, *The Faith of Our Pioneer Fathers* (Salt Lake City: Bookcraft, 1956), 207.

5. Boyd K. Packer, *Teach Ye Diligently* (Salt Lake City: Deseret Book, 1991), 20.

6. Robert D. Hales, "Gifts of the Spirit," *Ensign,* February 2002, 16.

7. Eliza R. Snow, "O My Father," in *Hymns of The Church of Jesus Christ of Latter-day Saints* (Salt Lake City: The Church of Jesus Christ of Latter-day Saints, 1985), no. 292.

8. George Q. Cannon, in *Millennial Star,* 23 April 1894, 260.

9. Wilford Woodruff, in *Millennial Star,* 9 April 1894, 229.

10. Hales, "Gifts of the Spirit," 16.

11. Thomas S. Monson, "May You Have Courage," *Ensign,* May 2009, 125–26.

12. Robert K Wagstaff, "When Should I Get My Patriarchal Blessing?" *New Era,* August 2009, 12.

13. Joseph Fielding Smith, *Answers to Gospel Questions,* comp. Joseph Fielding Smith, Jr., 5 vols. (Salt Lake City: Deseret Book, 1957–66), 5:138–39.

14. See John H. Groberg, *In the Eye of the Storm* (Salt Lake City: Bookcraft, 1993), 67.

15. Thomas S. Monson, "Decisions Determine Destiny," *New Era,* November 1979, 7.

16. *For the Strength of Youth* (Salt Lake City: The Church of Jesus Christ of Latter-day Saints, 2001), 38; emphasis added.

17. Joseph Smith, *Teachings of the Prophet Joseph Smith,* sel. Joseph Fielding Smith (Salt Lake City: Deseret Book, 1976), 246.

18. Ashton, "'There Are Many Gifts,'" 23.

CHAPTER 11: HOW CAN I TELL THE DIFFERENCE BETWEEN RIGHT AND WRONG?

1. George Albert Smith, in Conference Report, October 1945, 118.

2. Richard G. Scott, "Acquiring Spiritual Knowledge," *Ensign,* November 1993, 86.

3. Boyd K. Packer, "The Word of Wisdom: The Principle and the Promises," *Ensign,* May 1996, 17.

4. *For the Strength of Youth* (Salt Lake City: The Church of Jesus Christ of Latter-day Saints, 2001), 20.

5. Ibid., 17.

6. "Seeing more than your eye does," http://serendip.brynmawr.edu/bb/blindspot1.html.

7. M. Russell Ballard, "'When Shall These Things Be?'" *Ensign,* December 1996, 59.

8. David A. Bednar, "Receiving, Recognizing, and Responding to the Promptings of the Holy Ghost," BYU–Idaho Devotional, 31 August 1999; see http://www.byui.edu/Presentations/transcripts/devotionals/1999_08_31_bednar.htm.

9. See Chip and Dan Heath, *Made to Stick* (New York: Random House, 2007), 149–50.

10. Brigham Young, *Brigham Young,* in Teachings of President of the Church series [manual] (Salt Lake City: The Church of Jesus Christ of Latter-day Saints, 1997), 41; emphasis added.

11. See Paige Williams, "What makes our feet fall asleep," http://www.msnbc.msn.com/id/3076701.

CHAPTER 12: HOW CAN I SET STANDARDS THAT WILL KEEP ME SPIRITUALLY SAFE?

1. Thomas S. Monson, "Decisions Determine Destiny," CES Fireside for Young Adults, 6 November 2005, http://www.lds.org/library/display/0,4945,538-1-3310-1,00.html.

2. Richard G. Scott, "Do What Is Right," BYU Fireside, 3 March 1996, http://speeches.byu.edu/.

3. Spencer W. Kimball, *Teachings of Spencer W. Kimball,* ed. Edward L. Kimball (Salt Lake City: Bookcraft, 1982), 164.

4. Henry B. Eyring, "Teach with Spirit to get gospel into hearts of youth," *Church News,* 15 February 2003, 5; emphasis added.

5. Richard G. Scott, "To Acquire Spiritual Guidance," *Ensign,* November 2009, 8; emphasis added.

6. Richard G. Scott, "Do What Is Right," *Liahona,* March 2001, 16.

7. See http://en.wikipedia.org/wiki/Lindsey_Jacobellis.

8. *For the Strength of Youth* (Salt Lake City: The Church of Jesus Christ of Latter-day Saints, 2001), 27.

9. Henry B. Eyring, "Do Not Delay," *Ensign,* November 1999, 34.

CHAPTER 13: HOW CAN I STAY MORALLY CLEAN?

1. Gordon B. Hinckley, "A Prophet's Counsel and Prayer for Youth," *New Era,* January 2001, 12–13.

2. Spencer W. Kimball, *The Miracle of Forgiveness* (Salt Lake City: Bookcraft, 1969), 66.

3. Susan W. Tanner, "Make Dating Smooth Sailing," *New Era,* October 2004, 31.

4. *For the Strength of Youth* (Salt Lake City: The Church of Jesus Christ of Latter-day Saints, 2001), 26.

5. Gordon B. Hinckley, "To the Women of the Church," *Ensign,* November 2003, 115.

6. See Gene R. Cook, "The Eternal Nature of the Law of Chastity," Ricks College Devotional, 1989, 16.

7. Spencer W. Kimball, *The Teachings of Spencer W. Kimball,* ed. Edward L. Kimball (Salt Lake City: Bookcraft, 1982), 281.

8. David E. Sorensen, "You Can't Pet a Rattlesnake," *Ensign,* May 2001, 41; emphasis added.

9. *For the Strength of Youth,* 25.

10. Kimball, *Teachings of Spencer W. Kimball,* 287–88; emphasis added.

11. Bruce Monson, "Speaking of Kissing," *New Era,* June 2001, 36.

12. Gordon B. Hinckley, "A Prophet's Counsel and Prayer for Youth," 13; emphasis added; see also John Hilton III and Anthony Sweat, *Why? Powerful Answers and Practical Reasons for Living LDS Standards* (Salt Lake City: Deseret Book, 2009), 58–63.

13. *For the Strength of Youth,* 17.

14. Ibid., 15.

15. See also Hilton and Sweat, *Why?* 39–44.

16. See Joe S. McIlhaney Jr. and Freda McKissic Bush, *Hooked: New Science on How Casual Sex Is Affecting Our Children* (Chicago: Northfield Publishing, 2008), 80.

17. *For the Strength of Youth,* 28.

CHAPTER 14: HOW CAN I RESIST AND OVERCOME PORNOGRAPHY?

1. Richard G. Scott, "The Sanctity of Womanhood," *Ensign,* May 2000, 37.

2. H. David Burton, "Honoring the Priesthood," *Ensign,* May 2000, 39.

3. Julie B. Beck, "Teaching the Doctrine of the Family," Seminaries and Institutes of Religion Satellite Training Broadcast, 4 August 2009, http://www.lds.org/pa/rs/pdf/CES_2009_Beck_eng.pdf.

4. http://www.haverford.edu/biology/edwards/disease/viral_essays/redicanvirus.htm.

5. Name withheld, "Addicted to Romance Novels?" *Ensign,* July 2003, 59.

6. Joseph Smith, *Teachings of the Prophet Joseph Smith,* sel. Joseph Fielding Smith (Salt Lake City: Deseret Book, 1976), 181.

7. *For the Strength of Youth* (Salt Lake City: The Church of Jesus Christ of Latter-day Saints, 2001), 19.

8. Jeffrey R. Holland, "Personal Purity," *Ensign,* November 1998, 76.

9. LDS Bible Dictionary, 613, 614.

10. *For the Strength of Youth,* 19.

11. Gordon B. Hinckley, "Some Thoughts on Temple, Retention of Converts, and Missionary Service," *Ensign,* November 1997, 51.

12. List adapted from Dallin H. Oaks, "Pornography," *Ensign,* May 2005, 87; Gordon B. Hinckley "A Tragic Evil among Us," *Ensign,* November 2004, 59–62; Scott, "The Sanctity of Womanhood," 36–38; and *For the Strength of Youth,* 17–19.

13. See "Pornography Addiction May Cause Brain Damage in Kids," *Jakarta Globe,* November 2009, 15–21, http://addictionsawareness.com/2009/03/pornography-addiction-may-cause-brain-damage-in-kids/.

14. Thomas S. Monson, "Pornography, the Deadly Carrier," *Ensign,* July 2001, 2.

15. Richard G. Scott, "How Can I Find Happiness?" http://radio.lds.org/eng/programs/conversations-episode-6.

16. Gordon B. Hinckley, "Closing Remarks," *Ensign,* May 2005, 102.

17. M. Russell Ballard, "Be Strong in the Lord, and in the Power of His Might," 3 March 2002, http://speeches.byu.edu/.

18. *Let Virtue Garnish Thy Thoughts* (Salt Lake City: The Church of Jesus Christ of Latter-day Saints, 2006), 4.

19. Oaks, "Pornography," 90.

20. Joseph B. Wirthlin, "Press On," *Ensign,* November 2004, 102.

21. Gordon B. Hinckley, "A Tragic Evil among Us," *Ensign,* November 2004, 59.

CHAPTER 15: HOW CAN I HONOR MY PARENTS?

1. M. Russell Ballard, *When Thou Art Converted* (Salt Lake City: Deseret Book, 2001), 203.

2. M. Russell Ballard, "Fathers and Sons: A Remarkable Relationship," *Ensign,* November 2009, 48.

3. Ezra Taft Benson, "To the 'Youth of the Noble Birthright,'" *Ensign,* May 1986, 43.

4. Ballard, *When Thou Art Converted,* 203.

5. Adapted from Ardeth Greene Kapp, *The Joy of the Journey* (Salt Lake City: Deseret Book, 1992), 124–26.

6. Thomas S. Monson, "Be Thou an Example," *Ensign,* May 2005, 112.

7. *For the Strength of Youth* (Salt Lake City: The Church of Jesus Christ of Latter-day Saints, 2001), 10.

8. See Josephson Institute 2008, "The Ethics of American Youth," http://charactercounts.org/programs/reportcard/index
.html.

CHAPTER 16: HOW CAN I HAVE A FUN AND CLEAN DATE?

1. *For the Strength of Youth* (Salt Lake City: The Church of Jesus Christ of Latter-day Saints, 2001), 25.

2. Gordon B. Hinckley, "A Challenging Time—A Wonderful Time," Address to CES Religious Educators, 7 February 2003, 3.

3. *For the Strength of Youth,* 25.

4. Ibid.

5. See Dallin H. Oaks, "The Dedication of a Lifetime," CES Fireside for Young Adults, 1 May 2005, http://www.lds.org/
library/display/0,4945,538-1-3100-1,00.html.

CHAPTER 17: HOW CAN I HAVE MORE MEANINGFUL PRAYERS?

1. Henry B. Eyring, "The Lord Will Multiply the Harvest," in *Teaching Seminary: Preservice Readings* (Salt Lake City: The Church of Jesus Christ of Latter-day Saints, 2004), 95.

2. David A. Bednar, "'Quick to Observe,'" BYU Devotional, 10 May 2005, http://speeches.byu.edu/.

3. Richard G. Scott, "Learning to Recognize Answers to Prayer," *Ensign,* November 1989, 31; emphasis added.

4. Ibid., 30–31.

5. Dallin H. Oaks, "The Language of Prayer," *Ensign,* May 1993, 15.

6. F. Michael Watson, "His Servants, the Prophets," *Ensign,* May 2009, 108.

7. See David A. Bednar, "Pray Always," *Ensign,* November 2008, 42.

8. Bednar, "Pray Always," 42–43.

9. *The Tonight Show with Jay Leno,* 13 May 2005, http://www.flixxy.com/sms-text-messaging-vs-morse-code.htm.

10. Gordon B. Hinckley, *Teachings of Gordon B. Hinckley* (Salt Lake City: Deseret Book, 1997), 469.

11. M. Russell Ballard, *When Thou Art Converted* (Salt Lake City: Deseret Book, 2001), 67.

12. Matthew Eyring, in Gerald N. Lund, "Elder Henry B. Eyring: Molded by 'Defining Influences,'" *Ensign,* September 1995, 15.

13. Bruce R. McConkie, *Mormon Doctrine* (Salt Lake City: Bookcraft, 1966), 586.

14. J. Reuben Clark, Jr., in Conference Report, October 1944, 160; emphasis added.

15. Boyd K. Packer, "Prayer and Promptings," *Ensign,* November 2009, 46.

16. H. Burke Peterson, "Adversity and Prayer," *Ensign,* January 1974, 19.

17. Henry B. Eyring, *To Draw Closer to God* (Salt Lake City: Deseret Book, 1997), 70; emphasis added.

CHAPTER 18: HOW CAN I GET MORE FROM MY SCRIPTURE STUDY?

1. Howard W. Hunter, "Reading the Scriptures," *Ensign,* November 1979, 64.
2. *Preach My Gospel* (Salt Lake City: The Church of Jesus Christ of Latter-day Saints, 2004), 17.
3. Bruce R. McConkie, *A New Witness for the Articles of Faith* (Salt Lake City: Deseret Book, 1985), 399; emphasis added.
4. M. Russell Ballard, "'Be Strong in the Lord and in the Power of His Might,'" BYU Fireside, 3 March 2002, http://speeches .byu.edu/.
5. Hunter, "Reading the Scriptures," 64.
6. Anthony Sweat, "Reading Motivation: Factors Influencing Daily Scripture Study," unpublished paper for Utah State University, Logan, Utah, 2004, 12.
7. M. Russell Ballard, *When Thou Art Converted* (Salt Lake City: Deseret Book, 2001), 68.
8. First Presidency Letter, "Strengthening Families," 11 February 1999, http://www.lds.org/pa/display/0,17884,5154-1,00.html.
9. Henry B. Eyring, *To Draw Closer to God* (Salt Lake City: Deseret Book, 1997), 151; emphasis in original.
10. See Ann M. Dibb, "Hold On," *Ensign,* November 2009, 79.
11. David A. Bednar, "Understanding the Importance of Scripture Study," Ricks College Devotional, 6 January 1998, http:// www.byui.edu/Presentations/Transcripts/Devotionals/1998_01_06_Bednar.htm.
12. Jeffrey R. Holland, Summer 1992 CES Satellite Broadcast, 4.
13. D. Todd Christofferson, "When Thou Art Converted," *Ensign,* May 2004, 11.
14. *Preach My Gospel,* 22.

CHAPTER 19: HOW CAN I FIND ANSWERS IN THE SCRIPTURES?

1. Henry B. Eyring, "A Discussion on Scripture Study," *Ensign,* July 2005, 24.
2. Julie B. Beck, "My Soul Delighteth in the Scriptures," *Ensign,* May 2004, 108.
3. Thomas S. Monson, "Pathways to Perfection," *Ensign,* May 2002, 99.
4. David A. Bednar, "'Teach Them to Understand,'" Ricks College Campus Education Week Devotional, 4 June 1998, http://www.byui.edu/Presentations/Transcripts/EducationWeek/1998_06_04_Bednar.htm; emphasis added.
5. Richard G. Scott, "Acquiring Spiritual Knowledge," *Ensign,* November 1993, 86; emphasis added.
6. Gordon B. Hinckley, "The Light within You," *Ensign,* May 1995, 99; emphasis added.
7. "Time Spent Watching TV Continues Growing," http://www.msnbc.msn.com/id/27890381/.
8. William R. Bradford, "The Governing Ones," *Ensign,* November 1979, 37–38.
9. Henry B. Eyring, "Studying and Teaching the Old Testament," *Ensign,* January 2002, 32.
10. Brigham Young, *Discourses of Brigham Young,* comp. John A. Widtsoe (Salt Lake City: Deseret Book, 1954), 128.

CHAPTER 20: HOW CAN I KEEP THE SABBATH DAY HOLY?

1. See John Wells, in Conference Report, October 1927, 135.
2. *For the Strength of Youth* (Salt Lake City: The Church of Jesus Christ of Latter-day Saints, 2001), 32.
3. David A. Bednar, "'Heartfelt and Willing Obedience,'" BYU–Idaho Campus Education Week Devotional, 27 June 2002, http://www.byui.edu/Presentations/transcripts/educationweek/2002_06_27_bednar.htm.
4. *For the Strength of Youth,* 16.
5. James E. Faust, "The Lord's Day," *Ensign,* November 1991, 34.
6. Henry B. Eyring, "Education for Real Life," CES Fireside for Young Adults, 6 May 2001, http://www.lds.org/broadcast/ces050601/0,10483,538,00.html.
7. Ibid.
8. Joseph Fielding Smith, in Conference Report, October 1927, 143.
9. *For the Strength of Youth,* 33.
10. Ibid., 32–33.
11. Ibid., 32.
12. Ibid., 33.

CHAPTER 21: HOW CAN I GET MORE FROM MY CHURCH MEETINGS?

1. Gene R. Cook, in Gerry Avant, "Learning Gospel Is a Lifetime Pursuit," *Church News,* 24 March 1990, 10.

2. See Brian Wansink, *Mindless Eating* (New York: Bantam Books, 2006), 120–21.

3. See "Contagious Yawning," November 2003, http://faculty.washington.edu/chudler/yawnc.html.

4. Boyd K. Packer, *That All May Be Edified* (Salt Lake City: Deseret Book, 1982), 236.

5. Spencer W. Kimball, *The Teachings of Spencer W. Kimball,* ed. Edward L. Kimball (Salt Lake City: Bookcraft, 1982), 515; emphasis added.

6. Dallin H. Oaks, "The Gospel in Our Lives," *Ensign,* May 2002, 33.

7. Henry B. Eyring, *To Draw Closer to God* (Salt Lake City: Deseret Book, 1997), 16, 24.

8. Joseph B. Wirthlin, "Teaching by the Spirit," *Ensign,* January 1989, 15.

9. Richard G. Scott, "To Learn and to Teach More Effectively," BYU Education Week Devotional, 21 August 2007, http://speeches.byu.edu/; emphasis added.

10. Ibid.

11. Dallin H. Oaks, "Unselfish Service," *Ensign,* May 2009, 96.

12. M. Russell Ballard, "'Be Strong in the Lord, and in the Power of His Might,'" CES Fireside for Young Adults, 3 March 2002, http://www.lds.org/broadcast/ces030302/transcript/0,12845,395,00.html.

13. Ibid.

14. Scott, "To Learn and to Teach More Effectively."

CHAPTER 22: HOW CAN I KEEP A MEANINGFUL JOURNAL?

1. See M. Russell Ballard, "'Be Strong in the Lord and in the Power of His Might,'" BYU Fireside Address, 3 March 2002, http://speeches.byu.edu/.

2. Journal of Wilford Woodruff, February 12, 1862, see Wilford Woodruff, *Wilford Woodruff* (manual). In Teachings of President of the Church series (Salt Lake City: The Church of Jesus Christ of Latter-day Saints, 2004), 129.

3. Henry B. Eyring, "Remembrance and Gratitude," *Ensign,* November 1989, 13.

4. Spencer W. Kimball, *The Teachings of Spencer W. Kimball,* ed. Edward L. Kimball (Salt Lake City: Bookcraft, 1982), 350.

5. Meriwether Lewis and William Clark, *The Journals of Lewis and Clark: 200th Anniversary Edition,* ed. John Bakeless (New York: Signet Classics, 2002), 279.

6. Spencer W. Kimball, "President Kimball Speaks Out on Personal Journals," *Ensign,* December 1980, 61.

CHAPTER 23: HOW CAN I CREATE A LIVING AREA THAT INVITES THE HOLY GHOST?

1. See "Cleanliness Is Next to . . . Productivity," 1 November 1999, http://www.allbusiness.com/human-resources/employee-development-employee-productivity/374971-1.html; and "The Benefits of a Clean Office," 18 August 2009, http://www.articlealley.com/article_1038889_15.html.

2. Ibid.

3. "Q&A: Questions and Answers," *New Era,* March 2005, 16.

4. Spencer W. Kimball, "God Will Not Be Mocked," *Ensign,* November 1974, 4.

5. Gordon B. Hinckley, "'Be Ye Clean,'" *Ensign,* May 1996, 47.

6. LDS Bible Dictionary, "Temple," 781.

7. Ibid.

8. See Katie Liljenquist, in "Cleanliness Is Next to Godliness," 24 October 2009, physorg.com/news175585083.html.

9. Brigham Young, *Discourses of Brigham Young,* sel. and arr. by John A. Widtsoe (Salt Lake City: Deseret Book, 1954), 214.

10. Thomas S. Monson, "Principles from Prophets," BYU Devotional Address, 15 September 2009; http://speeches.byu.edu/.

11. Ezra Taft Benson, "Born of God," *Ensign,* November 1985, 6–7; emphasis added.

12. *Glimpses into the Life and Heart of Marjorie Pay Hinckley,* ed. Virginia H. Pearce (Salt Lake City: Deseret Book, 1999), 214.

13. Johann Wolfgang von Goethe, http://www.quoteworld.org/quotes/5588.

14. Keith M. Cottom, "Building a Good Home Library," *Ensign,* April 1982, 63.

15. M. Russell Ballard, "Let Our Voices Be Heard," *Ensign,* November 2003, 19.

16. Randal A. Wright, *25 Mistakes LDS Parents Make and How to Avoid Them* (Austin: National Family Institute; Salt Lake City: Deseret Book Distributors, 2006), 6.

17. Joseph B. Wirthlin, "The Unspeakable Gift," *Ensign,* May 2003, 28.

18. Howard W. Hunter, "'Exceeding Great and Precious Promises,'" *Ensign,* November 1994, 8.

19. Ezra Taft Benson, "Flooding the Earth with the Book of Mormon," *Ensign,* November 1988, 5.

20. Gordon B. Hinckley, "'Be Not Afraid, Only Believe,'" *Ensign,* February 1996, 5.

21. Benson, "Flooding the Earth with the Book of Mormon," 5.

22. M. Russell Ballard, "Creating a Gospel-Sharing Home," *Ensign,* May 2006, 85.

23. Ballard, "Let Our Voices Be Heard," 19.

24. *For the Strength of Youth* (Salt Lake City: The Church of Jesus Christ of Latter-day Saints, 2001), 10.

25. David O. McKay, *Steppingstones to an Abundant Life* (Salt Lake City: Deseret Book, 1971), 294.

26. David A. Bednar, "More Diligent and Concerned at Home," *Ensign,* November 2009, 17–18.

CHAPTER 24: HOW CAN I STAY FAITHFUL WHEN LIFE IS HARD?

1. Nick Vujicic, "Life without Limbs," www.lifewithoutlimbs.org/files/ministry_prospectus.pdf, 5.

2. Spencer W. Kimball, *The Teachings of Spencer W. Kimball,* ed. Edward L. Kimball (Salt Lake City: Bookcraft, 1982), 38–39; emphasis in original.

3. Boyd K. Packer, "The Choice," *Ensign,* November 1980, 21; emphasis added.

4. Richard G. Scott, "Trust in the Lord," *Ensign,* November 1995, 17.

5. Ibid.

6. Orson F. Whitney, quoted in Spencer W. Kimball, *Faith Precedes the Miracle* (Salt Lake City: Deseret Book, 1978), 98.

7. Scott, "Trust in the Lord," 16.

8. Joseph B. Wirthlin, "The Unspeakable Gift," *Ensign,* May 2003, 26.

9. Joseph B. Wirthlin, "'Choose the Right,'" BYU Fireside, 4 September 1994, http://speeches.byu.edu/.

10. See http://www.heartlandlibraries.org/news&clues/archive/S2002/columns.html.

11. "Seeing Burgon: Blind, deaf teen lives her life to the fullest," 20 September 2009, http://deseretnews.com/article/705331427/Blind-deaf-teen-lives-a-full-life.html?pg=6.

12. See Rich Bayer, "Gratitude and Mental Wellness," http://www.upperbay.org/articles/gratitude%20and%20mental%20wellness.pdf, 16.

13. See Catherine Price, "Stumbling Toward Gratitude," The Greater Good Science Center, Summer 2007, http://peacecenter.berkeley.edu/greatergood/archive/2007summer/price.pdf, 16.

14. Jeffrey R. Holland, "The Tongue of Angels," *Ensign,* May 2007, 18.

CHAPTER 25: HOW CAN I OVERCOME FEELINGS OF FEAR AND DOUBT?

1. Neil L. Andersen, "You Know Enough," *Ensign,* November 2008, 13.

2. Kevin W. Pearson, "Faith in the Lord Jesus Christ," *Ensign,* May 2009, 40.

3. See "Face Your Fears Today," http://faceyourfearstoday.com/Top_10_Fears.html.

4. Boyd K. Packer, *Mine Errand from the Lord* (Salt Lake City: Deseret Book, 2008), 63.

5. See http://www.phobialist.com/reverse.html.

6. Erik Weihenmayer, as cited in Joseph B. Wirthlin, "One Step after Another," *Ensign,* November 2001, 25; see also "Everest Grueling for Blind Man," *Deseret News,* 5 June 2001, A12; and Karl Taro Greenfeld, "Blind to Failure," *Time,* 18 June 2001.

7. Richard G. Scott, "To the Lonely and Misunderstood," BYU Devotional, 10 August 1982, http://speeches.byu.edu/.

8. Frederic W. Farrar, as cited in Carlos E. Asay, "Stay on the True Course," *Ensign,* May 1996, 60.

9. Dieter F. Uchtdorf, "The Reflection in the Water," CES Fireside for Young Adults, 1 November 2009, http://www.lds .org/.

10. http://www.phobialist.com/reverse.html.

11. Neal A. Maxwell, *Wherefore Ye Must Press Forward* (Salt Lake City: Deseret Book, 1977), 94.

12. *For the Strength of Youth* (Salt Lake City: The Church of Jesus Christ of Latter-day Saints, 2001), 42.

13. Brigham Young, in Loren C. Dunn, "Drink of the Pure Water," *Ensign,* June 1971, 81.

14. Neal A. Maxwell, *Men and Women of Christ* (Salt Lake City: Bookcraft, 1991), 105.

15. Boyd K. Packer, *Teach Ye Diligently* (Salt Lake City: Deseret Book, 1991), 102.

16. Thomas S. Monson, "Be of Good Cheer," *Ensign,* May 2009, 92.

CHAPTER 26: HOW CAN I HANDLE ANTI-MORMON TEACHINGS IN A CHRISTLIKE WAY?

1. *Encyclopedia of Mormonism,* 4 vols., ed. Daniel H. Ludlow (New York: Macmillan, 1992), 1:45.

2. Ezra Taft Benson, "The Book of Mormon Is the Word of God," *Ensign,* May 1975, 64.

3. Marion G. Romney, as cited in J. Richard Clarke, "'My Soul Delighteth in the Scriptures,'" *Ensign,* November 1982, 15.

4. Brigham Young, *Discourses of Brigham Young,* sel. John A. Widtsoe (Salt Lake City: Deseret Book, 1954), 351.

5. Bruce R. McConkie, in Conference Report, October 1962, 10.

6. Jeffrey R. Holland, "Our Consuming Mission," address to CES, 5 February 1999, 6.

CHAPTER 27: HOW CAN I SET MEANINGFUL PERSONAL GOALS?

1. Howard W. Hunter, *The Teachings of Howard W. Hunter* (Salt Lake City: Bookcraft, 1997), 259.

2. See http://thinkexist.com/quotation/i_find_the_great_thing_in_this_world_is_not_so/174881.html.

3. Ezra Taft Benson, "Do Not Despair," *Ensign,* October 1986, 5.

4. Richard G. Scott, "Learning to Succeed in Life," BYU Devotional, 15 September 1998, http://speeches.byu.edu/.

5. Jeffrey R. Holland, "'Cast Not Away Therefore Your Confidence,'" BYU Devotional, 2 March 1999, http://speeches.byu .edu/.

6. M. Russell Ballard, "Keeping Life's Demands in Balance," *Ensign,* May 1987, 14.

7. M. Russell Ballard, "Go for It!" *New Era,* March 2004, 7.

8. Jonah Lehrer, "Don't—The Secret of Self-Control," 18 May 2009, http://www.newyorker.comreporting/2009/05/18/090 518fa_fact_lehrer.

9. See George T. Doran, "There's a S.M.A.R.T. way to write management's goals and objectives," and Arthur F. Miller and James A. Cunningham, "How to avoid costly job mismatches," *Management Review,* November 1981, Volume 70, Issue 11.

10. Thomas S. Monson, *Favorite Quotations from the Collection of Thomas S. Monson* (Salt Lake City: Deseret Book, 1985), 61.

11. Ballard, "Keeping Life's Demands in Balance," 14.

12. Dallin H. Oaks, "Timing," BYU Devotional, 29 January 2002, http://speeches.byu.edu/.

13. See Gordon B. Hinckley, "A Testimony Vibrant and True," *Ensign,* August 2005, 2–6.

14. Jeffrey R. Holland, "The Best Is Yet to Be," *Ensign,* January 2010, 23; emphasis in original.

15. Monson, *Favorite Quotations from the Collection of Thomas S. Monson,* 61; emphasis added.

16. Bruce C. and Marie K. Hafen, "'Bridle All Your Passions,'" *Ensign,* February 1994, 16.

17. Ballard, "Go for It!" 4.

18. M. Russell Ballard, "Be Strong in the Lord, and in the Power of His Might," BYU Fireside, 3 March 2002, http://speeches .byu.edu/.

19. Henry Wadsworth Longfellow, http://quotationsbook.com/quote/35806.

20. Thomas S. Monson, "Choose You This Day," *Ensign,* November 2004, 68.

CHAPTER 28: HOW CAN I RESIST NEGATIVE PEER PRESSURE?

1. Gordon B. Hinckley, "Four Simple Things to Help Our Families and Our Nations," *Ensign,* September 1996, 7.
2. Robert D. Hales, "The Aaronic Priesthood: Return with Honor," *Ensign,* May 1990, 40.
3. Boyd K. Packer, "Counsel to Young Men," *Ensign,* May 2009, 50.
4. S. Michael Wilcox, *Don't Leap with the Sheep* (Salt Lake City: Deseret Book, 2001), 68.
5. See Carmen Rasmussen, *Staying in Tune* (Salt Lake City: Spring Creek Company, 2007), viii–xvi.
6. Chip and Dan Heath, *Made to Stick* (New York: Random House, 2007), 213; emphasis in original.
7. Thomas S. Monson, "Standards of Strength," *New Era,* October 2008, 2.
8. Thomas S. Monson, "Examples of Righteousness." *Ensign,* May 2008, 65.
9. Story told to authors in private conversation.

CHAPTER 29: HOW CAN I HELP FRIENDS AND FAMILY WHO ARE STRUGGLING WITH SERIOUS PROBLEMS?

1. Harold B. Lee, "Stand Ye in Holy Places," *Ensign,* July 1973, 123.
2. *For the Strength of Youth* (Salt Lake City: The Church of Jesus Christ of Latter-day Saints, 2001), 12.
3. Richard G. Scott, "Healing Your Damaged Life," *Ensign,* November 1992, 62.
4. Neal A. Maxwell, *All These Things Shall Give Thee Experience* (Salt Lake City: Deseret Book, 2007), 72, 81.
5. Robert L. Simpson, "'Strengthen Thy Brethren,'" *Ensign,* December 1971, 103.
6. See Richard G. Scott, "Now Is the Time to Serve a Mission!" *Ensign*, May 2006, 89.
7. See Spencer J. Condie, *Russell M. Nelson: Father, Surgeon, Apostle* (Salt Lake City: Deseret Book, 203), 26.
8. See Henry B. Eyring, "Elder David A. Bednar: Going Forward in the Strength of the Lord," *Ensign,* March 2005, 17.
9. Richard G. Scott, "To Help a Loved One in Need," *Ensign,* May 1988, 61.

CHAPTER 30: HOW CAN I BEAR A POWERFUL TESTIMONY?

1. See David Seastrand, "A study of Latter-day Saint high school seminary students' perceptions of their spirituality" (EO.D. diss., Brigham Young University, 1996).
2. See *Journal of Discourses,* 26 vols. (Liverpool: Latter-day Saints' Book Depot, 1854–86), 1:90–91.
3. Boyd K. Packer, "The Candle of the Lord," *Ensign,* January 1983, 55.
4. *Guide to the Scriptures,* "Testify," http://scriptures.lds.org/en/gs/t/17.
5. M. Russell Ballard, "Pure Testimony," *Ensign,* November 2004, 41.
6. Spencer W. Kimball, *The Teachings of Spencer W. Kimball,* ed. Edward L. Kimball (Salt Lake City: Bookcraft, 1982), 138.
7. Henry B. Eyring, "Witnesses for God," *Ensign,* November 1996, 32.
8. Ibid.
9. Ballard, "Pure Testimony," 41.
10. *Hymns of The Church of Jesus Christ of Latter-day Saints* (Salt Lake City: The Church of Jesus Christ of Latter-day Saints, 1985), no. 134.
11. Boyd K. Packer, "The Quest for Spiritual Knowledge," *New Era,* January 2007, 6; emphasis in original.
12. Harold B. Lee, *The Teachings of Harold B. Lee,* ed. Clyde J. Williams (Salt Lake City: Deseret Book, 1996), 603.
13. Spencer W. Kimball, "Personal Testimony," *Teachings of the President of the Church: Spencer W. Kimball* (Salt Lake City: The Church of Jesus Christ of Latter-day Saints, 2006); 76.
14. M. Russell Ballard, "Pure Testimony," *Ensign,* November 2004, 40–41.
15. Ibid., 41.

CHAPTER 31: HOW CAN I PREPARE AND GIVE A POWERFUL YOUTH TALK?

1. Seth Borenstein, "Study is a put off: Scientists research why procrastination is getting worse," *USA Today,* 12 January 2007, http://www.usatoday.com/tech/science/2007-01-12-procrastination-study_x.htm.

2. Piers Steel and William Knaus, in Seth Borenstein, "Study is a put off: Scientists research why procrastination is getting worse," *USA Today,* 12 January 2007, http://www.usatoday.com/tech/science/2007–01–12-procrastination-study_x .htm.

3. Richard G. Scott, "To Understand and Live Truth," Address to CES Religious Educators, 4 February 2005, 3; http://emp .byui.edu/WahlquistR/333Alltalks/RGSToUnderstandandLiveTruth.pdf.

4. Boyd K. Packer, "Little Children," *Ensign,* November 1986, 17.

CHAPTER 32: HOW CAN I SHARE THE GOSPEL WITH OTHERS?

1. Joseph Smith, *History of the Church,* (Salt Lake City: Deseret Book, 1976), 2:478.

2. M. Russell Ballard, "We Proclaim the Gospel," *Ensign,* November 1986, 32.

3. M. Russell Ballard, "Sharing the Gospel Using the Internet," *Ensign,* July 2008, 62; emphasis in original.

4. David A. Bednar, "Becoming a Missionary," *Ensign,* November 2005, 45; emphasis in original.

5. *For the Strength of Youth* (Salt Lake City: The Church of Jesus Christ of Latter-day Saints, 2001), 12–13.

6. Gordon B. Hinckley, "Opposing Evil," *Ensign,* November 1975, 38.

7. H. David Burton, "Courage to Hearken," *Ensign,* May 1994, 68.

8. David A. Bednar, "'Teach Them to Understand,'" Ricks College Campus Education Week Devotional, 4 June 1998, http://www.byui.edu/Presentations/Transcripts/EducationWeek/1998_06_04_Bednar.htm.

9. Dallin H. Oaks, "Sharing the Gospel," *Ensign,* November 2001, 9.

10. Ballard, "Sharing the Gospel Using the Internet," 62.

11. Bruce R. McConkie, in Conference Report, April 1961, 38.

12. *For the Strength of Youth,* 12–13.

13. M. Russell Ballard, "Creating a Gospel-Sharing Home," *Ensign,* May 2006, 87.

14. Ibid., 86.

15. Robert C. Oaks, "Sharing the Gospel," *Ensign,* November 2000, 81.

16. M. Russell Ballard, "The Essential Role of Member Missionary Work," *Ensign,* May 2003, 39–40.

17. Clayton M. Christensen, "Decisions for Which I've Been Grateful," BYU–Idaho Devotional, 8 June 2004, http://www .byui.edu/Presentations/Transcripts/Devotionals/2004_06_08_Christensen.htm.

CONCLUSION: THE HOLY GHOST WILL TELL YOU *HOW*

1. David A. Bednar, "Seek Learning by Faith" Address to CES Religious Educators, 3 February 2006, 5, http://www.lds .org/broadcast/misc/CES_2006_Eve_BednarDA_%20SeekLearningByFaith_00920_000.pdf.

2. http://www.lds.org/pa/flash/display/0,18519,8104-1-1,00.html.

3. see http://ldswhy.com/qa/category/personal-revelation/.

4. Julie B. Beck, "And upon the Handmaids in Those Days Will I Pour Out My Spirit," *Ensign,* May 2010, 11.

5. See John Hilton III, "Have Ye Inquired of the Lord?" *Ensign,* October 2008, 38–39.

About the Authors

John Hilton III is a religious educator with degrees from Brigham Young and Harvard Universities. John frequently speaks with Especially for Youth, Education Week, and Time Out for Women and Girls. He has published several titles with Deseret Book, including *Isn't Being Good Good Enough?* and *Please Pass the Scriptures*. John and his wife, Lani, have four children and live in Utah. For more information please visit johnhiltoniii.com

Anthony Sweat is a full-time religious educator and a speaker at Especially for Youth and Education Week conferences. He received his bachelor's degree from the University of Utah and his Master of Education degree from Utah State University. He and his wife, Cindy, are the parents of five children and reside in South Jordan, Utah.

Other Titles by John Hilton III

Dating and the Plan of Happiness: What Every Teenager Should Know (Audio CD)

The Dog Ate My Scriptures: Excuses, Agency, and Responsibility (Audio CD)

I Can Do Hard Things (Audio CD)

I Lost My Phone Number, Can I Have Yours? Pick-Up Lines That Don't Work,
   Scriptural Advice That Does

Isn't Being Good Good Enough? (DVD)

The Little Book of Book of Mormon Evidences

Please Pass the Scriptures

Why?

Other Titles by Anthony Sweat

I'm Not Perfect. Can I Still Go to Heaven?

Manly Book of Experiences

Why?

On sale now!

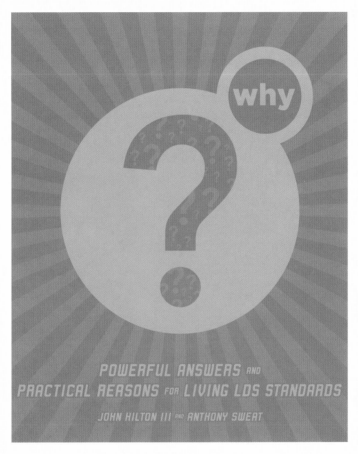

ISBN 978-1-60641-040-0 $32.95

Features answers to more than 100 questions!
Understand the doctrinal "whys" that help reinforce the
teachings found in the *For the Strength of Youth* pamphlet.

DESERET
BOOK